COLLINS

PHRASE BOOK & DICTIONARY

HarperCollins*Publishers*

Food section by Edite Vieira Phillips

Other languages in the *Collins Phrase Book & Dictionary* series:

FRENCH
GERMAN
GREEK
JAPANESE
PORTUGUESE
RUSSIAN
SPANISH

These titles are also published in a language pack containing 60-minute cassette and phrase book

First published 1998

Reprint 10 9 8 7 6 5 4 3 2 1 0
Printed in Italy by Amadeus SpA

ISBN 0 00-472074 1

INTRODUCTION

Your *Collins Phrase Book & Dictionary* is a handy, quick-reference guide that will help you make the most of your stay abroad. Its clear layout will save you valuable time when you need that crucial word or phrase.

There are three main sections in this book:

Practical topics arranged thematically with an opening section **KEY TALK** containing vital phrases that should stand you in good stead in most situations.

PHRASES

Short easy phrases that can be adapted for your situation

practical tips are highlighted in yellow boxes

SIGNS ARE IN GREEN BOXES

replies you might hear are highlighted in red boxes

FOOD SECTION

Phrases for ordering drinks and food
A region by region description of Italian food with a note on Italian wine and other popular drinks
Drinks
Menu reader

DICTIONARY

English-Italian | **Italian-English** **signs highlighted**

And finally, a short **GRAMMAR** section explaining how the language works.

So, just flick through the pages to find the information you need. Why not start with a look at pronouncing Italian on page 6. From there on the going is easy with your *Collins Phrase Book & Dictionary*.

CONTENTS

PRONOUNCING ITALIAN

We've tried to make the pronunciation under the phrases as clear as possible. We've split up the words to make them easy to read, but don't pause too long between syllables. Italian isn't really hard to pronounce and once you learn a few basic rules, it shouldn't be too long before you can read straight from the Italian.

Longer words are usually stressed on the next to last syllable, but we show all stressed syllables in **heavy type**, *so you won't be caught out by any exceptions.*

The spellings **c** *and* **ch** *might confuse you, because* **c** *is sometimes pronounced like English* **ch**, *while the Italian* **ch** *is pronounced like the English* **k**. *(Look at the English for kilogram and the Italian* **chilogramma**.*) So* **c'è** *(there is) is pronounced like English check without the final* **k** *sound, while* **che?** *(what?) is pronounced* **kay**. *The letter* **g** *behaves in a similar way. So when you see a* **ch** *or* **gh** *combination in Italian, remember to make the* **c** *and* **g** *hard.*

Sometimes Italian has two distinctive vowel sounds next to each other, in other words like **dei**, *shown in the pronunciation as* **day***-ee. These sounds merge with each other, so don't separate them with a long pause.*

Finally, pronounce all **r***'s when you see them in Italian words.*

Basic rules to remember are:

italian	*sounds like*	*example*	*pronunciation*
a	c**a**t	**pasta**	***pas**-ta*
e	b**e**t/d**ay**	**letto/per**	***let**-to/payr*
i	m**ee**t	**vino**	***vee**-no*
o	g**o**t	**sono**	***so**-no*
u	b**oo**t	**luna**	***loo**-na*
gli	mi**lli**on	**figlio**	***feel**-yo*
sc *(before* **e/i***)*	**sh**op	**sci**	*shee*
sc *(before* **a/o/u***)*	**sc**an	**scarpa**	***skar**-pa*

*Italian has two forms of address, formal and informal. The informal **tu** is used among family and friends. You will hear **ciao** (chow), meaning **hi** and **bye**, among friends and young people.*

yes
sì
see

no
no
no

that's fine
va bene
*va **be**-nay*

please
per favore
*payr fa-**vo**-ray*

thank you
grazie
***grat**-see-ay*

prego
***pray**-go*
don't mention it

hello
buon giorno
*bwon **jor**-no*

goodbye
arrivederci
*ar-ree-ve-**der**-chee*

good night
buona notte
***bwo**-na **not**-tay*

good afternoon/evening
buona sera
***bwo**-na **say**-ra*

that's very kind
molto gentile
***mol**-to jen-**tee**-lay*

excuse me/sorry
scusi
***skoo**-zee*

excuse me *(to get past people)*
permesso
*per-**mes**-so*

Here is an easy way to ask for something... just add **per favore**

a/an...
un... *('il' and 'lo' words)*
oon...

una... *('la' words)*
***oo**-na...*

an ice cream
un gelato
*oon jay-**la**-to*

a beer
una birra
***oo**-na **beer**-ra*

2 ice creams
due gelati
***doo**-ay jay-**la**-tee*

2 beers
due birre
***doo**-ay **beer**-ray*

a beer and two ice creams, please
una birra e due gelati, per favore
***oo**-na **beer**-ra ay **doo**-ay jay-**la**-tee payr fa-**vo**-ray*

KEY TALK

I'd like...
vorrei...
*vor-**ray**-ee...*

we'd like...
vorremmo...
*vor-**rem**-mo...*

I'd like an ice cream
vorrei un gelato
*vor-**ray**-ee oon jay-**la**-to*

we'd like to go to Pisa
vorremmo andare a Pisa
*vor-**rem**-mo an-**da**-ray a **pee**-za*

do you have...?
avete...?
*a-**vay**-tay...*

do you have any milk?
avete del latte?
*a-**vay**-tay del **lat**-tay*

do you have stamps?
avete dei francobolli?
*a-**vay**-tay **day**-ee fran-ko-**bol**-lee*

do you have a map?
avete una carta?
*a-**vay**-tay **oo**-na **kar**-ta*

do you have fruit?
avete della frutta?
*a-**vay**-tay **del**-la **froot**-ta*

how much is it?
quanto costa?
***kwan**-to **kos**-ta*

how much does ... cost?
quanto costa il/la...?
***kwan**-to **kos**-ta eel/la...*

how much is the wine?
quanto costa il vino?
***kwan**-to **kos**-ta eel **vee**-no*

how much is the ticket?
quanto costa il biglietto?
***kwan**-to **kos**-ta eel beel-**yet**-to*

how much is a kilo?
quanto costa al chilo?
***kwan**-to **kos**-ta al **kee**-lo*

how much is one?
quanto costa l'uno?
***kwan**-to **kos**-ta **loo**-no*

POMODORI..................al chilo	TOMATOES PER KILO
PERE ....al chilo	PEARS PER KILO
ARANCE ....al chilo	ORANGES PER KILO

where is...?
dov'è...?
*do-**ve**...*

where are...?
dove sono...?
***do**-vay **so**-no...*

where is the toilet?
dov'è la toilette?
*do-**ve** la twa-**let***

where are the children?
dove sono i bambini?
***do**-vay **so**-no ee bam-**bee**-nee*

DONNE	LADIES	**LIBERO**	FREE	**INGRESSO**	ENTRANCE
UOMINI	GENTS	**OCCUPATO**	OCCUPIED	**USCITA**	EXIT

is there?
c'è...?
che...

are there...?
ci sono...?
*chee **so**-no...*

is there a restaurant?
c'è un ristorante?
*che oon ree-sto-**ran**-tay*

where is there a chemist?
dove c'è una farmacia?
***do**-vay che **oo**-na far-ma-**chee**-a*

are there any children?
ci sono dei bambini?
*che **so**-no **day**-ee bam-**bee**-nee*

is there a swimming pool?
c'è una piscina?
*che **oo**-na pee-**shee**-na*

there is no...
non c'è...
non che...

there is no hot water
non c'è acqua calda
*non che **ak**-wa **kal**-da*

there is no bread
non c'è pane
*non che **pa**-nay*

I need...
ho bisogno di...
*o bee-**zon**-yo dee...*

I need a doctor
ho bisogno di un medico
*o bee-**zon**-yo dee oon **me**-dee-ko*

I need to phone
ho bisogno di telefonare
*o bee-**zon**-yo dee te-le-fo-**na**-ray*

KEY TALK

can I...?
posso...?
***pos**-so...*

can we...?
possiamo...?
*pos-see-**a**-mo...*

can I pay?
posso pagare?
***pos**-so pa-**ga**-ray*

can we go in?
possiamo entrare?
*pos-see-**a**-mo en-**tra**-ray*

where can I...?
dove posso...?
***do**-vay **pos**-so...*

where can I buy bread?
dove posso comprare il pane?
***do**-vay **pos**-so kom-**pra**-ray eel **pa**-nay*

where can I get tickets?
dove posso trovare i biglietti?
***do**-vay **pos**-so tro-**va**-ray ee beel-**yet**-tee*

si può comprare i biglietti dal tabaccaio
*see pwo kom-**pra**-ray ee beel-**yet**-tee dal ta-bak-**ka**-yo*
you can buy tickets at the tobacconist's

when?
quando?
***kwan**-do*

at what time...?
a che ora...?
*a kay **o**-ra...*

when does it leave?
quando parte?
***kwan**-do **par**-tay*

when does it arrive?
quando arriva?
***kwan**-do ar-**ree**-va*

when does it open?
a che ora apre?
*a kay **o**-ra **a**-pray*

when does it close?
a che ora chiude?
*a kay **o**-ra kee-**oo**-day*

yesterday
ieri
***ye**-ree*

today
oggi
***od**-jee*

tomorrow
domani
*do-**ma**-nee*

this morning
stamattina
*sta-mat-**tee**-na*

this afternoon
oggi pomeriggio
***od**-jee po-may-**reed**-jo*

tonight
stasera
*sta-**say**-ra*

ORARIO ESTIVO	SUMMER TIMETABLE
ORARIO INVERNALE	WINTER TIMETABLE
CHIUSO PER FERIE	CLOSED FOR HOLIDAYS
CHIUSO PER TURNO	CLOSED FOR RESTDAY

LUN.	MON
MAR.	TUE
MER.	WED
GIO.	THU
VEN.	FRI
SAB.	SAT
DOM.	SUN

is it open?
è aperto?
*e a-**payr**-to*

is it closed?
è chiuso?
*e kee-**oo**-zo*

APERTO	OPEN
CHIUSO	CLOSED
FERIALE	WEEKDAY *(Mon-Sat)*
FESTIVO	HOLIDAY/ SUNDAY

apre alle nove
***a**-pray **al**-lay **no**-vay*
it opens at 9

il museo è chiuso la domenica
*eel moo-**zay**-o e kee-**oo**-zo la do-**may**-nee-ka*
the museum is closed on Sundays

GETTING TO KNOW PEOPLE

*If you don't know a person's surname you can simply address them as **signore** (for a man) and **signora** (for a woman).*

how are you?
come sta?
***ko**-may sta*

fine, thanks. And you?
bene, grazie. E Lei?
***be**-nay **grat**-see-ay ay lay*

my name is...
mi chiamo...
*mee kee-**a**-mo...*

what is your name?
come si chiama?
***ko**-may see kee-**a**-ma*

I didn't understand
non ho capito
*non o ka-**pee**-to*

do you speak English?
parla inglese?
***par**-la een-**glay**-zay*

MONEY – changing

CAMBIO	BUREAU DE CHANGE
BANCOMAT	CASH DISPENSER

Banks are generally open from 8.30am-1.30pm Mon-Fri, and usually also for one hour in the afternoon (times vary). There are bureaux de change in towns and cities, and you can use your Eurocheque card at cashpoint machines with the Eurocheque logo.

where can I change money?
dove posso cambiare soldi?
***do**-vay **pos**-so kam-bee-**a**-ray **sol**-dee*

where is the bank?
dov'è la banca?
*do-**ve** la **ban**-ka*

where is the bureau de change?
dov'è il cambio?
*do-**ve** eel **kam**-bee-yo*

when does the bank open?
quando apre la banca?
***kwan**-do **a**-pray la **ban**-ka*

when does the bank close?
quando chiude la banca?
***kwan**-do kee-**oo**-day la **ban**-ka*

I want to cash these traveller's cheques
vorrei cambiare questi travellers cheque
*vor-**ray**-ee kam-bee-**a**-ray **kwes**-tee travellers cheque*

what is the rate?
quant'è il cambio?
*kwan-**te** eel **kam**-bee-yo*

for pounds
per sterline
*payr ster-**lee**-nay*

for dollars
per dollari
*payr **dol**-la-ree*

I want to change £50
vorrei cambiare cinquanta sterline
*vor-**ray**-ee kam-bee-**a**-ray cheen-**kwan**-ta ster-**lee**-nay*

where is there a cash dispenser?
dove c'è un bancomat?
***do**-ve che oon **ban**-ko-mat*

CASSA CASH DESK **IVA** VAT **COMPRESO** INCLUDED

Many shops and restaurants, and most hotels, will accept credit cards and Eurocheques. You must retain your receipt when you make any purchases.

how much is it?
quanto costa?
***kwan**-to **kos**-ta*

how much will it be?
quanto costerà?
kwan**-to kos-tay-**ra

I want to pay
vorrei pagare
*vor-**ray**-ee pa-**ga**-ray*

how much do I have to pay?
quanto devo pagare?
***kwan**-to **day**-vo pa-**ga**-ray*

can I pay by credit card?
posso pagare con la carta di credito?
***pos**-so pa-**ga**-ray kon la **kar**-ta dee **kre**-dee-to*

do you accept traveller's cheques?
accettate i travellers cheques?
*a-chet-**ta**-tay ee travellers cheques*

how much is it...?
quanto costa...?
***kwan**-to **kos**-ta...*

per person
per persona
*payr per-**so**-na*

per night
per notte
*payr **not**-tay*

per kilo
per chilo
*payr **kee**-lo*

I need a receipt
ho bisogno di una ricevuta
*oh bee-**zon**-yo dee **oo**-na ree-che-**voo**-ta*

do I need to pay a deposit?
devo pagare un deposito?
***day**-vo pa-**ga**-ray oon de-**po**-zee-to*

keep the change
tenga il resto
***ten**-ga eel **res**-to*

si paga alla cassa
*see **pa**-ga **al**-la **kas**-sa*
you pay at the cash desk

AIRPORT

ARRIVI	ARRIVALS
PARTENZE	DEPARTURES
RITIRO BAGAGLI	BAGGAGE RECLAIM
VOLO	FLIGHT
RITARDO	DELAY

to the airport, please
all'aeroporto, per favore
*a-lay-ro-**por**-to payr fa-**vo**-ray*

how do I get into town?
come si va in città?
ko**-may see va een cheet-**ta

where do I get the bus to the town centre?
da dove prendo l'autobus per il centro città?
*da **do**-vay **pren**-do **low**-to-boos payr eel **chen**-tro cheet-**ta***

how much is it...?
quanto costa...?
***kwan**-to **kos**-ta...*

to the centre
per il centro
*payr eel **chen**-tro*

to the airport
per l'aeroporto
*payr lay-ro-**por**-to*

where do I check in for...?
dov'è il check-in per...?
*do-**ve** eel check-in payr...*

which gate is it for the flight to...?
qual è l'uscita per il volo per...?
*kwal e loo-**shee**-ta payr eel **vo**-lo payr...*

l'imbarco sarà all'uscita numero...
*leem-**bar**-ko sa-**ra** al-loo-**shee**-ta **noo**-may-ro...*
boarding will take place at gate number...

l'ultima chiamata
***lool**-tee-ma kee-a-**ma**-ta*
the last call

il volo è in ritardo
*eel **vo**-lo e een ree-**tar**-do*
the flight is delayed

DOGANA	CUSTOMS
CITTADINI UE	EU CITIZENS

With the single European market, EU (European Union) citizens are subject only to highly selective spot checks and they can go through the blue customs channel (unless they have goods to declare). There is no restriction by quantity or value on goods purchased by travellers in another EU country provided they are for their own personal use (guidelines have been published). If unsure, check with customs officials.

I have nothing to declare
non ho niente da dichiarare
*non o nee-**en**-tay da dee-kee-a-**ra**-ray*

here is...
ecco...
***ek**-ko...*

my passport
il mio passaporto
*eel **mee**-o pas-sa-**por**-to*

my green card
la mia carta verde
*la **mee**-a **kar**-ta **ver**-day*

do I have to pay duty on this?
devo pagare la dogana per questo?
***day**-vo pa-**ga**-ray la do-**ga**-na payr **kwes**-to*

it's for my own personal use
è per il mio uso personale
*e payr eel **mee**-o **oo**-zo per-so-**na**-lay*

we're going to...
andiamo a...
*an-dee-**a**-mo a...*

the children are on this passport
i bambini sono su questo passaporto
*ee bam-**bee**-nee **so**-no soo **kwes**-to pas-sa-**por**-to*

I'm...
sono...
***so**-no...*

British *(m/f)*
inglese
*een-**glay**-zay*

Australian *(m/f)*
australiano(a)
*ow-stra-lee-**a**-no(a)*

ASKING THE WAY – questions

excuse me
scusi
***skoo**-zee*

where is...?
dov'è...?
*do-**ve**...*

where is the nearest...?
dov'è il/la ... più vicino(a)?
*do-**ve** eel/la ... pee-**yoo** vee-**chee**-no(a)*

how do I get to...?
per andare a...?
*payr an-**da**-ray a...*

is this the right way to...?
questa è la strada giusta per...?
***kwes**-ta e la **stra**-da **joos**-ta payr...*

the...
il/la...
eel/la...

is it far?
è lontano?
*e lon-**ta**-no*

can I walk there?
si può andare a piedi?
*see pwo an-**da**-ray a pee-**ay**-dee*

is there a bus that goes there?
c'è un autobus che ci va?
*che oon **ow**-to-boos kay chee va*

we're looking for...
cerchiamo...
*cher-kee-**a**-mo...*

we're lost
ci siamo persi
*chee see-**a**-mo **per**-see*

can you show me on the map?
mi può indicare sulla cartina?
*mee pwo een-dee-**ka**-ray **sool**-la kar-**tee**-na*

answers – ASKING THE WAY

It's no use being able to ask the way if you're not going to understand the directions you get. We've tried to anticipate the likely answers, so listen carefully for these key phrases.

continui sempre dritto
*kon-**tee**-noo-ee **sem**-pray **dreet**-to*
keep going straight ahead

bisogna tornare indietro
*bee-**zon**-ya tor-**na**-ray een-dee-**ay**-tro*
you have to turn round

giri...
***gee**-ree...*
turn...

a destra
*a **des**-tra*
right

a sinistra
*a see-**nee**-stra*
left

va...
va...
go...

verso...
***ver**-so...*
towards...

continui...
*kon-**tee**-noo-ee...*
keep going...

fino a...
***fee**-no a...*
as far as...

prenda...
***pren**-da...*
take...

la prima strada a destra
*la **pree**-ma **stra**-da a **des**-tra*
the first road on the right

la seconda strada a sinistra
*la se-**kon**-da **stra**-da a see-**nee**-stra*
the second road on the left

attraversi...
*at-tra-**ver**-see...*
cross...

la piazza
*la pee-**at**-sa*
the square

è dopo il semaforo
*e **do**-po eel se-**ma**-fo-ro*
it's after the traffic lights

BUS

Buy your bus tickets in advance at newspaper kiosks, tobacconists and bars showing the bus company logo. On boarding the bus you must immediately stamp your ticket in a machine which is usually beside the front or rear doors. You may be able to save money by buying tickets which are valid for a whole day or a week's travel.

where is the bus station?
dov'è la stazione degli autobus?
*do-**ve** la stats-**yo**-nay **del**-yee **ow**-to-boos*

I want to go...
voglio andare...
***vol**-yo an-**da**-ray...*

to the station
alla stazione
***al**-la stats-**yo**-nay*

to the museum
al museo
***al** moo-**zay**-o*

to Piazza Cavour
a Piazza Cavour
*a pee-**at**-sa ka-**voor***

to the Vatican
al Vaticano
*al va-tee-**ka**-no*

does this bus go to...?
questo autobus va a...?
***kwes**-to **ow**-to-boos va a...*

which bus do I take?
quale autobus devo prendere?
***kwa**-lay **ow**-to-boos **day**-vo **pren**-day-ray*

where does the bus go from?
da dove parte l'autobus?
*da **do**-vay **par**-tay **low**-to-boos*

how often are the buses?
ogni quanto ci sono gli autobus?
***on**-yee **kwan**-to chee **so**-no lyee **ow**-to-boos*

can you please tell me when to get off?
può dirmi quando devo scendere?
*pwo **deer**-mee **kwan**-do **day**-vo **shen**-day-ray*

UNDERGROUND

METROPOLITANA (M)	UNDERGROUND
ENTRATA / USCITA	ENTRANCE / EXIT
INGRESSO ABBONATI	SEASON TICKET/CARD HOLDERS

*There is an underground system (**Metro**) in Rome and Milan. Tickets are available at the same outlets as bus tickets as well as in the underground stations. In Milan Metro tickets are valid for 75 minutes and can also be used on buses and trams.*

where is the metro station?
dov'è la stazione della metropolitana?
*do-**ve** la stats-**yo**-nay **del**-la met-ro-po-lee-**ta**-na*

a block of tickets, please
un blocco di biglietti, per favore
*oon **blok**-ko dee beel-**yet**-tee payr fa-**vo**-ray*

do you have an underground map?
avete una piantina della metro?
*a-**vay**-tay **oo**-na pee-an-**tee**-na **del**-la **met**-ro*

I want to go to...
voglio andare a...
***vol**-yo an-**da**-ray a...*

can I go by underground?
si può andare colla metro?
*see pwo an-**da**-ray **kol**-la **met**-ro*

do I have to change?
devo cambiare?
***day**-vo kam-bee-**a**-ray*

where?
dove?
***do**-vay*

which line do I take?
quale linea prendo?
***kwa**-lay **lee**-nay-a **pren**-do*

which is the station for the cathedral?
qual è la stazione per il duomo?
*kwal e la stats-**yo**-nay payr eel **dwo**-mo*

TRAIN

SUPER RAPIDO	HIGH SPEED INTERCITY
RAPIDO *(EuroCity /InterCity)*	SUPPLEMENT PAYABLE
BIGLIETTERIA	TICKETS AND INFORMATION
PARTENZE	DEPARTURES
ARRIVI	ARRIVALS
BINARIO	PLATFORM
RTD	DELAYED

Travel by train is relatively cheap in Italy and there are different kinds of trains, ranging from the ***Pendolino*** *(very high speed) to the* ***Locale****, which stops at all stations. The* ***Pendolino*** *and some other high-speed trains must be booked in advance, and some also require the payment of a supplement,* ***un supplemento****. Check in advance, as supplements bought on the train will cost more.*

where is the station?
dov'è la stazione?
*do-**ve** la stats-**yo**-nay*

to the main station, please
alla stazione centrale, per favore
***al**-la stats-**yo**-nay chen-**tra**-lay payr fa-**vo**-ray*

a single to...
un andata per...
*oon an-**da**-ta payr...*

2 singles to...
due andate per...
***doo**-ay an-**da**-tay payr...*

a return to...
un andata e ritorno per...
*oon an-**da**-ta ay ree-**tor**-no payr...*

2 returns to...
due andata e ritorno per...
***doo**-ay an-**da**-ta ay ree-**tor**-no payr...*

a child's return to...
un andata e ritorno ridotto per...
*oon an-**da**-ta ay ree-**tor**-no ree-**dot**-to payr...*

Ist/2nd class
prima/seconda classe
***pree**-ma/se-**kon**-da **klas**-say*

smoking
fumatori
*foo-ma-**to**-ree*

non smoking
non fumatori
*non foo-ma-**to**-ree*

do I have to pay a supplement?
devo pagare un supplemento?
__day__-vo pa-__ga__-ray oon soop-play-__men__-to

is my pass valid for this journey?
è valida la tessera per il viaggio?
e __va__-lee-da la __tes__-say-ra payr eel vee-__ad__-jo

I want to book...
voglio prenotare...
__vol__-yo pray-no-__ta__-ray...

a seat
un posto
oon __pos__-to

a couchette
una cuccetta
__oo__-na koo-__chet__-ta

where is the timetable?
dov'è l'orario dei treni?
do-__ve__ lo-__rar__-yo __day__-ee __tray__-nee

do I need to change?
devo cambiare?
__day__-vo kam-bee-__a__-ray

where?
dove?
__do__-vay

which platform does it leave from?
da quale binario parte?
da __kwa__-lay bee-__nar__-yo __par__-tay

does the train to ... leave from this platform?
il treno per ... parte da questo binario?
eel __tray__-no payr ... __par__-tay da __kwes__-to bee-__nar__-yo

is this the train for...?
è questo il treno per...?
e __kwes__-to eel __tray__-no payr...

where is the left-luggage?
dov'è il deposito bagagli?
__do__-ve eel de-__po__-zee-to ba-__gal__-yee

is this seat taken?
è occupato?
e ok-koo-__pa__-to

TAXI

As a rule taxis should be picked up at a taxi stance rather than hailed in the street. Be sure to take an official taxi (yellow in Rome, white in Florence) as pirate cab operators are likely to overcharge. Tipping is normally from 10-15% of the fare.

to the airport, please
all'aeroporto, per favore
*al-lay-ro-**por**-to payr fa-**vo**-ray*

please take me to this address
per favore mi porti a questo indirizzo
*payr fa-**vo**-ray mee **por**-tee a **kwes**-to een-dee-**reet**-so*

how much will it cost?
quanto verrà a costare?
*__kwan__-to ver-**ra** a kost-**ta**-ray*

it's too much
è troppo
*e **trop**-po*

how much is to the centre?
quanto costa per il centro?
*__kwan__-to **kos**-ta payr eel **chen**-tro*

where can I get a taxi?
dove posso trovare un taxi?
*__do__-vay **pos**-so tro-**va**-ray oon **tak**-see*

please order me a taxi
per favore mi chiami un taxi
*payr fa-**vo**-ray mee kee-**a**-mee oon **tak**-see*

can I have a receipt?
posso avere una ricevuta?
*__pos__-so a-**vay**-ray **oo**-na ree-che-**voo**-ta*

I've nothing smaller
non ho moneta
*non o mon-**ay**-ta*

keep the change
tenga il resto
*__ten__-ga eel **res**-to*

BOAT

*In the city of Venice public transport is by waterbus (**vaporetto**). The best one to take for sightseeing is the no.1 as it travels the length of the Grand Canal (**Canal Grande**) from the Rialto Bridge to St. Mark's Square. Tickets may be purchased in advance at landing stages or from some tobacconists, shops and bars and should be punched before boarding (prices vary depending on the line travelled). Most journeys within the city, however, can be covered on foot. There are also links by boat to the islands in the lagoon.*

1 ticket	**2 tickets**	**single**	**round trip**
un biglietto	due biglietti	andata	andata e ritorno
*oon beel-**yet**-to*	***doo**-ay beel-**yet**-tee*	*an-**da**-ta*	*an-**da**-ta ay ree-**tor**-no*

is there a tourist ticket?
c'è un biglietto turistico?
*che oon beel-**yet**-to too-**rees**-tee-ko*

are there any boat trips?
ci sono delle gite in battello?
*chee **so**-no **del**-lay **jee**-tay een bat-**tel**-lo*

when does the boat leave?
quando parte il battello?
***kwan**-do **par**-tay eel bat-**tel**-lo*

do you have a time table?
ha l'orario?
*a lo-**rar**-yo*

is there a restaurant on board?
c'è un ristorante sul battello?
*che oon rees-to-**ran**-tay sool bat-**tel**-lo*

can we hire a boat?
possiamo noleggiare una barca?
*pos-see-**a**-mo no-led-**ja**-ray **oo**-na **bar**-ka*

CAR – driving/parking

TUTTE LE DIREZIONI	ALL ROUTES
USCITA	EXIT
AUTOSTRADA	MOTORWAY
PEDAGGIO	TOLL
DIVIETO DI SOSTA	NO PARKING
CENTRO CITTÀ	CITY CENTRE

*To drive in Italy visitors must be at least 18 years old and have a valid pink EU licence. Tolls are payable on most sections of the motorway (**autostrada**), and you can pay by **Viacard** which you can buy at motorway service stations, toll booths and some tourist offices. Parking can be difficult and there are often tight restrictions on parking in the centre of Italy's historic towns.*

can I park here?
posso parcheggiare qui?
***pos**-so par-ked-**ja**-ray kwee*

where can I park?
dove posso parcheggiare?
***do**-vay **pos**-so par-ked-**ja**-ray*

do I need a parking disk?
è necessario il disco orario?
*e ne-ches-**sar**-yo eel **dee**-sko o-**ra**-ree-o*

is there a car park?
c'è un parcheggio?
*che oon par-**ked**-jo*

where can I get a parking disk?
dove posso trovare un disco orario?
***do**-vay **pos**-so tro-**va**-ray oon **dee**-sko o-**rar**-yo*

how long can I park here?
per quanto tempo posso stare qui?
*payr **kwan**-to **tem**-po **pos**-so **sta**-ray kwee*

we're going to....
andiamo a...
*an-dee-**a**-mo a...*

is the pass open?
il passo è aperto?
*eel **pas**-so e a-**payr**-to*

what's the best route?
qual è la strada migliore?
*kwal e la **stra**-da meel-**yo**-ray*

SUPER	4 STAR
SENZA PIOMBO	UNLEADED
GASOLIO	DIESEL
BENZINA	PETROL

Motorway petrol stations are usually open 24 hours a day, but off the motorway opening hours are restricted and petrol stations may close for long lunch times and on Sundays and public holidays.

is there a petrol station near here?
c'è una stazione di servizio qui vicino?
*che **oo**-na stats-**yo**-nay dee ser-**veets**-yo kwee vee-**chee**-no*

fill it up, please
il pieno, per favore
*eel pee-**ay**-no payr fa-**vo**-ray*

unleaded
senza piombo
***sent**-sa pee-**om**-bo*

fifty thousand lire of 4-star
cinquanta mila lire di super
*cheen-**kwan**-ta **mee**-la **lee**-ray dee **soo**-per*

where is the air line?
dov'è la canna dell'aria?
***do**-vay la **kan**-na del-**la**-ree-a*

please check...
per favore controlli...
*payr fa-**vo**-ray kon-**trol**-lee...*

the tyre pressure
la pressione delle gomme
*la pres-**yo**-nay **del**-lay **gom**-may*

the oil
l'olio
***lol**-yo*

the water
l'acqua
***lak**-wa*

tutto a posto
***toot**-to a **pos**-to*
everything is ok

quale pompa?
***kwa**-lay **pom**-pa*
which pump?

CAR – problems/breakdown

If you break down on the motorway you can use one of the emergency phones situated every 2 km to call 116 for assistance, and your car will be towed free of charge to the nearest garage. Italian law requires drivers to carry a warning triangle.

I've broken down
la mia macchina è rotta
*la **mee**-a **ma**-kee-na e **rot**-ta*

I'm on my own *(female)*
sono da sola
***so**-no da **so**-la*

there are children in the car
ci sono bambini nella macchina
*chee **so**-no bam-**bee**-nee **nel**-la **ma**-kee-na*

where is the nearest garage?
dov'è il garage più vicino?
*do-**ve** eel ga-**raj** pee-**yoo** vee-**chee**-no*

is it serious?
è una cosa seria?
*e **oo**-na **ko**-za **say**-ree-a*

can you repair it?
può ripararlo?
*pwo ree-pa-**rar**-lo*

when will it be ready?
quando sarà pronta?
***kwan**-do sa-**ra** **pron**-ta*

how much will it cost?
quanto costerà?
kwan**-to kos-tay-**ra

the car won't start
la macchina non parte
*la **ma**-kee-na non **par**-tay*

I have a flat tyre
ho una foratura
*o **oo**-na fo-ra-**too**-ra*

the engine is overheating
il motore si surriscalda
*eel mo-**to**-ray see soor-rees-**kal**-da*

the battery is flat
la batteria è scarica
*la bat-te-**ree**-a e **ska**-ree-ka*

have you the parts?
avete i pezzi di ricambio?
*a-**vay**-tay ee **pet**-see dee ree-**kamb**-yo*

can you replace the windscreen?
può cambiare il parabrezza
*pwo kam-bee-**a**-ray eel pa-ra-**bret**-sa*

AUTONOLEGGIO CAR HIRE

To hire a car in Italy you must be over 21 and have held a full driver's licence for at least a year. Car hire is quite expensive and it may be cheaper to make your arrangements before you go.

I want to hire a car
vorrei noleggiare una macchina
*vor-**ray**-ee no-led-**ja**-ray **oo**-na **ma**-kee-na*

for one day
per un giorno
*payr oon **jor**-no*

for ... days
per ... giorni
*payr ... **jor**-nee*

does the price include fully comprehensive insurance?
il prezzo è inclusivo della polizza a casco?
*eel **pret**-so e een-kloo-**see**-vo **del**-la po-**leet**-sa a **kas**-ko*

I want...
vorrei...
*vor-**ray**-ee...*

a large car
una macchina grande
***oo**-na **ma**-kee-na **gran**-day*

a small car
una macchina piccola
***oo**-na **ma**-kee-na **peek**-kol-la*

an automatic
una automatica
***oo**-na ow-to-**ma**-tee-ka*

what do we do if we break down?
che cosa facciamo se ci capita un guasto?
*kay **ko**-za fa-chee-**a**-mo say chee **ka**-pee-ta oon **gwas**-to*

must I return the car here?
devo riportare la macchina qui?
***day**-vo ree-por-**ta**-ray la **ma**-kee-na kwee*

by what time?
per che ora?
*payr kay **o**-ra*

I'd like to leave it in...
vorrei lasciarla a...
*vor-**ray**-ee la-**shar**-la a...*

where are the documents?
dove sono i documenti?
***do**-vay **so**-no ee do-koo-**men**-tee*

SHOPPING – holiday

APERTO OPEN
CHIUSO CLOSED
CASSA CASH DESK
SALDI SALE

Shops are usually open 8.30am-1.30pm and 3.30-7.30pm Mon-Sat, though hours vary from region to region and in some places shops are closed one weekday as well as on Sunday. Large department stores such as ***Upim*** *and* ***Standa*** *often open from 9am to 8pm Mon-Sat and provide excellent value for money.*

do you sell...?
vendete...?
*ven-**day**-tay...*

stamps
francobolli
*fran-ko-**bol**-lee*

batteries for this
pile per questo
***pee**-lay payr **kwes**-to*

where can I buy...?
dove posso comprare...?
***do**-vay **pos**-so kom-**pra**-ray...*

a colour film
una pellicola a colori
***oo**-na pel-**lee**-ko-la a ko-**lo**-ree*

10 stamps
dieci francobolli
*dee-**ay**-chee fran-ko-**bol**-lee*

for postcards
per cartoline
*payr kar-to-**lee**-nay*

to Britain
per la Gran Bretagna
*payr la gran bre-**tan**-ya*

a tape for this video camera, please
una cassetta per questa videocamera, per favore
***oo**-na kas-**set**-ta payr **kwes**-ta vee-**day**-o-ka-**may**-ra payr fa-**vo**-ray*

I'm looking for a present
cerco un regalo
***cher**-ko oon ray-**ga**-lo*

it's a gift
è un regalo
*e oon ray-**ga**-lo*

is there a market?
c'è un mercato?
*che oon mer-**ka**-to*

have you something cheaper?
ha qualcosa di meno caro?
*a kwal-**ko**-za dee **may**-no **ka**-ro*

please wrap it up
può incartarlo, per favore
*pwo een-kar-**tar**-lo payr fa-**vo**-ray*

which day?
quale giorno?
***kwa**-lay **joor**-no*

WOMEN		MEN		SHOES			
UK	EU	**UK**	EU	**UK**	EU	**UK**	EU
8	36	**36**	46	**2**	35	**7**	41
10	38	**38**	48	**3**	36	**8**	42
12	40	**40**	50	**4**	37	**9**	43
14	42	**42**	52	**5**	38	**10**	44
16	44	**44**	54	**6**	39	**11**	45
18	46	**46**	56	**7**	41	**12**	46

can I try this on?
posso provarlo?
__pos__-so pro-__var__-lo

it's too big
è troppo grande
e __trop__-po __gran__-day

it's too small
è troppo piccolo
e __trop__-po __peek__-ko-lo

it's too expensive
è troppo caro
e __trop__-po __ka__-ro

I'll take this one
prendo questo
__pren__-do __kwes__-to

I take a size ... shoe
porto il numero...
__por__-to eel __noo__-may-ro...

I like it
mi piace
mee pee-__a__-chay

have you a smaller one?
ha uno più piccolo?
a __oo__-no pee-__yoo__ __peek__-ko-lo

have you a larger one?
ha uno più grande?
a __oo__-no pee-__yoo__ __gran__-day

can you give me a discount?
mi può fare uno sconto?
mee pwo __fa__-ray __oo__-no __skon__-to

che taglia porta?
kay __tal__-ya __por__-ta
what size are you?

che numero di scarpe porta?
kay __noo__-may-ro dee __skar__-pay __por__-ta
what shoe size do you take?

SHOPPING – food

PANIFICIO	BAKER'S	**SUPERMERCATO**	SUPERMARKET
MACELLERIA	BUTCHER'S	**ALIMENTARI**	GROCER'S

Most towns will have a market at least one day a week where you can buy fresh fruit, vegetables and other local produce. They are usually open from early morning till about 1.30pm. The price of food is fixed, but you may be able to bargain for other goods.

where can I buy...?
dove posso comprare...?
*do-vay **pos**-so kom-**pra**-ray...*

fruit
la frutta
*la **froot**-ta*

bread
il pane
*eel **pa**-nay*

milk
il latte
*eel **lat**-tay*

where is the supermarket?
dov'è il supermercato?
*doh-**ve** eel **soo**-per-mer-**ka**-to*

where is the market?
dov'è il mercato?
*doh-**ve** eel mer-**ka**-to*

when is the market?
quando c'è il mercato?
***kwan**-do che eel mer-**ka**-to*

it's me next
tocca me
***tok**-ka me*

that's enough
basta così
bas**-ta ko-**zee

6 bread rolls
sei panini
*say pa-**nee**-nee*

a ciabatta
una ciabatta
***oo**-na cha-**bat**-ta*

a litre of...
un litro di...
*oon **lee**-tro dee...*

milk
latte
***lat**-tay*

beer
birra
***beer**-ra*

mineral water
acqua minerale
***ak**-wa mee-nay-**ra**-lay*

a bottle of...
una bottiglia di...
***oo**-na bot-**teel**-ya dee...*

wine
vino
***vee**-no*

still water
acqua naturale
***ak**-wa na-too-**ra**-lay*

sparkling water
acqua gassata
***ak**-wa gas-**za**-ta*

a can of...
una lattina di...
***oo**-na lat-**tee**-na dee...*

coke
coca
***ko**-ka*

tonic water
acqua tonica
***ak**-wa **to**-nee-ka*

beer
birra
***beer**-ra*

4 oz of... *(approx.)*
un etto di...
*oon **et**-to dee...*

salami
salami
*sa-**la**-mee*

grated parmesan
parmigiano grattugiato
*par-mee-**ja**-no grat-too-**ja**-to*

cooked ham
prosciutto cotto
*pro-**shoot**-to **kot**-to*

Parma ham
prosciutto crudo
*pro-**shoot**-to **kroo**-do*

half a pound of... *(approx.)*
due etti e mezzo di...
***doo**-ay **et**-tee ay **med**-zo dee...*

butter
burro
***boor**-ro*

cheese
formaggio
*for-**mad**-jo*

a kilo of...
un chilo di...
*oon **kee**-lo dee...*

potatoes
patate
*pa-**ta**-tay*

apples
mele
***may**-lay*

two slices of pizza
due fette di pizza
***doo**-ay **fet**-tay dee **peet**-sa*

three slices of focaccia
tre fette di focaccia
*tray **fet**-tay dee fo-**ka**-cha*

a portion of...
una porzione di...
***oo**-na ports-**yo**-nay dee...*

Russian salad
insalata russa
*een-sa-**la**-ta **roos**-sa*

lasagne
lasagne
*la-**zan**-yay*

a packet of...
un pacchetto di...
*oon pak-**ket**-to dee...*

biscuits
biscotti
*bee-**skot**-tee*

sugar
zucchero
***tsook**-ke-ro*

a tin of...
una scatola di...
***oo**-na **ska**-to-la dee...*

tomatoes
pelati
*pay-**la**-tee*

peas
piselli
*pee-**zel**-lee*

a jar of...
un vaso di...
*oon **va**-zo dee...*

honey
miele
*mee-**ay**-lay*

olives
olive
*oo-**lee**-vay*

mi dica?
*mee **dee**-ka*
can I help you?

altro?
*al-**tro***
anything else?

è tutto?
*e **toot**-to*
is that everything?

SIGHTSEEING

AZIENDA DI TURISMO TOURIST OFFICE

Local tourist offices can provide free maps, help with booking accommodation, and advise on attractions and excursions. Museum opening hours are very variable so it is best to check before you visit. Churches open early in the morning and usually close at noon for three or four hours, opening again from about 4-7pm. Visitors should observe a strict dress code: skirts and shorts should be below the knee; torsos and upper arms should also be covered.

where is the tourist office?
dov'è l'ufficio turistico?
*do-**ve** loof-**fee**-cho too-**rees**-tee-ko*

we want to visit...
vogliamo visitare...
*vol-**ya**-mo vee-zee-**ta**-ray...*

do you have a town guide?
ha una guida della città?
*a **oo**-na **gwee**-da **del**-la cheet-**ta***

we want to go to...
vogliamo andare a...
*vol-**ya**-mo an-**da**-ray a...*

when does it leave?
quando parte?
***kwan**-do **par**-tay*

how much is it to get in?
quanto costa l'ingresso?
***kwan**-to **kos**-ta leen-**gres**-so*

is it open to the public?
è aperto al pubblico?
*e a-**payr**-to al poob-**blee**-ko*

have you any leaflets?
ha degli opuscoli?
*a **del**-yee o-**poos**-ko-lee*

in English
in inglese
*een een-**glay**-zay*

are there any excursions?
ci sono delle gite?
*chee **so**-no **del**-lay **jee**-tay*

where does it leave from?
da dove parte?
*da **do**-vay **par**-tay*

BEACH

VIETATO IL BAGNO	NO SWIMMING
VIETATO TUFFARSI	NO DIVING
PERICOLO	DANGER

*At popular beaches you may be able to hire cabins, beach umbrellas and deck chairs. Many have a bar on site and are patrolled by a lifeguard (**bagnino**). A red flag means it is unsafe to swim in the sea. Most lakes and some beach resorts have facilities for watersports.*

can you recommend a quiet beach?
ci può consigliare una spiaggia tranquilla?
*chee pwo kon-seel-**ya**-ray **oo**-na spee-**ad**-ja tran-**kweel**-la*

is there a swimming pool?
c'è una piscina?
*che **oo**-na pee-**shee**-na*

can we swim in the lake?
si può fare il bagno nel lago?
*see pwo **fa**-ray eel **ban**-yo nel **la**-go*

is the water clean?
l'acqua è pulita?
***lak**-wa e poo-**lee**-ta*

is the water deep?
l'acqua è profonda?
***lak**-wa e pro-**fon**-da*

is the water cold?
l'acqua è fredda?
***lak**-wa e **fred**-da*

is it dangerous?
c'è pericolo?
*che pe-**ree**-ko-lo*

are there currents?
ci sono delle correnti?
*chee **so**-no **del**-lay kor-**ren**-tee*

where can we...?
dove si può...?
***do**-vay see pwo...*

windsurf
fare il surfing
***fa**-ray eel surfing*

waterski
fare lo sci nautico
***fa**-ray lo shee **now**-tee-ko*

hire a beach umbrella
noleggiare un ombrellone
*no-led-**ja**-ray oon om-brel-**lo**-nay*

SPORT

Most tourist offices have information on local sports facilities.

where can we...?
dove si può...?
***do**-vay see pwo...*

play tennis
giocare a tennis
*jo-**ka**-ray a **ten**-nees*

play golf
giocare a golf
*jo-**ka**-ray a golf*

hire bikes
noleggiare le biciclette
*no-led-**ja**-ray lay bee-chee-**kle**-tay*

go fishing
pescare
*pes-**ka**-ray*

go riding
andare a cavallo
*an-**da**-ray a ka-**val**-lo*

how much is it...?
quanto costa...?
***kwan**-to **kos**-ta...*

per hour
all'ora
*al-**lo**-ra*

per day
al giorno
*al **jor**-no*

how do I book a court?
come si prenota il campo da tennis?
***ko**-may see pray-**no**-ta eel **kam**-po da **ten**-nees*

do I need a fishing permit?
devo avere una licenza da pesca?
***day**-vo a-**vay**-ray **oo**-na lee-**chen**-za da **pes**-ka*

can I hire...?
posso noleggiare...?
***pos**-so no-led-**ja**-ray...*

raquets
le racchette
*lay rak-**ket**-tay*

golf clubs
le mazze da golf
*lay **mat**-say da golf*

is there a football match?
c'è una partita di calcio?
*che **oo**-na par-**tee**-ta dee **kal**-cho*

where is there a sports shop?
dove c'è un negozio di articoli sportivi?
***da**-vay che oon nay-**gots**-yo dee ar-**tee**-ko-lee spor-**tee**-vee*

SKIING

The best known ski-resorts are in the Dolomites but there are also skiing facilities in Sicily and the Apennines.

can I hire skis?
posso noleggiare gli sci?
__pos__-so no-led-__ja__-ray lyee shee

how much is a pass?
quanto costa lo skipass?
__kwan__-to __kos__-ta lo skee-pass

I'm a beginner
sono un principiante
__so__-no oon preen-chee-pee-__an__-tay

which is an easy run?
qual è la pista facile?
kwal e la __pees__-ta __fa__-chee-lay

what is the snow like today?
com'è la neve oggi?
ko-__me__ la __nay__-vay __od__-jee

is there a map of the ski runs?
avete una piantina delle piste?
a-__vay__-tay __oo__-na pee-an-__tee__-na __day__-lay __pees__-tay

my skis are...
i miei sci sono...
ee mee-__ay__-ee shee __so__-no...

too long
troppo lunghi
__trop__-po __loon__-gee

too short
troppo corti
__trop__-po __kor__-tee

my bindings are...
i miei attacchi sono...
ee mee-__ay__-ee at-__tak__-kee __so__-no...

too loose
troppo larghi
__trop__-po __lar__-gee

too tight
troppo stretti
__trop__-po __stret__-tee

where can we go cross-country skiing?
dove si può andare a fare lo sci di fondo?
__do__-vay see pwo an-__da__-ray a __fa__-ray lo shee dee __fon__-do

quale numero di scarponi porta?
__kwa__-lay __noo__-may-ro dee skar-__po__-nee __por__-ta
what is your boot size?

c'è pericolo di valanghe
che pe-__ree__-ko-lo dee va-__lan__-gay
there is danger of avalanches

NIGHTLIFE – popular

You can buy tickets for rock concerts at record stores see publicity for details. Note that the price you pay to get into clubs in Italy normally includes the cost of your first drink. The final phrase is just in case you are asked to sing at a karaoke, now becoming very popular in Italy.

what is there to do at night?
che cosa c'è da fare di sera?
*kay **ko**-za che da **fa**-ray dee **say**-ra*

which is a good bar?
qual è un bel bar?
kwal e oon bel bar

which is a good disco?
qual è una bella discoteca?
*kwal e **oo**-na **bel**-la dee-sko-**te**-ka*

where do local people go at night?
dove va la gente del posto di sera?
***do**-vay va la **jen**-tay del **pos**-to dee **say**-ra*

are there any concerts?
ci sono dei concerti?
*chee **so**-no **day**-ee kon-**cher**-tee*

no thanks, I don't want to
no grazie, non voglio
*no **grat**-see-ay non **vol**-yo*

is it in a safe area?
è in una zona sicura?
***e** een oona **zo**-na see-**koo**-ra*

is it expensive?
è caro?
*e **ka**-ro*

I sing badly
canto male
***kan**-to **ma**-lay*

vuoi ballare?
***vwo**-ee bal-**la**-ray*
do you want to dance?

come ti chiami?
***ko**-may tee kee-**a**-mee*
what's your name?

mi chiamo Marco
*mee kee-**a**-mo **mar**-ko*
I'm Marco

A list of cultural events should be available from the tourist office, and it's always worth checking the local newspaper. Opera lovers should book their seats well in advance, preferably some months before the performance. Theatre bookings are usually made in person at the box office rather than over the phone.

is there a list of cultural events?
c'è un programma degli spettacoli?
*che oon pro-**gram**-ma **del**-yee spet-**ta**-ko-lee*

are there any local festivals?
ci sono delle feste locali?
*chee **so**-no **del**-lay **fes**-tay lo-**ka**-lee*

we'd like to go...
vogliamo andare...
*vol-**ya**-mo an-**da**-ray...*

to the theatre
a teatro
*a tay-**a**-tro*

to the opera
all'opera
*al-**lo**-pay-ra*

to the ballet
al balletto
*al bal-**let**-to*

to a concert
a un concerto
*a oon kon-**cher**-to*

what's on?
che cosa c'è?
*kay **ko**-za che*

do I need to book?
devo prenotare?
***day**-vo pray-no-**ta**-ray*

how much are the tickets?
quanto costano i biglietti?
***kwan**-to **kos**-ta-no ee beel-**yet**-tee*

2 tickets...
due biglietti...
***doo**-ay beel-**yet**-tee...*

for tonight
per stasera
*payr sta-**say**-ra*

for tomorrow night
per domani sera
*payr do-**ma**-nee **say**-ra*

when does the performance end?
a che ora finisce lo spettacolo?
*a kay **o**-ra fee-**nee**-shay lo spet-**ta**-ko-lo*

HOTEL

CAMERE VACANCIES (B & B)

Tourist offices will be able to give you information on accommodation and help you make a booking.

have you a room for tonight?
avete una camera per stanotte?
*a-**vay**-tay **oo**-na **ka**-may-ra payr sta-**not**-tay*

a single room
una camera singola
*oo-na **ka**-may-ra seen-**go**-la*

a double room
una camera doppia
*oo-na **ka**-may-ra **dop**-ya*

a family room
una camera per una famiglia
*oo-na **ka**-may-ra payr **oo**-na fa-**meel**-ya*

with bathroom
con bagno
*kon **ban**-yo*

with shower
con doccia
*kon **do**-cha*

how much is it?
quanto costa?
***kwan**-to **kos**-ta*

is breakfast included?
comprende la colazione?
*kom-**pren**-day la ko-lats-**yo**-nay*

I booked a room
ho prenotato una camera
*o pray-no-**ta**-to **oo**-na **ka**-may-ra*

my name is...
mi chiamo...
*mee kee-**a**-mo...*

I'd like to see the room
vorrei vedere la camera
*vor-**ray**-ee ve-**day**-ray la **ka**-may-ra*

is there anything cheaper?
c'è qualcosa di meno caro?
*che kwal-**ko**-za dee **may**-no **ka**-ro*

what time is...?
a che ora c'è...?
*a kay **o**-ra che...*

breakfast
la colazione
*la ko-lats-**yo**-nay*

dinner
la cena
*la **chey**-na*

we'll be back late tonight
ritorniamo tardi stasera
*ree-tor-nee-**a**-mo **tar**-dee sta-**say**-ra*

the key, please
la chiave, per favore
*la kee-**a**-vay payr fa-**vo**-ray*

can you keep these in the safe?
può tenere questi nella cassaforte?
*pwo te-**ne**-ray **kwes**-tee **nel**-la kas-sa-**for**-tay*

come in!
avanti!
*a-**van**-tee*

please come back later
ritorni più tardi per favore
*ree-**tor**-nee pee-**yoo** **tar**-dee payr fa-**vo**-ray*

can we have breakfast in our room?
possiamo avere la colazione in camera?
*pos-see-**a**-mo a-**vay**-ray la ko-lats-**yo**-nay een **ka**-may-ra*

please bring...
per favore mi porti...
*payr fa-**vo**-ray mee **por**-tee...*

ashtray
un portacenere
*oon por-ta-**chay**-nay-ray*

soap
il sapone
*eel sa-**po**-nay*

towels
degli asciugamani
***del**-yee a-shoo-ga-**ma**-nee*

a glass
un bicchiere
*oon beek-**ye**-ray*

please clean...
può pulire per favore...
*pwo poo-**lee**-ray payr fa-**vo**-ray...*

my room
la camera
*la **ka**-may-ra*

the bathroom
il bagno
*eel **ban**-yo*

I would like a wake-up call...
vorrei la sveglia...
*vor-**ray**-ee la **svel**-ya...*

at 7 o'clock
alle sette
***al**-lay **set**-tay*

is there a laundry service?
c'è il servizio lavanderia?
*che eel ser-**veets**-yo la-van-day-**ree**-a*

I'm leaving tomorrow
parto domani
***par**-to do-**ma**-nee*

please prepare the bill
ci prepari il conto
*chee pray-**pa**-ree eel **kon**-to*

SELF-CATERING

The voltage in Italy is 220, so if you plan to take any electrical appliances, such as an electric kettle, with you, make sure you have an adaptor.

which is the key for this door?
qual è la chiave di questa porta?
*kwal e la kee-**a**-vay dee **kwes**-ta **por**-ta*

where are the fuses?
dove sono i fusibili?
***do**-vay **so**-no ee foo-**zee**-bee-lee*

can you show us how this works?
può farci vedere come funziona questo?
*pwo **far**-chee ve-**day**-ray **ko**-may foonts-**yo**-na **kwes**-to*

how does ... work?
come funziona...?
***ko**-may foonts-**yo**-na...*

the dishwasher
la lavastoviglia
*la la-va-sto-**veel**-ya*

the washing machine
la lavatrice
*la la-va-**tree**-chay*

the waterheater
lo scaldabagno
*lo **skal**-da-**ban**-yo*

the cooker
la cucina
*la koo-**chee**-na*

whom do I speak to if there are any problems?
con chi devo parlare se ci sono dei problemi?
*kon kee **day**-vo par-**la**-ray say chee **so**-no **day**-ee prob-**lay**-mee*

where do I put the rubbish?
dove lascio la spazzatura?
***do**-vay **la**-sho la spat-sa-**too**-ra*

the gas has run out
è finito il gas
*e fee-**nee**-to eel gaz*

what do I do?
che cosa devo fare?
*kay **ko**-za **day**-vo **fa**-ray*

CAMPING & CARAVANNING

Off-site camping is allowed in Italy provided you have the permission of the landowner, but you are not allowed to camp in national parks or state forests. A car towing a caravan or trailer must not exceed 50 kph in built-up areas, 70 kph outside built-up areas and 80 kph on motorways.

we're looking for a campsite
cerchiamo un campeggio
*cher-kee-**a**-mo oon kam-**ped**-jo*

have you a list of campsites?
ha una lista dei campeggi?
*a **oo**-na **lees**-ta **day**-ee kam-**ped**-jee*

have you any vacancies?
avete dei posti?
*a-**vay**-tee **day**-ee **pos**-tee*

how much is it per night?
quanto costa per notte?
***kwan**-to **kos**-ta payr **not**-tay*

we'd like to stay for ... nights
vorremmo restare per ... notti
*vor-**rem**-mo res-**ta**-ray payr ... **not**-tee*

is the campsite sheltered?
il campeggio è riparato?
*eel kam-**ped**-jo e ree-pa-**ra**-to*

can we have a more sheltered site?
possiamo avere un posto più riparato?
*pos-see-**a**-mo a-**vay**-ray oon **pos**-to pee-**yoo** ree-pa-**ra**-to*

this site is very muddy
questo posto è molto fangoso
***kwes**-to **pos**-to e **mol**-to fan-**go**-zo*

is there another site?
c'è un altro posto?
*che oon **al**-tro **pos**-to*

can we park our caravan here overnight?
possiamo mettere la nostra roulotte qui per la notte?
*pos-see-**a**-mo **met**-te-ray la **nos**-tra roo-**lot** kwee payr la **not**-tay*

can we put our tent here?
possiamo mettere la tenda qui?
*pos-see-**a**-mo **met**-te-ray la **ten**-da kwee*

CHILDREN

Children are well catered for in Italy and are welcome everywhere including bars and restaurants. There are many reductions available on transport, in hotels, etc. Note that when travelling by car, children under 4 must have a suitable restraint system. Children between 4 and 12 must have a suitable restraint system when travelling in the front seat.

a child's ticket
un biglietto ridotto
*oon beel-**yet**-to ree-**dot**-to*

he/she is ... years old
ha ... anni
*a ... **an**-nee*

is there a reduction for children?
c'è una riduzione per bambini?
*che **oo**-na ree-doots-**yo**-nay payr bam-**bee**-nee*

is there a children's menu?
c'è un menù per bambini?
*che oon me-**noo** payr bam-**bee**-nee*

do you have...?
avete...?
*a-**vay**-tay...*

a high chair
un seggiolone
*oon sed-jo-**lo**-nay*

a cot
un lettino
*oon let-**tee**-no*

is it ok to bring children?
si può portare i bambini?
*see pwo por-**ta**-ray ee bam-**bee**-nee*

what is there for children to do?
che cosa c'è da fare per i bambini?
*kay **ko**-za che da **fa**-ray payr ee bam-**bee**-nee*

is it safe for children?
va bene per bambini?
*va **be**-nay payr bam-**bee**-nee*

is it dangerous
c'è pericolo?
*che pe-**ree**-ko-lo*

I have two children
ho due figli
*o **doo**-ay **feel**-yee*

do you have children?
ha dei figli?
*a **day**-ee **feel**-yee*

Provision for the disabled has been low in the past but is gradually improving. Some churches and museums will have access ramps or lifts, but many do not. Many Intercity trains have facilities for the disabled.

is it possible to visit ... with a wheelchair?
si può visitare ... con la sedia a rotelle?
*see pwo vee-zee-**ta**-ray kon la **sed**-ya a ro-**tel**-lay*

do you have toilets for the disabled?
ci sono le toilette per i disabili?
*chee **so**-no lay twa-**let** payr ee dee-**za**-bee-lee*

I need a bedroom on the ground floor
ho bisogno di una camera al pian terreno
*o bee-**zon**-yo dee **oo**-na ka-**may**-ra al **pee**-an ter-**ray**-no*

is there a lift?
c'è l'ascensore?
*che la-shen-**so**-ray*

where is the lift?
dov'è l'ascensore?
*do-**ve** la-shen-**so**-ray*

are there many steps?
ci sono tanti gradini?
*chee **so**-no **tan**-tee gra-**dee**-nee*

is there an entrance for wheelchairs?
c'è l'accesso per la sedia a rotelle?
*che la-**ches**-so payr la **sed**-ya a ro-**tel**-lay*

is there a place on this train for a wheelchair?
c'è un posto su questo treno per una sedia a rotelle?
*che oon **pos**-to soo **kwes**-to **tray**-no payr **oo**-na **sed**-ya a ro-**tel**-lay*

is there a reduction for the disabled?
c'è una riduzione per i disabili?
*che **oo**-na ree-doots-**yo**-nay payr ee dee-**za**-bee-lee*

EXCHANGE VISITORS

*These phrases are intended for families hosting Italian-speaking visitors. We have used the informal **tu** form for these phrases.*

did you sleep well?
hai dormito bene?
***a**-ee dor-**mee**-to **be**-nay*

would you like to take a shower?
vuoi fare la doccia?
***vwo**-ee **fa**-ray la **do**-cha*

what would you like for breakfast?
che cosa prendi per colazione?
*kay **ko**-za **pren**-dee payr ko-lats-**yo**-nay*

what would you like to eat/drink?
che cosa vuoi da mangiare/bere?
*kay **ko**-za **vwo**-ee da man-**ja**-ray/**be**-ray*

do you eat...?
mangi...?
***man**-jee...*

do you drink...?
bevi...?
***be**-vee...*

what would you like to do today?
che cosa vuoi fare oggi?
*kay **ko**-za **vwo**-ee **fa**-ray od-jee*

would you like to go shopping?
vuoi andare a fare la spesa?
***vwo**-ee an-**da**-ray a **fa**-ray la **spay**-za*

I will pick you up at...
vengo a prenderti alle...
***ven**-go a **pren**-der-tee **al**-lay...*

did you enjoy yourself?
ti sei divertito(a)?
*tee **say**-ee dee-ver-**tee**-to(a)*

take care
sta attento(a)
*sta at-**ten**-to(a)*

please be back by...
devi essere a casa per le...
***day**-vee **es**-say-ray a **ka**-za payr lay...*

we'll be in bed when you get back
saremo a letto quando ritorni
*sa-**ray**-mo a **let**-to **kwan**-do ree-**tor**-nee*

EXCHANGE VISITORS

*These phrases are intended for those people staying with Italian-speaking families. We have used the formal **lei** form for these phrases.*

I like...
mi piace...
*me pee-**a**-chay...*

I don't like...
non mi piace...
*non mee pee-**a**-chay*

that was delicious
era buonissimo
***ay**-ra bwo-**nees**-see-mo*

may I phone home?
posso telefonare a casa?
***pos**-so te-le-fo-**na**-ray a **ka**-za*

may I make a local call?
posso fare una telefonata?
***pos**-so **fa**-ray **oo**-na te-le-fo-**na**-ta*

can I have a key?
posso avere la chiave di casa?
***pos**-so a-**vay**-ray la kee-**a**-vay dee **ka**-za*

can you take me by car?
mi può portare in macchina?
*mee pw**o** por-**ta**-ray een **ma**-kee-na*

can I borrow...?
mi può prestare...?
*mee pw**o** pres-**ta**-ray...*

an iron
un ferro da stiro
*oon **fer**-ro da **stee**-ro*

a hairdryer
un fon
oon fon

what time do I have to get up?
a che ora devo alzarmi?
*a kay **o**-ra **day**-vo alt-**sar**-mee*

please would you call me at...?
per favore mi chiama alle...?
*payr fa-**vo**-ray mee kee-**a**-ma **al**-lay...*

whom are you staying with?
con chi sta?
kon kee sta

I'm staying with...
sono ospite di...
***so**-no **os**-pee-tay dee...*

how long are you staying?
quanto tempo resta?
***kwan**-to **tem**-po **res**-tah*

I'm leaving in a week
parto tra una settimana
***par**-to tra **oo**-na set-tee-**ma**-na*

thanks for everything
grazie di tutto
*grat-**see**-ay dee **toot**-to*

I've had a great time
mi sono divertito(a) proprio
*mee **so**-no dee-ver-**tee**-to(a) **pro**-pree-o*

PROBLEMS

can you help me?
può aiutarmi?
*pwo a-yoo-**tar**-mee*

do you speak English?
parla inglese?
***par**-la een-**glay**-zay*

I'm lost
mi sono smarrito(a)
*mee **so**-no smar-**ree**-to(a)*

I'm late
sono in ritardo
***so**-no een ree-**tar**-do*

I don't speak Italian
non parlo italiano
*non **par**-lo ee-tal-lee-**a**-no*

does anyone speak English?
c'è qualcuno che parla inglese?
*che kwal-**koo**-no kay **par**-la een-**glay**-zay*

how do I get to...?
come si fa per andare a...?
***ko**-may see fa payr an-**da**-ray a...*

I need to get to...
devo andare a...
***day**-vo an-**da**-ray a...*

I've missed...
ho perso...
*o **per**-so...*

my plane
l'aereo
*la-**e**-ray-o*

my connection
la coincidenza
*la ko-een-chee-**dent**-sa*

I've lost...
ho perso...
*o **per**-so...*

my money
i soldi
*ee-**sol**-dee*

my passport
il passaporto
*eel pas-sa-**por**-to*

my camera
la macchina fotografica
*la **ma**-kee-na fo-to-**gra**-fee-ka*

my keys
le chiavi
*lay kee-**a**-vee*

my suitcase isn't here
non c'è la mia valigia
*non che la **mee**-a va-**lee**-ja*

I have no money
non ho soldi
*non o **sol**-dee*

I've left my bag in...
ho lasciato la mia borsa nel/nella...
*o lash-**a**-to la **mee**-a **bor**-sa nel/**nel**-la...*

on the coach
sul pullman
*sool **pool**-man*

leave me alone!
mi lasci in pace!
*mee **la**-shee een **pa**-chay*

go away!
se ne vada!
*say nay **va**-da*

the light
la luce
la ***loo****-chay*

the toilet
il water
eel ***va****-ter*

the telephone
il telefono
*eel te-****le****-fo-no*

the heating
il riscaldamento
*eel ree-skal-da-****men****-to*

...doesn't work
...non funziona
*...non foonts-****yo****-na*

the room is dirty
la camera è sporca
*la ka-****may****-ra e* ***spor****-ka*

the bath is dirty
il bagno è sporco
eel ***ban****-yo e* ***spor****-ko*

I don't like the room
non mi piace la camera
*non mee pee-****a****-chay la ka-****may****-ra*

it's too noisy
c'è troppo rumore
che ***trop****-po roo-****mo****-ray*

I didn't order this
non ho ordinato questo
*non o or-dee-****na****-to* ***kwes****-to*

I want to complain
voglio fare un reclamo
vol*-yo* ***fa****-ray oon rek-****la****-mo*

I want a refund
voglio un rimborso
vol*-yo oon reem-****bor****-so*

we've been waiting for a very long time
aspettiamo da molto
*as-pet-tee-****a****-mo da* ***mol****-to*

we're in a hurry
abbiamo fretta
*ab-bee-****a****-mo* ***fret****-ta*

there is a mistake
c'è un errore
*che oon er-****ro****-ray*

this is broken
questo è rotto
kwes*-to e* ***rot****-to*

can you repair it?
può ripararlo?
*pwo ree-pa-****rar****-lo*

EMERGENCIES

CARABINIERI / POLIZIA	POLICE
VIGILI DEL FUOCO	FIRE BRIGADE
PRONTO SOCCORSO	CASUALTY DEPARTMENT

The number for all emergency services is 113.

help!
aiuto!
*a-**yoo**-to*

can you help me?
può aiutarmi?
*pwo a-yoo-**tar**-mee*

there's been an accident
c'è stato un incidente
*che **sta**-to oon een-chee-**den**-tay*

someone is injured
qualcuno si è fatto male
*kwal-**koo**-no see e **fat**-to **ma**-lay*

please call...
per favore chiamate...
*payr fa-**vo**-ray kee-a-**ma**-tay...*

the police
la polizia
*la po-leet-**see**-a*

an ambulance
un'ambulanza
*oon am-boo-**lant**-sa*

he was going too fast
andava troppo forte
*an-**da**-va **trop**-po **for**-tay*

that man keeps following me
quell'uomo mi segue
*kwel **wo**-mo mee **seg**-way*

where's the police station?
dov'è la questura?
***do**-vay la kwes-**too**-ra*

I want to report a theft
voglio denunciare un furto
***vol**-yo den-oon-**cha**-ray oon **foor**-to*

I've been robbed
mi hanno derubato
*mee **an**-no de-roo-**ba**-to*

I've been attacked
mi hanno assalito
*mee **an**-no as-sa-**lee**-to*

my car has been broken into
hanno svaligiato la mia macchina
***an**-no sva-lee-**ja**-to la **mee**-a **ma**-kee-na*

my car has been stolen
mi hanno rubato la macchina
*mee **an**-no roo-**ba**-to la **ma**-kee-na*

I've been raped
mi hanno violentata
*mee **an**-no vee-o-len-**ta**-ta*

I need a report for my insurance
ho bisogno di un verbale per la mia assicurazione
*o bee-**zon**-yo dee oon ver-**ba**-lay payr la **mee**-a as-see-koo-rats-**yo**-nay*

how much is the fine?
quant'è la multa?
*kwan-**te** la **mool**-ta*

where do I pay it?
dove devo pagarla?
***do**-vay **day**-vo pa-**gar**-la*

I would like to phone the British Consulate
vorrei telefonare il Consolato Britannico
*vo-**ray**-ee te-le-fo-**na**-ray eel kon-so-**la**-to bree-**tan**-nee-ko*

I have no money
sono senza soldi
***so**-no **sent**-sa **sol**-dee*

arriviamo
*ar-ree-vee-**a**-mo*
we're on our way

HEALTH

FARMACIA	PHARMACY
OSPEDALE	HOSPITAL
PRONTO SOCCORSO	ACCIDENT AND EMERGENCY DEPARTMENT

EU citizens are entitled to free emergency care in Italy. You should take with you form E111, completed and stamped at a post office in the UK before your trip. However you will need to take out a medical insurance policy to cover non-emergency treatment.

have you something for...?
può darmi qualcosa per...
*pwo **dar**-mee kwal-**ko**-za payr...*

car sickness
il mal d'auto
*eel mal **dow**-to*

diarrhoea
la diarrea
*la dee-ar-**ray**-a*

is it safe to give children?
va bene per i bambini?
*va **be**-nay payr ee bam-**bee**-nee*

I feel ill
mi sento male
*mee **sen**-to **ma**-lay*

I need a doctor
ho bisogno di un medico
*o bee-**zon**-yo dee oon **me**-dee-ko*

my son/my daughter is ill
mio figlio/mia figlia non sta bene
__mee__-o __feel__-yo/__mee__-a __feel__-ya non sta __be__-nay

(s)he has a temperature
ha la febbre
*a la **feb**-bray*

I'm on this medication
sto prendendo queste medicine
*sto pren-**den**-do **kwes**-tay me-dee-**chee**-nay*

I have high blood pressure
ho la pressione alta
*o la pres-**yo**-nay **al**-ta*

I'm diabetic
sono diabetico(a)
__so__-no dee-a-__be__-tee-ko(a)

I'm pregnant
sono incinta
__so__-no een-__cheen__-ta

I'm on the pill
prendo la pillola
__pren__-do la __peel__-lo-la

I'm allergic to penicillin
sono allergico(a) alla penicillina
so-no al-ler-jee-ko(a) al-la pe-nee-cheel-lee-na

my blood group is...
il mio gruppo sanguigno è...
eel mee-o groop-po san-gween-yo e...

I'm breastfeeding
sto allattando al seno
sto al-lat-tan-do al say-no

is it safe to take?
si può prenderlo?
see pwo pren-der-lo

will he/she have to go to hospital?
deve andare in opsedale?
day-vay an-da-ray een o-spe-da-lay

I need to go to casualty
devo andare al pronto soccorso
day-vo an-da-ray al pron-to sok-kor-so

where is the hospital?
dov'è l'ospedale?
do-ve los-pe-da-lay

when are visiting hours?
qual è l'orario di visita?
kwal e lo-rar-yo dee vee-zee-ta

which ward?
quale riparto?
kwal-lay ree-par-to

I need a dentist
ho bisogno di un dentista
o bee-zon-yo dee oon den-tee-sta

I have toothache
ho mal di denti
o mal dee den-tee

the filling has come out
è uscita l'otturazione
e oo-shee-ta lot-too-rats-yo-nay

I have an abscess
ho un ascesso
o oon a-shes-so

it hurts
fa male
fa ma-lay

can you repair my dentures?
può riparare la mia dentiera?
pwo ree-pa-ra-ray la mee-a den-tee-e-ra

do I have to pay now?
devo pagare subito?
day-vo pa-ga-ray soo-bee-to

BUSINESS

Most firms shut down for the month of August when Italians take their main holiday. Beaches can be very crowded.

I am...
sono...
***so**-no...*

here's my card
ecco il mio bigiletto da visita
***ek**-ko eel **mee**-o beel-**yet**-to da **vee**-zee-ta*

I'm from the Smith Company
sono della ditta Smith
***so**-no **del**-la **deet**-ta Smith*

I'd like to arrange an appointment
vorrei fissare un appuntamento
*vor-**ray**-ee fees-**sa**-ray oon ap-poon-ta-**men**-to*

with Mr/Ms...
con il Signor/la Signora...
*kon eel seen-**yor**/la seen-**yo**-ra...*

for April 4th at 11 o'clock
per il quattro aprile alle undici
*payr eel **kwat**-tro a-**pree**-lay **al**-lay **oon**-dee-chee*

can we meet at a restaurant?
possiamo incontrarci in un ristorante?
*pos-see-**a**-mo een-kon-**trar**-chee een oon rees-to-**ran**-tay*

I will send a fax to confirm
mando un fax per confermare
***man**-do oon fax payr kon-fayr-**ma**-ray*

I'm staying at Hotel...
sono all'Hotel...
***so**-no al-lo-**tel**...*

how do I get to your office?
come si arriva al suo ufficio?
***ko**-may see ar-**ree**-va al **soo**-o oo-**fee**-cho*

here is some information about my company
ecco delle informazioni sulla mia ditta
***ek**-ko **day**-lay een-for-mats-**yo**-nay **sool**-la **mee**-a **deet**-ta*

I have an appointment with...
ho un appuntamento con...
*o oon ap-poon-ta-**men**-to kon...*

at ... o'clock
alle...
***al**-lay...*

delighted to meet you!
molto piacere!
***mol**-to pee-a-**chay**-ray*

my Italian isn't very good
parlo poco l'italiano
***par**-lo **po**-ko lee-tal-ee-**a**-no*

what is the name of the managing director
come si chiama il direttore?
***ko**-may see kee-**a**-ma eel dee-ret-**to**-ray*

I would like some information about your company
vorrei delle informazioni sulla sua ditta
*vor-**ray**-ee **del**-lay een-for-mats-**yo**-nee **sool**-la **soo**-a **deet**-ta*

do you have a press office?
avete l'ufficio stampa?
*a-**vay**-tay loof-**fee**-cho **stam**-pa*

I need an interpreter
ho bisogno di un interprete
*o bee-**zon**-yo dee oon een-**ter**-pray-tay*

can you photocopy this for me?
mi può fare una fotocopia?
*mee pwo **fa**-ray **oo**-na fo-to-**ko**-pee-a*

is there a business centre?
c'è un centro per gli affari?
*che oon **chen**-tro payr lyee af-**fa**-ree*

ha un appuntamento?
*a oon ap-poon-ta-**men**-to*
do you have an appointment?

a che ora?
*a kay **o**-ra*
at what time?

PHONING

*Coin-operated payphones take 200- and 500-lire coins, and older payphones take **gettoni** (tokens) which you can buy from post offices, tobacconists, bars and newspaper kiosks for 200 lire each. However card-operated machines are becoming much more common – you can buy phonecards from the same outlets which sell **gettoni**. To call abroad, dial 00 before the country code. To call the UK, dial 00 44 then the area code without the first 0.*

a phonecard
una scheda telefonica
***oo**-na **skay**-da te-le-**fo**-nee-ka*

Mr Ponti, please
il signor Ponti, per favore
*eel seen-**yor** Ponti payr fa-**vo**-ray*

can I speak to...?
posso parlare con...?
***pos**-so par-**la**-ray kon...*

I'll call back later
richiamo più tardi
*ree-kee-**a**-mo pee-**yoo** **tar**-dee*

I want to make a phone call
vorrei fare una telefonata
*vor-**ray**-ee **fa**-ray **oo**-na te-le-**fon**-na-ta*

extension ..., please
interno ..., per favore
*een-**ter**-no ... payr fa-**vo**-ray*

this is Jim Brown
sono Jim Brown
***so**-no Jim Brown*

I'll call back tomorrow
richiamo domani
*ree-kee-**a**-mo do-**ma**-nee*

can I have an outside line, please
posso avere la linea, per favore
***pos**-so a-**vay**-ray la **lee**-nay-a payr fa-**vo**-ray*

pronto
***pron**-to*
hello

la linea è occupata
*la **lee**-nay-a e ok-koo-**pa**-ta*
it's engaged

vuole lasciare un messaggio?
***vwo**-lay la-**sha**-ray oon mes-**sad**-jo*
do you want to leave a message?

chi parla?
*kee **par**-la*
who is calling?

può richiamare più tardi?
*pwo ree-kee-a-**ma**-ray pee-**yoo** **tar**-dee*
can you call back later?

I want to send a fax
vorrei mandare un fax
*vor-**ray**-ee man-**da**-ray oon fax*

what's your fax number?
qual è il suo numero di fax?
*kwal e eel **soo**-o **noo**-may-ro dee fax*

please resend your fax
per favore ci rimandi il suo fax
*payr fa-**vo**-ray chee ree-**man**-dee eel **soo**-o fax*

your fax is constantly engaged
il suo fax è sempre occupato
*eel **soo**-o fax e **sem**-pray ok-koo-**pa**-to*

where can I send a fax from?
da dove posso mandare un fax?
*da **do**-vay **pos**-so man-**da**-ray oon fax*

did you get my fax?
ha ricevuto il mio fax?
*a ree-chay-**voo**-to eel **mee**-o fax*

I want to send an e-mail
vorrei mandare un e-mail
*vor-**ray**-ee man-**da**-ray oon **ee**-mail*

what's your e-mail address?
qual è il suo indirizzo per l'e-mail?
*kwal e eel **soo**-o een-dee-**reet**-so payr **lee**-mail*

did you get my e-mail?
ha ricevuto il mio e-mail?
*a ree-**chay**-voo-to eel **mee**-o **ee**-mail*

do you have a fax?
avete il fax?
*a-**vay**-tay eel fax*

I can't read it
non riesco a leggerlo
*non ree-**es**-ko a **led**-jer-lo*

il mio indirizzo per l'e-mail è...
*eel **mee**-yo een-dee-**reet**-so payr **lee**-mail...*
my e-mail address is...

NUMBERS

0	**zero**	***tsay**-ro*
1	**uno**	***oo**-no*
2	**due**	***doo**-ay*
3	**tre**	*tray*
4	**quattro**	***kwat**-tro*
5	**cinque**	***cheen**-kway*
6	**sei**	***say**-ee*
7	**sette**	***set**-tay*
8	**otto**	***ot**-to*
9	**nove**	***no**-vay*
10	**dieci**	*dee-**ay**-chee*
11	**undici**	***oon**-dee-chee*
12	**dodici**	***do**-dee-chee*
13	**tredici**	***tray**-dee-chee*
14	**quattordici**	*kwat-**tor**-dee-chee*
15	**quindici**	***kween**-dee-chee*
16	**sedici**	***say**-dee-chee*
17	**diciasette**	*dee-chas-**set**-tay*
18	**didiotto**	*dee-**chot**-to*
19	**diciannove**	*dee-chan-**no**-vay*
20	**venti**	***ven**-tee*
21	**ventuno**	*ven-**too**-no*
22	**ventidue**	*ven-tee-**doo**-ay*
30	**trenta**	***tren**-ta*
40	**quaranta**	*kwa-**ran**-ta*
50	**cinquanta**	*cheen-**kwan**-ta*
60	**sessanta**	*ses-**san**-ta*
70	**settanta**	*set-**tan**-ta*
80	**ottanta**	*ot-**tan**-ta*
90	**novanta**	*no-**van**-ta*
100	**cento**	***chen**-to*
110	**cento dieci**	*chent-to-dee-**ay**-chee*
500	**cinquecento**	*cheen-kway-**chen**-to*
1,000	**mille**	*meel-lay*
2,000	**duemila**	*doo-ay-**mee**-la*
1,000,000	**un milione**	*oon meel-**yo**-nay*

1st	**primo**	***pree**-mo*
2nd	**secondo**	*se-**kon**-do*
3rd	**terzo**	***tert**-so*
4th	**quarto**	***kwar**-to*
5th	**quinto**	***kween**-to*
6th	**sesto**	***ses**-to*
7th	**settimo**	***set**-tee-mo*
8th	**ottavo**	*ot-**ta**-vo*
9th	**nono**	***no**-no*
10th	**decimo**	***de**-chee-mo*

DAYS & MONTHS

Key words to look out for on timetables are ***feriale*** *meaning weekday (ie Mon-Sat) and* ***festivo*** *meaning Sundays and public holidays. Timetables vary according to whether they are* ***estivo*** *(summer) or* ***invernale*** *(winter).*

GENNAIO	JANUARY
FEBBRAIO	FEBRUARY
MARZO	MARCH
APRILE	APRIL
MAGGIO	MAY
GIUGNO	JUNE
LUGLIO	JULY
AGOSTO	AUGUST
SETTEMBRE	SEPTEMBER
OTTOBRE	OCTOBER
NOVEMBRE	NOVEMBER
DICEMBRE	DECEMBER

LUNEDÌ	MONDAY
MARTEDÌ	TUESDAY
MERCOLEDÌ	WEDNESDAY
GIOVEDÌ	THURSDAY
VENERDI	FRIDAY
SABATO	SATURDAY
DOMENICA	SUNDAY

what's the date?
qual è la data?
*kwal e la **da**-ta*

which day?
quale giorno?
***kwal**-lay **jor**-no*

which month?
quale mese?
***kwal**-lay **me**-zay*

it's the 5th of March 1998
è il cinque marzo millenovecentonovantotto
*e eel **cheen**-kway **mart**-so **meel**-lay-no-vay-**chen**-to-no-van-**tot**-to*

on Saturday
sabato
***sa**-ba-to*

on Saturdays
il sabato
*eel **sa**-ba-to*

every Saturday
ogni sabato
***on**-yee **sa**-ba-to*

this Saturday
questo sabato
***kwes**-to **sa**-ba-to*

next Saturday
sabato prossimo
***sa**-ba-to **pros**-see-mo*

last Saturday
sabato scorso
***sa**-ba-to **skor**-so*

TIME

Note that throughout Europe the 24-hour clock is used much more widely than in the UK.

excuse me, what time is it?
scusi, che ore sono?
***skoo**-zee kay **o**-ray **so**-no*

am
di mattina
*dee mat-**tee**-na*

pm
di pomeriggio/sera
*dee po-may-**reed**-jo/**say**-ra*

at midday
a mezzogiorno
*a med-zo-**jor**-no*

at midnight
a mezzanotte
*a med-za-**not**-tay*

it's 1 o'clock
è l'una
*e **loo**-na*

it's six o'clock
sono le sei
***so**-no lay **say**-ee*

it's half past 8
sono le otto e mezza
***so**-no lay o**ot**-to ay **med**-za*

an hour
un'ora
*oon **o**-ra*

half an hour
una mezz'ora
***oo**-na med-**zo**-ra*

until 8 o'clock
fino alle otto
***fee**-no **al**-lay **ot**-to*

it is half past 10
sono le dieci e mezza
***so**-no lay dee-**ay**-chee ay **med**-za*

at 10 o'clock
alle dieci
***al**-lay dee-**ay**-chee*

at 2200
alle ore ventidue
***al**-lay **o**-ray ven-tee-**doo**-ay*

soon
fra poco
*fra **po**-ko*

later
più tardi
***pee**-yoo **tar**-dee*

FOOD

ORDERING DRINKS

*You can get a snack in most bars. Look out for **panini** (bread rolls), **al prosciutto** (with ham), **al formaggio** (with cheese), toast (toasted sandwiches), **tramezzini** (sandwiches made with sliced bread). Remember, if you just want a quick coffee (or any other drink), it is cheaper to drink it standing at the bar rather than seated.*

an espresso
un caffè
*oon kaf-**fe***

a cappuccino
un cappuccino
*oon kap-poo-**chee**-no*

2 cappuccinos
due cappuccini
***doo**-ay kap-poo-**chee**-nee*

a tea
un tè
oon te

with milk
al latte
*al **lat**-tay*

with lemon
al limone
*al lee-**mo**-nay*

a lager
una birra
***oo**-na **beer**-ra*

small
piccola
***pee**-kol-la*

large
grande
***gran**-day*

a bottle of mineral water
una bottiglia di acqua minerale
***oo**-na bot-**teel**-ya dee **ak**-wa mee-nay-**ra**-lay*

sparkling
gassata
*gas-**za**-ta*

still
naturale
*na-too-**ra**-lay*

would you like a drink?
prende qualcosa da bere?
***pren**-day kwal-**ko**-za da **be**-ray*

what will you have?
che cosa prende?
*kay **ko**-za **pren**-day*

the wine list, please
la lista dei vini, per favore
*la **lee**-sta **day**-ee **vee**-nee payr fa-**vo**-ray*

a bottle of house wine
una bottiglia di vino della casa
***oo**-na bot-**teel**-ya dee **vee**-no **del**-la **ka**-za*

a glass of wine
un bicchiere di vino
*oon bee-kee-**e**-ray dee **vee**-no*

a bottle of wine
una bottiglia di vino
***oo**-na bot-**teel**-ya dee **vee**-no*

red
rosso
***ros**-so*

white
bianco
*bee-**an**-ko*

ORDERING FOOD

where is there a good local restaurant?
dove c'è un buon ristorante locale?
__do__-vay che oon bwon rees-to-__ran__-tay lo-__ka__-lay

I'd like to book a table
vorrei prenotare una tavola
__vor__-ray-ee pray-no-__ta__-ray __oo__-na __ta__-vo-la

for ... people
per ... persone
payr ... per-__so__-nay

do you have a table?
avete una tavola?
a-__vay__-tay __oo__-na __ta__-vo-la

for tonight
per stasera
payr sta-__say__-ra

at 8 pm
alle otto
__al__-lay __ot__-to

the menu, please
il menù, per favore
eel me-__noo__ payr fa-__vo__-ray

is there a dish of the day?
c'è un piatto del giorno?
che oon pee-__at__-to del __jor__-no

have you a set-price menu?
c'è un menù turistico?
che oon me-__noo__ too-__rees__-tee-ko

I'll have this
prendo questo
__pren__-do __kwes__-to

I'll just have the first course
prendo solo il primo
__pren__-do __so__-lo eel __pree__-mo

I'll just have the main course
prendo solo il secondo
__pren__-do __so__-lo eel se-__kon__-do

what do you recommend?
che cosa ci consiglia?
kay __ko__-za chee kon-__seel__-ya

I don't eat meat
non mangio carne
non __man__-jo __kar__-nay

do you have any vegetarian dishes?
avete dei piatti per vegetariani?
a-__vay__-tay __day__-ee pee-__at__-tee payr ve-jay-ta-ree-__a__-nee

excuse me!
scusi!
__skoo__-zee

please bring...
ci porti...
chee __por__-tee...

more bread
altro pane
__al__-tro __pa__-nay

another bottle
un'altra bottiglia
oon __al__-tra bot-__teel__-ya

some butter
del burro
del __boor__-ro

the bill, please
il conto, per favore
eel __kon__-to payr fa-__vo__-ray

ITALIAN FOOD

Italian food is rich in all the wonderful flavours of the Mediterranean – olives, fresh fish, fruit and vegetables, pasta and aromatic herbs. Up in the north of the country, however, Italian cooking also reveals the influence of its northern neighbours – France, Austria, Switzerland and Slovenia. The further south you go, the lighter and more colourful the food becomes.

Despite these north-south variations, there are some features common to most of Italy – **polenta** (coarse corn meal cooked as thick porridge), pasta, pizza, salt cod, salami and **prosciutto** (ham). The marked variations in regional cooking no doubt have their roots in the culinary traditions of past invaders, traditions whose influence was preserved by Italy's independent states, which came together as a single nation only in the latter half of the nineteenth century. These regional differences are now less noticeable, but one can still see, for example, a preference for the use of butter in the north, whereas in the central areas lard is used, and the south is definitely olive oil country. It also seems fair to say that there has been a kind of 'invasion' of southern cooking throughout the whole of Italy. But after a period when the old gastronomic values were challenged and modern, lighter meals came into fashion, there is now, happily, a revival of traditional dishes, at least in the less internationally minded restaurants. This is partly in response to the demand by tourists for real Italian regional cuisine, which is met by trattorias (usually traditional family-run restaurants) with the sign **piatti tipici** (typical dishes of the region). Head for those if you are interested in tradition.

In Italy a main meal with all the trimmings starts with **antipasto** (hors d'œuvre), consisting of cured meats or, depending on the occasion, elegant mini dishes like **insalata di mare** (seafood salad) or **tortine al tartufo** (little tarts with truffles). This is followed by the first course (**il primo**), which may be soup, risotto or pasta, and then the second course (**il secondo**), which will be fish or meat, usually served with vegetables or salad. A grand dinner will finish with cheese and ice cream (in which the Italians excel), or a tart, fruit salad, or simply fruit. For everyday eating, desserts consist mainly of fresh fruit only. But to round off any meal a small cup of strong coffee (**espresso**) is obligatory.

THE MAIN CHARACTERISTICS OF THE REGIONS

PIEDMONT (Turin)

Piedmont and Valle d'Aosta is a prosperous, very industrialised and lively region, with Turin at its centre. Agriculture flourishes, producing most staple foods. An abundance of wheat, barley, maize and rice means wholesome soups to counteract the cold winters. White truffles are a feature of this region and when in season they enhance almost any dish. Good wine and game are an essential part of wonderful meals here and the French influence is very apparent, not least in the use of snails, frogs' legs and butter. A warming meat dish is **bollito misto**, consisting of different kinds of meat cooked with vegetables.

Country festivals with an emphasis on wine and food keep the rural areas busy. Excellent beef, butter and cheese are characteristic of the area, which also offers a great variety of sausages, salamis, venison and pâtés. Vermouth originated in Piedmont and is a popular **aperitivo**. Meals are heavy, starting with a rich collection of **antipasto** followed by robust dishes and crowned with pastries and sweet desserts, the best in Italy.

One of the most typical Piemontese delicacies is the **fritto misto**, which is a tempting platter of fried food. Ingredients, including small portions of meat and vegetables, or even fruit, are dipped in egg and breadcrumbs and deep fried. You can probably buy **fritto misto** from the street stalls, but you will also find it included on the most elegant menus. Other special dishes not to be missed are **anatra di Palmina** (duck cooked in wine) and **fagiano** or **lepre in salmi** (pheasant or hare, also cooked in wine).

Marsala is used in various concoctions, including the divine **zabaione** (zabaglione), a warm creamy dessert made with egg yolks and sugar, which is served at the end of a special meal. Chocolate is served hot at any time and the region is famous for its chocolate confectionery.

The main cheeses are **Tomini**, the strong **Bross**, **Castelmagno** (also strong and herby), **Robiola**, a soft cheese, and the best known, **Fontina**, quite rich and delicious. The region offers curious mixtures with different kinds of cheeses creamed and laced with spirits.

LOMBARDY (Milan)

Lombardy is blessed with rivers, mountains, valleys and plains. This lovely area has everything, from the stunning scenery of the Alps to the fertile plains of the river Po. Milan, the main industrial city, gives its name to various dishes, such as **ossobuco alla milanese** (large marrow-bone veal steak, cooked in wine, butter, garlic and herbs). Although the people here are too busy working outside the home to slave over the stove, the regional gastronomy is rich and includes many specialities. This is the home of **panettone** (a large cork-shaped yeast cake eaten during the Christmas season). Butter is used in preference to other fats, then comes lard, but lately there has been a movement towards adopting a healthier style of diet, with more olive oil and pasta, from the south.

Polenta is made in many different ways in Lombardy, and used to be the main food in rural communities. It is still part of the region's repertoire, and is served with **Gorgonzola** (a local cheese), with mushrooms, meat, or on its own. Lombardy grows most of the rice in Italy, so it is not surprising that rice is the staple food here. Try **risotto alla milanese** (a simple rice dish flavoured with saffron and sprinkled liberally with Parmesan), and **risotto con pesce persico** (rice with fish caught in Lake Como). With so many rivers and lakes the region boasts many fresh water fish dishes as well as salted dried fish such as **missultitt** (grilled dried fish from Lake Como).

All kinds of meat are plentiful, and found in excellent dishes like **risotto con le quaglie** (quails served with risotto).

Minestre (soups) are a warming and nutritious easy way to feed the family. Soups are generally thick, enriched with rice and/or pasta, and can serve as a main dish, for example **minestrone alla milanese**, with tomatoes, pulses, pork, vegetables, rice, cheese and herbs.

Lombardy produces more milk than any other region, so it is no surprise that the regional cheeses are among the best in Italy. For example, the creamy **Bel Paese** and **Robiola**, the outstanding **Gorgonzola** (blue cheese, with herbs), **grana** (which is similar to Parmesan) and the very rich cream cheese **mascarpone** which is used in many desserts. But there are dozens of other varieties as well. Desserts in Lombardy are not to be missed, especially **albicocche ripiene** (stuffed apricots), chocolate tarts and mouthwatering **torrone** (almond nougat with honey).

TRENTINO-ALTO ADIGE (Bolzano)

Trentino – Alto Adige, where the mighty Dolomites rise, is the region where apples grow most abundantly, and are used in dishes like **vitello alla mele renette** (veal with apples). **Polenta** is, as in all northern regions, a staple food, served in imaginative dishes, for example **polenta carbonara** (polenta, onions and salami, with plenty of butter and cheese). The area is rich in freshwater fish (mainly trout) from the hundreds of lakes. The Austrian influence is very strong, both in the language and the cooking, especially north of Trento. Although Trentino itself is Italian-speaking, some of the food is Germanic in origin. Try Tyrolean dumplings (**canederli tirolesi**), which can either be served with soup or eaten by themselves. **Grigliata di cervo** are venison steaks grilled after being marinated in olive oil, wine, cinnamon and other seasonings. Despite the abundance of trout (try **trote alla panna acida**, prepared with sour cream), salt cod is also popular, for example **baccalà dei frati** (cooked in milk and served with tomato and anchovies). Wine is used a lot in cooking and the region is very rich in wild mushrooms: one of the outstanding local dishes featuring both ingredients is a delicious mushroom stew (**misto di funghi**). Potatoes are also widely used. There are many Austrian-inspired cakes, such as strudel, fruit tarts and **sachertorte** (chocolate cake).
Beer is preferred to wine in some parts of the region.

VENETO (Venice)

Veneto is again **polenta** land, but rice is very much a staple as well, prepared with a wide range of fish, meat and vegetables. Venice dominates the region gastronomically, a legacy from its golden, cosmopolitan past, but Venetian cooking is simple, based on fish from the sea, lagoons and rivers. This is fried as soon as it is caught and sold immediately. A favourite dish is **fegato alla veneziana**, calves' liver cooked with onions. Another Venetian speciality is **risi e bisi** (a thick pea and rice soup). Splendid vegetable soups are served all over the region – try **pasta e fagioli**, a bean soup with pasta. The northern part has more meat dishes, especially offal and all kinds of poultry. A famous dish is **paparelle e fegatini**, chicken livers with pasta. Veneto also uses dried cod (**stoccafisso**) and salt cod (**baccalà**) in dishes accompanied with **polenta**.

For dessert, local ice creams are excellent, and cakes are delicious too, for example **torta sabiosa**, a light cake flavoured with aniseed. Fritters are popular here but the crown of glory has to go to **tiramisù**, which was allegedly created in Veneto. It is a rich dessert made with mascarpone cheese, strong coffee, chocolate, sponge fingers and Marsala. The local cheeses are from the north, the best being **Vezzena** and **Asiago**, which is strongly flavoured.

FRIULI-VENEZIA GIULIA (Trieste)

Friuli–Venezia Giulia is a very small region which shares a border with Slovenia and Austria. Consequently, the language and food are less Italian than in most other areas. This does not prevent **polenta** from being an important staple (white **polenta**, in this case). The area is mountainous and difficult but there are excellent cured meats here, such as **prosciutto** (ham), perhaps the best, lean and sweet, named after the city of San Daniele. Game is plentiful and welcome in the autumn. Snails and frogs' legs are also appreciated. The food is generally simple and filling, with thick soups playing a major role. There are many rice dishes, but potatoes are used a lot, especially in **gnocchi** (dumplings). **Frittatas** are popular and consist of pan-fried food, from omelettes to onions. Wild mushrooms give an elegant touch to peasant dishes. The use of sugar and cinnamon in some savoury recipes such as **cialzons alla carnia** (pasta squares filled with spinach, chocolate and cinnamon) is an obvious Slavic influence. There are good cakes, like the delicious **torta di castagne**, made with chestnuts.

LIGURIA (Genoa)

Liguria is a narrow strip of mountainous country sweeping down to the Ligurian Sea. This region is blessed with a wonderful climate and, despite its size, grows an amazing variety of fruits, vegetables, herbs and olives, which are all used in the tasty cooking. The olive oil here is of the best quality. Fish is, of course, eaten much more than meat (try the local red mullet, **triglia**, and **cappon magro**, an elaborate seafood and vegetable salad from Genoa) but vegetables are important too. **Pesto**, the famous sauce made with fresh basil leaves, pine kernels, pecorino, garlic and olive oil, comes from Liguria. It is used to flavour pasta dishes and soups, such as **trenette al pesto alla genovese**, a potato and noodle dish, or **minestrone alla genovese**, a thick soup with **pesto**. **Focaccia** (flat bread brushed with olive oil, garlic and herbs) is another Ligurian creation. **Ravioli**, stuffed with cheese, vegetables or eggs, are also a local speciality. Desserts are based on chocolate, almonds and dried fruits.

EMILIA-ROMAGNA (Bologna)

Emilia–Romagna's main city is Bologna and everybody is familiar with the famous sauce, **ragù alla bolognese**, made with minced meat, wine and tomato. This is a rich gastronomic region, where pasta of every shape reigns. Fresh egg pasta is made here, more than in any other Italian region. **Lasagne** is a local speciality. Parmesan (**parmigiano reggiano**) originated here and is widely used: any dish marked **alla parmigiana** will be served with Parmesan cheese. Parma ham (**prosciutto di Parma**) also comes from here, and there are many other excellent cold meats, such as **zampone** (a sausage from Modena) and **salami da sugo** (a special salami). Look out for salami from Felino as well, considered the best, and **mortadella**. As in Piedmont, **fritto misto** is a speciality not to be missed. People here have big appetites and will serve several dishes at each meal – from soup, to pasta and/or rice, followed by meat. If you are having **arrosti** (roast meat), try **porchetta** (roast suckling pig). Game, mushrooms and white truffles abound too. The city of Modena has many specialities, but one of the best is the fashionable **aceto balsamico** (balsamic vinegar) which is used both in sweet and savoury dishes. Fish is splendid, and locally prepared in mixed grills (**mistigriglia**).
There are some good desserts, like **pan pepato**, a sweet loaf with all kinds of nuts.

TUSCANY (Florence)**, the MARCHES** (Ancona) **and UMBRIA** (Perugia)

Tuscany, the Marches and Umbria form a 'middle Italy' with some culinary similarities. The Marches, bordering the Adriatic, are an area of rural tranquility, with a rich truffle harvest and excellent olives. The main cheese is sheep's **pecorino**. But the sea is the real provider. There are wonderful fish dishes, like the **brodetto di pesce**, a soup made with many varieties of fish.

Umbria, in the centre, is completely landlocked, but there is fish from the lakes, generally served grilled. Meat is important and cooking is identical to that of Tuscany, with wonderful grills. Truffles are again abundant here. Sausages and other pork products are of high quality – try **lonza**, an excellent salami. **Porchetta** is crisply cooked pork, sold at roadside stalls. Desserts include **coccio**, a yeast cake with dried fruits.

Tuscany (Toscana) is a peaceful region where splendid olive oil is produced, to go with an uncomplicated local cuisine. Florence, the capital, is a model of frugality. Good olive oil, good wine, good vegetables (spinach dishes are a speciality in Florence) and herbs form the basis of many dishes, as well as chestnuts and pulses. Meat is mainly lean pork, duck, chicken and rabbit. Try **pappardelle al sugo di lepre** (ribbon noodles with a hare, wine and tomato sauce). There is a special breed of cattle here called **Chianina**, and not surprisingly, one of the most relished Tuscan dishes is steak (**bistecca**). **Crostini di fegatini**, another speciality, is a pâté of chicken livers on toast. Red mullet is prepared with chillies (**triglie alla livornese**) and eels are, as in many other Italian regions, a great delicacy. Nutty biscuits (**cantucci**) are served with sweet wine (**vino santo**) for dessert.

LATIUM (Rome)

Latium (**Lazio**) is really Rome, in the sense that everything concentrates on and is dominated by the capital. The cooking is simple, and uses the excellent local produce to full advantage. The region grows many vegetables and the preferred meats are pork and lamb. Many typical dishes are based on spring lamb, like **abbacchio arrosto** (roast lamb) or **abbacchio alla cacciatora**, a rich lamb stew. Offal and cheap cuts of meat are carefully cooked in wholesome dishes. **Trippa alla romana** (tripe stew) and **coda alla vaccinara** (an oxtail stew) are two examples. A very famous Roman dish is **saltimbocca alla romana**, veal escalopes with ham, sage and wine.

In Rome many pasta dishes are served not with Parmesan cheese, but with the milder **pecorino** and tomato sauce. One of the best ever pasta dishes is **spaghetti all'amatriciana**, with bacon, onion and tomato sauce. **Fettucine al ragù** are fresh ribbon noodles with **bolognese** sauce. **Gnocchi alla romana** (dumplings) are made with semolina and

Parmesan, not potato, and are delicious.
With such good vegetables available, there is an emphasis on salads and raw vegetables served with olive oil (**pinzimonio**). Good fish and shellfish are served along the coast.

The cheeses are generally made from ewe's milk but **mozzarella** (from buffalo's milk) is also produced locally. **Budino di ricotta** is an excellent cake made with ricotta cheese.

ABRUZZI (L'Aquila) and MOLISE (Campobasso)

Abruzzi and Molise are mountainous regions where tender lamb is the main ingredient in a number of distinctive dishes. Three examples are **agnello all'arrabbiata**, made with a hot sauce of chillies and tomato, **costolette di agnello alla brace**, lamb chops marinated and grilled, and **cosciotto d'agnello all'abruzzese**, which is braised lamb with garlic, rosemary, tomatoes and wine. **Maccheroni alla chitarra** is a square-shaped pasta usually served with lamb in a chilli and tomato sauce. Barbecued goat's meat (**capretto**) is also eaten here, as well as suckling pig roasted whole (**porchetta**). The region produces very good hams and salamis. Cooks here like to use hot chillies, often in fish dishes, such as **brodetto alla pescarese**. Many generations of good cooks come from this region and there is a famous cookery school in Villa Santa Maria.
Liqueurs, as in most Italian regions, are served with dessert, perhaps with **confetti** (sugared almonds) or nut cakes.

CAMPANIA (Naples)

Naples is the principal city of Campania, a region renowned for the vitality of its people. The food is based mainly on flour, with an immense variety of **pasta** and **pizza**. This really is pasta land and is, of course, the place where pizza was created. Although there is a fertile plain, the land is not very rich and the people of Campania have always had to make do with the minimum. This makes for imaginative dishes enhanced with the ubiquitous tomato. **Sartù di riso** is a rice dish, more like a pie, with meat and herbs. Fish is eaten mainly along the coast, and octopus is a speciality – try **polpo affogato**, octopus cooked in a tomato, herb and garlic sauce. Vegetables are treated with respect in lovely recipes, like the **parmigiana di melanzane** (sliced aubergines cooked in the oven with tomato sauce and Parmesan). Soups (**minestre**) are filling, with different kinds of pulses, vegetables and pasta. But there is no getting away from pasta and pizza dishes in Campania. One must try **lasagne alla napoletana** (a lavish lasagne dish with mozarella, meatballs, hardboiled eggs and ricotta cheese), **maccheroni ai quatro formaggi** (pasta with four cheeses), **calzone imbottito** (folded pizzas with cheese and ham filling). The region is also good for sweets, like the **sfogliatelle frolle** (puff pastry cakes filled with ricotta cheese).

PUGLIA (Bari), BASILICATA (Potenza) and CALABRIA (Reggio di Calabria)

Apulia, Basilicata and Calabria form the southernmost part of the Italian peninsula and here too, pasta is much in evidence. Apulia is, as it were, the heel of the boot and enjoys a long coastline, so fish is prominent in regional dishes. Try the local red mullet, called **triglie**, which is usually served grilled. Octopus is prepared in a special way **polpi arricciati** ('curled' octopus) in Bari, the main city. Shellfish is excellent here, with lovely oysters and mussels. Try **cozze arraganate** (grilled mussels) and the rich **zuppa di pesce** (fish soup) with a large variety of seafood, tomatoes and wine. The land is fertile and the main product is olive oil, which is used in most dishes. Plenty of vegetables and fruit are grown as well. Meat is not eaten in large amounts, but there is game, pork and lamb. Try **braciole al ragù**, which includes different kinds of meat stewed with lots of tomatoes and wine. The best bread is the flat **focaccia** which is brushed with olive oil, garlic and flavoured with herbs Apulia grows almonds which go into special cakes. In Basilicata (once known as Lucania) and Calabria, pasta is again used very often in dishes enriched with **ragù** (bolognese sauce). Another addition to most dishes in Basilicata is the locally grown **peperoncino** (red chilli pepper). Even the fish is cooked with these peppers, which can be very hot or quite mild. Pork is the mainstay in this inland region and cooks here are famous for their sausages, some kept in olive oil. Try **soppressato** (a type of salami/ham with pistacchio nuts) and **capocello** (a smoked salami preserved in olive oil). Potatoes, again with red chilli peppers (**patate con diavolicchio**) are very popular. A special chicken dish is **pollo alla lucana** (chicken stuffed with its own liver, pecorino cheese and eggs). **Erbe alla lucana** is a vegetable dish similar to ratatouille but with plenty of basil. Aubergines, peppers and tomatoes go into many simple and tasty dishes. Basilicata is well-known for its cheeses. **Burrini**, a creamy cheese, is one of the best. Calabria is a wild and mountainous region, but olives, vegetables and fruit grow in abundance. Aubergines are plentiful and mushrooms a speciality. They are even preserved in olive oil (**funghi sott'olio**). The local **pitta** bread is stuffed with all kinds of food for a quick meal. One of Calabria's specialities is roast kid with herbs (**capretto ripieno al forno**). Pork is the main meat however. Desserts may be figs, fresh or dried, and there are cakes made with honey and almonds.

SICILY (Palermo)

Sicily is a wonderful place to visit. The people are very warm and outgoing, and the delicious food adds to the atmosphere of conviviality. Fish, olive oil and pasta are the main ingredients. The island's culinary heritage is treasured, representing as it does an exotic mix of different traditions, rich in the strong flavours of anchovies, hot peppers and garlic, and the more subtle flavours of fruit and herbs (chiefly basil and mint). Although there are many dishes which are extremely simple, as is the case with **orecchiette ai broccoli** (pasta with broccoli) or **annelletti** (baked squid or cuttle fish rings), there are more elaborate ones such as the stuffed sardines and stuffed baby squid (**sarde a beccafico** and **calamaretti imbottiti**). Tuna and swordfish are very plentiful and popular (try **pesce spada alla siciliana**, a swordfish stew). Pasta is of course a staple ingredient in Sicilian dishes as well, and is often eaten with sardines (**pasta con le sarde**, layers of fried sardines and pasta in a rich sardine and anchovy sauce baked in the oven). If you enjoy rice dishes, try **peperoni ripieni di riso** (peppers stuffed with rice, cooked with plenty of tomato). Vegetables are an important part of the diet, especially aubergines. There are pigs (and good sausages), sheep, goats and some cattle, but Sicilians are not big meat eaters. Curiously, various meat dishes are of the sweet and sour variety, like **ficatu all'agru e duci** (calves' liver in a sweet and sour sauce made with vinegar and sugar).The Sicilians have a great love for good desserts and have created the famous **cassata**, a sponge cake covered with ricotta cheese, candied fruit and chocolate. Candied fruit is in fact another big speciality of the island. They make good cheeses, the main ones being **ricotta**, **pecorino** and **caciocavallo**.

SARDINIA (Cagliari)

Sardinia is an interesting mixture of ancient tradition in the mountains, and modern tourist developments around the coast. While the rural interior is the true Sardinia, where life centres on tending the animals and cultivating what the land will allow (not an easy task), the coast is cosmopolitan and quite separate. One eats meat, the other fish and seafood, and they do not mix. The island offers a great variety of dishes, some introduced by past conquerors, many of whom seem to have stayed on, and preserved by the rivalry between villages, keen to keep their traditions alive. Wheat for pasta is grown, and enough vegetables, olive oil and fruit to sustain the people. Meat usually means lamb or pork, but there is also game in the mountains. Wild boar is plentiful and cured boar ham is a speciality (**prosciutto di cinghiale**). Pork sausages are highly seasoned and used a lot in the cooking. Suckling pig (**porceddu**) is one of the best specialities of the interior. **Agnello con olive** (tender lamb served with plenty of olives) is another delicious treat. The meat has a delicious flavour which comes from the animals' diet of wild herbs in the mountains. The shepherds make many kinds of cheese which they eat with pasta and bread. Bread and cakes are another Sardinian speciality, each village and town producing several kinds. One of the most interesting breads is the very thin and crispy **carta di musica**. It can be eaten as it is, but is also used as a cooking ingredient or warmed up with olive oil. Other breads, in a variety of artistic shapes, are made for festivities. In the restaurants along the coast, lobster and crayfish are the main attractions, but there are all kinds of splendid fish dishes, some Sicilian, others French or Catalonian in origin. Fresh tuna is delicious here, grilled, baked or fried with onions. Some of the specialities are **filotrottas** (grilled eels), **spaghetti al sugo di granchio** (spaghetti with a crab sauce), **pasta con frutti di mare** (pasta with a great variety of seafood) and **bottarga** (fish roe).

The main cheeses are **fetta**, **formaggio fiore**, excellent **pecorino** and **ricotta**. Cheese is used to make cakes of all sorts, such as **sebadas**. Another important dairy product is **gioddu** (yoghurt).

SWITZERLAND (Ticino)

Much of northern Italy borders with Switzerland but only Ticino is really influenced by the Italian language and Italian food, because the regions of Piedmont, Valle d'Aosta and Lombardy are influenced by Switzerland, rather than the other way round – a legacy perhaps of their shared history. In Ticino (a name that, in itself, is suggestive of Italian), **minestre** (soups) are a feature, for example **minestra calanchina** (a vegetable and rice soup, served with bread and cheese), and the classic **minestrone**, which has become popular all over Europe. Tripe is a speciality in the Ticino area – try **busecca**, a rich tripe soup served with Sbrinz cheese and rolls. Potato **gnocchi** are dumplings made with mashed potato and flour.
In Ticino desserts are sometimes based on cakes like **torta di pane**, made with bread, milk, eggs and lots of spices. **Zabaglione**, a hot mixture of egg yolks, white wine and sugar, is popular. Peaches in Merlot and Marsala wines with sugar make another nice dessert, as does **cavolatte**, a rich custard pudding. **Amaretti** are little almond biscuits.

FESTIVE FOOD

As in most European countries, especially Latin ones, each village or town in Italy has its own annual celebrations, mainly based on the religious calendar and the harvests (**sagre**). Cakes and pastries are baked throughout Italy to celebrate these special events.

Christmas is the most important festival and people usually eat a traditional meal of fish on Christmas Eve. In Piedmont, this meal includes **bagna cauda**, a strong hot mixture of anchovies, garlic and truffles, eaten as a dip. Baked fish, shellfish salads and other fish dishes appear throughout the country. To round off the meal, different kinds of cake (like the famous **panettone**, with dried fruits) and a huge variety of nuts are spread on the table. On Christmas Day, lunch is a rich meal including turkey and other roast meat with vegetables, and a variety of desserts.

Carnival, which is celebrated in most of Italy, has its own specialities. Taking place just before Lent, **Carnevale** offers a splendid opportunity to indulge. Try the **lasagne alla napoletana**, richly prepared with ham cooked in Marsala and cream. **Castagnole** and **chiacchiero** are little sugared cakes specially baked for this jolly occasion.

At Easter time, the whole of Italy goes chocolate-crazy (Italy makes wonderful Easter eggs). On Easter Sunday, a rich lunch is served with pasta, roast lamb (or goat), with regional dishes like **torta pasqualina** from Genoa, made with eggs, artichokes and cheese. Desserts are of course obligatory, such as the popular almond **colomba**, a yeast cake made in the shape of a dove.

Religious festivals are greeted everywhere with regional cakes and tasty morsels sold at street stalls. **Sagre** (harvest festivals) are usually celebrated at weekends. Visitors get the chance to enjoy delicacies made with the crop which has just been gathered in – cherries, grapes, chestnuts or truffles, for example.

EATING PLACES AND TYPES OF FOOD SERVED

There is no difficulty in finding a place to eat in Italy. Italians love to go out for a meal and to take away meals and snacks to eat elsewhere. This means that there is a great variety of establishments and prices to suit everyone's tastes and needs. If you are keen on trying a special restaurant, it is a good idea to book in advance to avoid waiting in a queue, especially at peak times. The Italians spend a lot of time in bars which are open all day from 6 am until late. They have a vast range of drinks, alcoholic or not, plus coffee, snacks and light meals. Coffee is a national institution. If you order just coffee (**caffè**), you will be given a small cup of strong **espresso**. A **cappuccino** is the familiar frothy white coffee, served for breakfast (**colazione**) at a bar, with a **brioche** (croissant) or a roll (**panino**). **Caffè americano** means a black filter coffee, while **caffè corretto** is coffee with a dash of local **grappa** (brandy). Bar food consists of hamburgers, pizza, sandwiches and hot dogs. Space permitting, they will have some tables outside, and you can pay a little more to eat your food out in the sunshine.

A popular food shop is the **friggitoria**, especially common in southern Italy, where all kinds of fried food and pizzas are sold. **Rosticceria** and **tavola calda** are more or less the same and they sell food to eat there, self-service style, or to take away. The menu will cover basic pasta and various other dishes, so you can have a complete meal, with drinks and dessert. **Pizzeria** specialise in pizzas and **calzoni** (filled pizzas), with a few other dishes. They may be open for lunch (**pranzo**) and dinner (**cena**) but usually just for dinner, and are very good places to take children. The other pizza shops are the **pizza rustica**, or **pizza a taglio**, which offer slices of pizza sold by weight, normally to take away.

There are also tavern-style food and wine shops, with simple dishes, where people can sit for long hours. They are called **bottiglieria** or **fiaschetteria** and sometimes **cantina**. A **birreria** is a beer house inspired by similar Austrian establishments and serving the sort of dishes you would expect to find in Austria, such as sauerkraut and sausages.

A **gelateria** is the place to find all those marvellous ice creams the Italians are so good at. You can eat them there, or take them away. These shops are open from before lunch time until the evening. **Trattoria** are family-run restaurants which tend to have good home cooking at reasonable prices, although some trattoria are more elegant and expensive.

A **ristorante** is a restaurant, and can be of any size and degree of refinement. Italians are very friendly towards children and will be happy to give them half portions. As to prices, it is always best to look at the menus before entering.

READING THE MENU

Menus will look different, according to the type of establishment and what is available. At proper restaurants there will be sections with the different courses comprising a main meal, although it is not necessary to order something from each section. One or even two courses can be omitted, especially if the main dish (**secondo**) is heavy.

Antipasto *starters/appetizers.*
Primo *first course, which can be soup, pasta or rice*
Secondo *main course, with meat or fish*
Contorno *vegetable accompaniments, served separately from the main course*
Formaggi *selection of cheeses.*
Dolce *fruit, ice cream, dessert*

DRINKS

WINES

Most of Italy has grown grapes and made wine since time immemorial. Italians consider wine an indispensable part of their meals; they don't talk much about it, they just partake of it as something natural, a part of life. Most eating places (perhaps with the exception of elegant restaurants) will serve a carafe of local wine (**vino in caraffa**), which is usually good and cheap. This is house wine (**vino della casa**), which is also called **vino ordinario**, **vino da tavola** or **vino da banco**. If you want something different, ask for the wine list (**lista dei vini**) and don't forget to specify **bianco** (white) or **rosso** (red), when ordering. Other useful expressions are **secco** (dry), **abbocato** or **amabile** (medium sweet) or **dolce** (sweet).
As in other wine-producing countries, wine in Italy is controlled by law and classified into two main categories: **Denominazione di Origine Controllata** (DOC) and **Denominazione di Origine Controllata e Garantita** (DOCG). These categories are displayed on the bottles, giving the buyer a guarantee of quality.
Apart from these outstanding wines, there are lots of others which, although more ordinary, are not necessarily uninteresting. On the contrary, they can be excellent.
Some of the most important wine regions are: Piedmont, Lombardy, Trentino, Veneto, Friuli, Liguria, Tuscany, Emilia–Romagna, Umbria, Lazio, Apulia, Campania, Sicily (producing the famous sweet Marsala and Moscato) and Sardinia. Italy also produces some sparkling wines, the best being **Asti spumante,** sparkling, sweet or semi-sweet white wine, often drunk for celebrations and produced in the Asti district of Piedmont.
Here is a selection of well-known wines:

Barbaresco *dry, full-bodied red wine from Piedmont*
Barbera *dry, spicy red wine from Piedmont*
Bardolino *light, dry red or rosé wine from the Veneto*
Barolo *good, full-bodied red wine from Piedmont*
Brunello di Montalcino *superior, strong red wine from Tuscany*
Chianti *full, fruity red wine from Tuscany*
Chiaretto *light, rosé-style wine from the Veneto*
Cinqueterre *dry, light and fragrant white wine from Liguria*

Est! Est! Est! *crisp, fruity white wine from a region near Rome*
Frascati *crisp, fresh, dry to off-dry white wine from a region near Rome*
Lacrima christi *full-bodied wine from Campania and Sicily*
Lambrusco *slightly sparkling wine from Emilia–Romagna*
Marsala *dark dessert wine from Sicily*
Merlot *good, dry red wine from north-east Italy*
Montepulciano *dry or sweet red wine from Tuscany*
Moscato *sweet, aromatic white wine from north-west Italy*
Nebbiolo *light red wine from Piedmont*
Orvieto *crisp, smooth, dry white wine from Umbria*
Pinot bianco *dry white wine from north-east Italy*
Savuto *dry red wine from Calabria*
Soave *dry white wine from the Veneto*
Valpolicella *light, fruity red wine from the Veneto*
Verdicchio *fresh, dry white wine from the Marches*
Verduzzo *dry, tangy white wine from north-east Italy*
Vernaccia di San Gimignano *dry white wine from Tuscany*
Vino da tavola *table wine*
Vino della casa *house wine*
Vin santo *golden, scented wine ranging from sweet to dry (made from dried grapes)*

OTHER DRINKS (aperitifs, liqueurs, spirits and soft drinks)

acqua brillante *tonic water*
acqua minerale *mineral water; this can be still (**naturale**), with gas (**effervescente**), or with artificial gas (**gassata**)*
Amaretto di Saronno *almond liqueur*
amaro *bitter-sweet liqueur (herbal)*
analcolico *non-alcoholic, slightly bitter drink served as an aperitif*
anice *aniseed liqueur*
anisetta *powerful aniseed liqueur*
aperitivo *aperitif*
Aperol *aperitif made with the essence of various plants*
aranciata *orangeade*
birra *beer; draught beer (**birra alla spina**) is also available*
bitter *non-alcoholic bitter drink served as an aperitif*

DRINKS

caffè *coffee - if you ask for* **un caffè** *you'll be served* **un espresso** *(small, strong, black)*
caffè americano *black filter coffee*
caffè corretto *coffee laced with* **grappa** *(strong spirit)*
caffè doppio *a large coffee (twice normal size)*
caffèllatte *milky coffee*
camomilla *camomile tea*
Campari *bitter-tasting aperitif made with herbs and fruit*
cappuccino *frothy white coffee*
Centerbe *herbal liqueur*
China *bitter liqueur*
chinotto *fizzy soft drink with taste of bitter orange*
Cinzano *popular aperitif*
cioccolata calda *rich hot chocolate, often served* **con panna**
crodino *slightly bitter, non-alcoholic aperitif*
Cynar *bitter aperitif (curiously made from artichokes)*
digestivo *slightly bitter, herb-flavoured liqueur to help digestion*
Filu Ferru *very strong liqueur from Sardinia*
frullato di frutta *milk shake made with fruits*
Fuoco dell'Etna *very strong liqueur from Sicily*
gazzosa *fizzy bottled lemonade*
granita *flavoured crushed ice drink*
granita di caffè *coffee drink with crushed ice and cream*
granita di limone *lemon drink with crushed ice*
grappa *strong spirit from grape pressings, often added to coffee*
latte *milk*
lemonsoda *fizzy drink with taste of real lemons*
limonata *bottled lemon drink*
Martini *famous Italian aperitif*
orzata *cool, milky drink made from barley*
Sambuca *aniseed liqueur, served with coffee beans and set alight*
spremuta *freshly squeezed fruit juice*
spremuta di pompelmo *fresh grapefruit juice*
Strega *strong herb-flavoured liqueur*
succo di frutta *bottled fruit juice*
tè *tea. It is not very popular in Italy and normally served with lemon (***al limone***). If you want it with milk you must ask for* **tè al latte**.
Vecchia Romagna *Italian cognac*
Vermut *aperitif made from herbs and wine; very popular*

abbacchio *suckling or milk-fed lamb, usually eaten at Easter. Roasted with garlic and rosemary*
abbacchio alla cacciatora *lamb cooked in olive oil, garlic and rosemary*
acciughe *anchovies: fresh, salted or in olive oil*
acciughe ripiene *fresh anchovies filled with fillets of salted anchovies and cream cheese and fried in oil*
aceto *vinegar*
aceto balsamico *balsamic vinegar*
acqua cotta *literally 'cooked water', a traditional Tuscan soup made from onions, peppers, celery and tomato. Beaten eggs and parmesan are added just before serving*
affettato misto *selection of cold meats: ham, salami, mortadella, etc*
affogato *poached*
affumicato *smoked*
aglio *garlic*
aglio, olio e peperoncino *garlic, olive oil and hot chilli sauce*
agnello *lamb*
agnello al forno *roast lamb with vegetables*
agnello all'arrabbiata *lamb cooked in a tomato and chilli sauce*
agnello arrosto *roast lamb*
agnollotti *pasta squares filled with white meat and cheese. Usually served with bolognese sauce*
agoni *small fish from Italian lakes. Usually marinated in vinegar and herbs*
agrodolce *sweet and sour sauce made from sugar, water, vinegar, wine, pine-nuts and sultanas, often served with vegetables or meat such as rabbit or duck*
ai ferri *grilled*
a, al, alla, *etc means with, or in the style of: eg* **pasta al sugo** *is pasta with tomato sauce, and* **pollo alla cacciatora** *is chicken hunter-style*
...al burro *fried in butter*
...al dente *pasta cooked so that it is still quite firm to the bite*
...al forno *cooked in the oven*
...al pesto *with* **pesto** *(thick sauce made from fresh basil, garlic, pine-nuts, olive oil and pecorino cheese)*
...al pomodoro *classic tomato sauce (same as* **sugo***)*
...al ragù *minced meat, tomato and garlic (same as* **bolognese***)*
...al sugo *same as* ***al pomodoro***
...al tonno *with a sauce made of tuna fish and tomatoes*
albicocche *apricots*

MENU READER

albicocche ripeine *stuffed apricots*
alici *anchovies, often served dipped in flour and fried*
...all'amatricana *bacon, tomato and onion sauce*
...all'arrabbiata *tomato sauce with bacon, tomatoes, onion and hot chillies*
...alla bolognese *with tomato and minced meat sauce, served with parmesan*
...alla boscaiola *with mushroom and ham sauce*
...alla cacciatora *meat or game, hunter-style, meaning cooked with tomato, herbs, garlic and wine*
...alla carbonara *smoked bacon, egg, cream and parmesan*
...alla ciociara *with mushroom, cream and ham sauce*
...alla finanziera *with chicken livers, mushrooms and wine sauce*
...alla italiana *platters with mixed cured meats/cheeses, olives and savoury things like anchovies and pickles*
...alla milanese *normally applied to veal cutlets which are dipped in egg and breadcrumbs before frying*
...alla mugnaia *usually applies to fish dusted in flour then fried in butter*
...alla norma *a sauce from Sicily, with tomatoes and aubergines*
...alla parmigiana *with parmesan cheese*
...alla pizzaiola *cooked with tomatoes, garlic and herbs*
...alla puttanesca *tomato, garlic, hot chilli, anchovies and capers*
...alle vongole *clam, parsley, garlic and olive oil*
...allo spiedo *spit-roasted, or on skewer, kebab-style*
alloro *bayleaf*
amarene *dark morello cherries*
amaretti *macaroons, biscuits with a strong almond flavour*
ananas *pineapple*
anatra *duck*
anatra di Palmina *duck cooked in wine*
anatra in porchetta *roast duck stuffed with its liver and ham*
anguille *eel*
anguille alla comácchio *stewed eel*
anguille carpionate *fried eels*
anguille in umido *eel stewed in tomato sauce*
anguria *watermelon*
annelletti *baked squid or cuttlefish rings*
antipasto *starters/appetizers.*

antipasto misto *selection of cold starters such as ham, salami, russian salad and pickles*
aragosta *crayfish*
aragosta allo spiedo *crayfish cooked kebab-style*
arance *oranges*
arancini di riso *rice croquettes filled with minced veal and peas*
arrosto *roast meat, usually cooked in casserole with wine and herbs*
arrosto di maiale *roast pork*
arrosto di manzo *roast beef*
arrosto di vitello *roast veal*
asparagi *asparagus*
asparagi alla parmigiana *lightly boiled asparagus baked with Parmesan*
astice *lobster*
baccalà *salt cod, popular in Italy*
bacalà alla vicentina *salt cod cooked in milk with anchovies, onion, garlic, parsley and herbs*
baccalà alla livornese *salt cod cooked in a tomato sauce*
baccalà alla milanese *Milanese salt cod fritters, served with lemon*
bagna cauda *hot garlic and anchovy dip. Literally means 'hot bath' because raw vegetable such as pepper, celery and artichokes are dipped into it*
banana *banana*
basilico *basil*
Bel Paese *soft creamy mild cheese*
besciamella *béchamel sauce*
bianco, in *literally white, pasta or rice served with melted butter, garlic, sage and parmesan sauce*
bietola *beetroot*
biscotti *biscuits*
bistecca *steak*
bistecca alla fiorentina *thickly cut, charcoal-grilled steak*
bistecca alla pizzaiola *fried steak in a tomato and herb sauce*
bistecchini di cinghiale *wild boar steaks in a sweet and sour sauce*
bocconcini di vitello *little pieces of veal cooked in wine and butter*
bollito *boiled*
bollito misto *different kinds of meat and vegetables cooked together. There are many regional variations*
bonet *chocolate pudding with caramel*
borlotti *dried red haricot beans*

bottarga *preserved tuna or mullet roes, served in thin slices as a starter (speciality from Sardinia)*
brace, alle *grilled*
braciola *rib steak/chop*
braciole al ragù *chops cooked in tomato sauce*
brasato *beef stew*
bresaola *dried cured beef, cut very finely and served with black pepper and olive oil*
broccoletti *leafy green vegetable similar to turnip tops*
broccoli *broccoli*
brodetto di pesce *usually a substantial fish soup made with different kinds of fish*
brodo *bouillon or broth often served with meat-stuffed pasta such as ravioli (***in brodo***)*
bruschetta *thickly-sliced bread rubbed with garlic and olive oil, often served topped with cheese and tomato*
bucatini *a type of pasta like thick spaghetti with a hole running through it*
budino *a blancmange-type pudding*
budino di ricotta *pudding made from ricotta cheese*
buridda *famous Genoese fish soup using a variety of fish*
burrini *a creamy cheese from Basilicata*
burro *butter*
burro e salvia *butter and sage sauce*
busecca *rich tripe and cheese soup*
cacciatora, alla *literally hunter-style, cooked with wine, onion and tomato*
cachi *persimmons*
caciocavallo *cow's cheese which is quite strong when mature*
calamaretti imbottiti *baby squid stuffed with breadcrumbs and anchovies*
calamari *squid*
calamari fritti *squid rings dipped in batter and fried*
calzone *folded over pizza with filling. There are lots of local variations*
canederli tirolesi *Tyrolean dumplings made with bacon and sausage*
cannella *cinnamon*
cannellini *small white beans*
cannelloni *meat-filled tubes of pasta covered with béchamel sauce and baked until golden brown. Vegetarian options may be filled with spinach and ricotta*
cantucci *nutty biscuits*
capocello *smoked salami preserved in olive oil*

caponata *Sicilian dish of aubergines cooked in a sweet and sour sauce*
cappelletti *literally 'little hats' filled with ricotta cheese, can be served with bolognese meat sauce*
capperi *capers*
cappon magro *an elaborate cold seafood and cooked vegetable salad*
capretto *baby goat (kid)*
capretto arrosto *kid roasted in the oven with vegetables and wine*
caprino *soft goat's cheese usually eaten with a sprinkling of olive oil and freshly ground black pepper*
carbonade *beef cooked in wine; the classic accompaniment is polenta*
carciofi *globe artichokes*
carciofi alla Giudia *young globe artichokes, flattened and deep-fried*
carciofi alla romana *globe artichokes stuffed with breadcrumbs, parsley and anchovies*
carciofi ripieni *artichokes stuffed with mozarella, parmesan and anchovies*
cardi *cardoons (vegetable similar to fennel)*
carne *meat*
carote *carrots*
carpaccio *raw sliced lean beef eaten with lemon juice, olive oil and thickly grated parmesan cheese*
carpione *carp*
carpione, in *pickled in vinegar, wine and lemon juice. Fish is often served this way and fried*
casalinga, alla *home-made*
cassata *layers of ice cream with candied fruits*
cassata siciliana *sponge dessert with ricotta and candied fruits*
cassoeula *substantial pork and vegetable casserole*
castagnaccio *chestnut cake*
castagne *chestnuts*
cavolatte *rich custard pudding*
cavolfiore *cauliflower*
cavolo *cabbage*
ceci *chickpeas*
cena *dinner*
cervelle *calves' brains usually fried*
cetriolo *cucumber*
cialzons alla carnia *pasta squares filled with spinach, chocolate and cinnamon*

ciambella *ring-shaped fruit cake*
ciambellini *ring-shaped aniseed biscuits*
cicoria *chicory*
ciliege *cherries*
cinghiale *wild boar*
cioccolatini *chocolates*
cioccolato *chocolate*
cipolle *onions*
cipolle ripiene *stuffed onions*
coccio *a yeast cake with dried fruit*
cocco *coconut*
cocomero *watermelon*
coda alla vaccinara *famous Roman dish, consisting of oxtail stewed with tomatoes and herbs*
coda di bue *oxtail*
conchiglie *shell-shaped pasta*
confetti *sugared almonds*
coniglio *rabbit*
coniglio all'ischitana *rabbit stewed in wine*
coniglio in umido *rabbit stew*
contorni *vegetable side dishes*
cosciotto d'agnello all'abruzzese *braised lamb with garlic, rosemary, tomatoes and wine*
costeletta *cutlet/chop*
costoletta al prosciutto *veal cutlet with a slice of Parma ham*
costoletta alla bolognese *veal cutlet topped with ham and cheese*
costoletta alla milanese *veal cutlet dipped in egg and breadcrumbs then fried. Served with lemon wedges*
costoletta alla valdostana *breaded veal chop stuffed with cheese*
costoletta di vitello *veal cutlet*
costolette di abbacchio *lamb chops*
costolette di agnello alla brace *marinated and grilled lamb chops*
cotechino *spicy pork sausage usually cooked with lentils*
cotto *cooked, cured*
cozze *mussels*
cozze arraganate *grilled mussels*
crema di... *cream soup or sauce/custard*
crêpe *pancake*

crocchette di patate *potato croquettes*
crostata *tart which is usually filled with fruit and glazed*
crostata di frutta *fruit tart*
crostini di fegatini *chicken liver pâté on toast*
dolce *dessert*
dolcelatte *soft, creamy blue cheese*
dragoncello *tarragon*
entrecote *steak*
fagiano *pheasant*
fagiano con funghi *pheasant with porcini mushrooms*
fagiano in salmi *pheasant stewed in wine*
fagioli *type of bean*
fagioli al tonno *haricot beans with tuna fish in olive oil*
fagioli con cotiche *bean stew with pork*
fagioli nel fiasco *haricot beans cooked in a flask*
fagiolini *runner beans*
faraona *guinea fowl*
farcito *stuffed*
farfalle *butterfly-shaped pasta*
farsu magru *veal stuffed and rolled up, cooked in wine (Sicilian speciality)*
fave *broad beans*
fave al guanciale *broad beans cooked with bacon and onion*
fegatini di pollo *chicken livers*
fegato *liver (mainly calves')*
fegato alla veneziana *calves' liver fried in butter and onion*
fettuccine *fresh ribbon pasta*
ficatu all'agru e duci *calves' liver in sweet and sour sauce*
fichi *figs*
filetto *fillet steak*
filetto di tacchino alla bolognese *turkey breast served with a slice of ham and cheese*
finocchio *fennel*
fiori di zucchini *courgette flowers fried in batter*
focaccia *flat bread brushed with garlic, salt and olive oil, sprinkled with herbs or onions. There are many variations*
fonduta al parmigiano *cheese fondue made with Fontina cheese, eggs, butter and truffles. Eaten with crusty bread*
fontina *mild to strong cow's milk cheese from northern Italy*
formaggio *cheese*

fragole *strawberries*
frittata *omelette, usually with different ingredients*
fritto *fried*
fritto misto *platter of deep-fried food including different kinds of meat and vetables*
fritto misto di mare *fried/grilled selection of seafood*
frutta *fruit*
frutti di mare *shellfish/seafood*
funghi *mushrooms, very popular and varied in Italy. In autumn many Italians take to the woods in search of the prized porcini*
funghi trifolati *sliced mushrooms fried with garlic and parsley*
fusilli *spiral-shaped pasta*
gamberi *prawns*
gamberoni *giant prawns*
gelato *ice cream*
gelato misto *a selection of different flavoured ice creams*
gioddu *yoghurt*
girasole *sunflower*
gnocchi *small dumplings made from potato and flour; can be made with spinach. Boiled and served with tomato sauce or ragù*
gnocchi alla romana *dumplings made from semolina, butter and parmesan, baked in the oven*
gnocchi verdi *spinach and cheeese dumplings, usually cooked in melted butter, garlic and sage*
Gorgonzola *a strong blue cheese made from cows' milk*
granchio *crab*
grana *hard cows' milk cheese; generic name given to Parmesan cheese*
granseola *large crab*
grigliata di cervo *grilled venison steaks*
grigliata mista *mixed grill consisting of various barbecued meats*
grissini *breadsticks provided along with bread on the table*
guanciale *streaky bacon made from pig's cheek*
gulasch *spicy beef stew*
impepata di cozze *peppery mussels*
insalata *salad*
insalata caprese *tomato, basil and mozarella salad*
insalata di mare *mixed seafood salad*
insalata di pomodori *tomato salad*

insalata mista *mixed salad*
insalata russa *cold diced cooked vegetables served with mayonnaise*
insalata verde *green salad*
involtini *rolls of veal or pork stuffed with chicken liver, pork sausage and parmesan*
lamponi *raspberries*
lasagne *layers of pasta with bolognese and béchamel sauces, baked until golden*
lasagne verdi *layers of green (spinach) pasta filled with bolognese and béchamel sauces. May be made with ricotta filling*
lattuga *lettuce*
lenticchie *lentils usually cooked with pork sausage*
lepre *hare*
lepre in salmi *hare stewed in wine*
limone *lemon*
linguine *thin strips of pasta*
lombata di maiale *pork chop*
lonza *type of salami*
luccio *pike*
lumache *snails*
maccheroni *macaroni*
maccheroni ai quattro formaggi *pasta with four cheeses*
maccheroni alla chitarra *square-shaped pasta often served with lamb in chilli and tomato sauce*
macedonia (con panna) *fresh fruit salad (with cream)*
macinata *mince*
magro, di *a meatless dish (often a fish alternative)*
maiale *pork*
maionese *mayonnaise*
mandorle *almonds*
manzo *beef*
mascarpone *rich cream cheese used in desserts such as tiramisù*
mela *apple*
melanzane *aubergines – found in a great variety of regional dishes*
melanzane alla Parmigiana *layers of aubergine baked with tomato or meat sauce, parma ham and grated parmesan cheese*
melanzane ripiene *stuffed aubergines*
melograno *pomegranate*
melone *melon*

menta *mint*
merengata *meringue and ice cream dessert*
merluzzo *cod*
miele *honey*
minestra *soup*
minestra calanchina *vegetable and rice soup served with cheese*
minestrone *thick vegetable, bean and pasta soup with many regional variations*
minestrone al pesto *minestrone flavoured with pesto sauce*
missultitt *grilled dried fish from Lake Como, often eaten with* **polenta**
misto di funghi *mushroom stew*
more *blackberries*
mortadella *type of salami*
mostarda *fruit pickled in syrup and mustard sauce. Served with* **bollito** *(boiled meats)*
mozzarella *cheese traditionally made from buffalo milk but increasingly made from cow's milk. Usually preserved in liquid and used on pizza*
mozzarella in carozza *mozarella sandwiched between slices of bread dipped in egg and breadcrumbs and then fried*
nocciole *hazelnuts*
nocciole d'agnello *noisette of lamb*
nocepesca *nectarine*
noci *walnuts*
olio *oil*
olio d'oliva *olive oil*
olive *olives*
orecchiette *ear-shaped pasta*
orecchiette ai broccoli *pasta with broccoli*
origano *oregano*
ossobucco *marrow-bone veal steak cooked in tomato and wine sauce*
ostriche *oysters*
paglia e fieno *literally straw and grass; a combination of green and plain ribbon pasta cooked with mushrooms sausage and cream*
pan pepato *sweet loaf with mixed nuts*
pancetta *streaky bacon*
pandoro *a large yeast cake rich in butter and eggs, traditionally eaten at Christmas*
pane *bread*
pane e coperto *cover charge*

panettone *a large cork-shaped yeast cake with dried fruit, rich in eggs and butter. Traditionally eaten at Christmas*
panforte *a hard dried fruit and nut cake*
panna *cream*
pansôti (di Rapallo) *literally 'pot-bellied', pasta squares filled with spinach and egg and served in a walnut and parmesan sauce*
panzerotti *ravioli stuffed with mozzarella, salami and ham. Usually fried*
paparelle e fegatini *chicken livers with pasta*
pappardelle *wide ribbon-shaped pasta*
pappardelle al sugo di lepre *wide ribbon pasta with hare, wine and tomato sauce*
parmigiana di melanzane *layers of aubergine cooked in the oven with tomato sauce and parmesan cheese*
parmigiano *parmesan cheese. A hard cow's milk cheese used extensively in Italian cooking. It is always best to use freshly grated parmesan*
pasta *the dry variety takes between 10 and 15 minutes to cook. The fresh variety just 3 or 4 minutes*
pasta all'uovo *fresh pasta made from flour and eggs*
pasta asciutta *pasta served with a sauce such as* **spaghetti al sugo** *and not in a soup form such as* **ravioli in brodo** (ravioli in bouillon)
pasta con le sarde *a baked dish of layers of pasta and fried sardines*
pasta fresca *fresh pasta*
pasticcio *pie*
patate *potatoes*
patate fritte *chips*
pecorino *hard tangy cheese made from ewe's milk. Used in pesto*
penne *quill-shaped pasta*
penne rigate *ribbed quill-shaped pasta*
peperonata *sweet peppers cooked with tomatoes and olive oil*
peperoncino *hot chilli pepper*
peperoni ripieni *stuffed peppers (the filling depends on the region)*
pere *pears*
pesca *peach*
pesce *fish*
pesce arrosto *baked fish (whole)*
pesce persico *perch*
pesce spada *swordfish, often grilled or served in a tomato sauce*
pesce spada alla siciliana *swordfish cooked with orange and lemon juice*

pesto *sauce traditionally made from fresh young basil leaves pounded with garlic, pine-nuts, olive oil and pecorino cheese.*
petto di pollo *chicken breast*
pezzenta *variety of salad*
piatto *dish*
piatto del giorno *dish of the day*
piatti tipici *regional dishes*
piccatine al limone *tender thinly sliced veal in butter and lemon*
pietanze *main courses*
pinoli *pine-nuts*
piselli *peas*
pistacchio *pistachio*
pizza *originally from Naples and cooked in wood-burning ovens. The most basic is* **pizza margherita** *with tomato, basil and mozarella*
pizza ai funghi *mushroom pizza*
pizza alla Siciliana *pizza with tomato, anchovy, black olives and capers*
pizza margherita *created after the first queen of a united Italy symbolising the colours of the Italian flag: red (tomatoes), green (basil) and white (mozarella)*
pizza quattro formaggi *a pizza divided into four sections, each with a different type of cheese topping*
pizza quattro stagioni *literally four seasons: the pizza is divided into four sections with a selection of toppings on each section*
pizzocheri *pasta noodles made from buckwheat flour and cooked in the oven with cabbage, potatoes and melted cheese*
polenta *coarse corn or maize meal porridge which solidifies and can be cut into slices. Considered rather bland by those who have not grown up with it, it is a perfect accompaniment to stews. Can be dipped in egg, breadcrumbs, grated parmesan and then fried*
polenta e osei *polenta with song birds. Not for the squeamish*
polenta uncia *polenta cooked with butter, garlic and Fontina cheese*
pollame *poultry/fowl*
pollo *chicken*
pollo alla diavola *chicken grilled with herbs and chilli pepper*
pollo alla marengo *chicken cooked in wine,served with eggs and prawns*
pollo alla romana *chicken with tomatoes and peppers*
pollo arrosto *roast chicken*
polpette *meatballs made from minced lean beef with grated parmesan and parsley*

polpo *octopus, served in salad (cold) or tomato sauce*
polpo affogato *octopus cooked in tomato sauce*
pomodori da sugo *plum tomatoes*
pomodori *tomatoes*
pompelmo *grapefruit*
porceddu *suckling pig*
porchetta *roast suckling pig*
porcini *prized cep mushrooms which are often dried.*
porri *leeks*
pranzo *lunch*
prezzemolo *parsley*
prima colazione *breakfast*
primo *first course*
prosciutto *ham*
prosciutto cotto *boiled ham*
prosciutto crudo *cured Parma ham which is sliced off the bone*
prosciutto di cinghiale *cured ham made from wild boar*
prosciutto e melone *Parma ham and melon slices*
provolone *creamy cow's milk cheese, mild to strong*
prugne *plums*
quaglie *quails*
radicchio *red-leaf lettuce*
ragù alla bolognese *bolognese sauce*
rana pescatrice *monkfish*
rane *frogs' legs*
ravioli *pasta cushions filled with meat or cheese and spinach*
ribes *blackcurrants*
ricotta *soft white cheese used as filling for pasta as well as in desserts*
rigatoni *ribbed tubes of pasta*
risi e bisati *rice cooked with eel – a traditional Venetian dish*
risi e bisi *thick rice and pea soup (almost liquid risotto) cooked with bacon*
riso *rice*
riso alla pilota *rice cooked with sausage, nutmeg and cinnamon*
risotto *rice cooked in broth with different ingredients added*
risotto ai funghi *risotto with porcini mushrooms*
risotto al nero di seppie *risotto made with cuttlefish and its ink*

risotto alla milanese *rich yellow risotto flavoured with saffron, parmesan and butter. The risotto is cooked in meat broth*
risotto alla pescatora *seafood rice*
risotto alle seppie *Venetian speciality, risotto cooked with squid. Its ink turns the rice black*
risotto con le quaglie *quails with risotto*
robiola *creamy cheese with a mild taste*
rognone *kidney*
rosmarino *rosemary*
salame *salami (there are many types)*
sale *salt*
salmone *salmon*
salsa *sauce*
salsa verde *sauce made of olive oil, breadcrumbs, anchovies, hard boiled egg and parsley. Usually served with boiled meat or fish*
salsicce *sausages: there are many regional variations but they are mainly thick pork sausages which can be boiled or grilled*
saltimbocca alla romana *veal cooked in white wine with parma ham*
salvia *sage*
sarde *sardines*
sarde e beccafico *sardines stuffed with breadcrumbs, anchovies, sultanas and pine-nuts*
sarde in saour *sardines marinated in vinegar, sultanas and pine-nuts*
sartù di riso *rice and meat timbale (rather like a pie)*
scaloppine *veal escalopes*
scaloppine al limone *veal escalopes cooked in lemon juice*
scaloppine al marsala *veal escalopes cooked in marsala*
scamorza *a cheese similar to mozarella but smoked*
scampi *scampi*
secondo *main dish, usually meat or fish.*
sedano *celery*
semifreddo *chilled dessert made with ice cream*
senape *mustard*
seppie coi piselli *squid cooked with peas*
servizio compreso *service included*
sfogliatelle frolle *puff pastry cakes filled with ricotta cheese*
sgavecio *fried fish served cold with vinegar and seasonings*
sgombro *mackerel*
soffritto *pig's offal with tomatoes and spices*

sogliola *sole*
sopa cauda *soup made from bread and pigeon meat*
soppressata *type of salami, with pistachio*
sott'oglio *in olive oil*
spaghetti *spaghetti*
spaghetti aglio, olio e peperoncino *spaghetti with garlic, chilli pepper and olive oil sauce*
spaghetti all'amatriciana *spaghetti with bacon, onion and tomato sauce*
spaghettini aromatici *very fine spaghetti cooked in anchovy, garlic, black olive and caper sauce*
spezzatine *stew, usually with tomato sauce*
spiedini *meat kebabs*
spinaci *spinach*
spinaci alla piemontese *spinach cooked with anchovies and garlic*
stoccafisso *stoccafisso (bacalà, as opposed to baccalà) is dried, not salted cod and needs still more soaking before cooking*
stracciatella *consommé with egg stirred in and grated parmesan*
stracotto *braised beef which is cooked with vegetables for over three hours so that the meat becomes very tender. Often served with polenta*
sugo *sauce, often refers to the basic tomato, basil and garlic sauce (same as* ***al pomodoro****)*
tacchino *turkey*
tagliatelle *ribbon-like pasta often served in cream sauce*
Taleggio *soft, creamy cheese similar to Camembert*
tartine *canapés*
tartufo *truffles: both white (bianco) and black (nero) used extensively in risotto and game dishes*
tartufo di cioccolato *a rich chocolate ice cream shaped like a truffle*
teglia *earthenware casserole dish*
tiella di sardine *baked sardines with cheese*
timballo *a baked dish*
timballo di melanzane *baked dish of aubergines, egg, cheese and parma ham*
timo *thyme*
tinche *tench*
tiramisù *dessert made with mascarpone, sponge, coffee and marsala*
tonno *tuna fish*
tonno e fagioli *tuna and bean salad*
torrone *nougat, traditionally eaten at Christmas*

torta *cake/flan/tart*
tortellini *meat filled pasta cushions reputedly modelled on Venus' navel*
tortellini panna e prosciutto *tortellini cooked with cream and ham*
tortine al tartufo *little savoury tarts with truffles*
trenette *long thin strips of pasta, traditionally served with pesto sauce*
triglie *red mullet*
triglie alla livornese *red mullet fried with chillies in tomato sauce*
trippa *tripe, often cooked with tomatoes and onions*
trota *trout*
trote alla panna acida *trout in soured cream*
ucelli scappati *pork kebabs*
uova *eggs*
uova alla fiorentina *poached eggs on spinach tarts*
uva *grapes*
uva passa *raisins*
vaniglia *vanilla*
verdure *vegetables*
vermicelli *very thin pasta*
verza *Savoy (green) cabbage*
vitello *veal*
vongole *clams*
wurstel *Frankfurter sausages*
zabaglione *frothy dessert made with egg yolks and sugar beaten with marsala over heat*
zafferano *saffron, used in* **risotto alla milanese**
zampone *spicy sausage in shape of a pig's trotter, sliced and served hot*
zucca *marrow*
zucchero *sugar*
zucchini *courgettes*
zuccotto *rich cream and nut pudding in the shape of a pumpkin*
zuppa *soup*
zuppa di cozze *mussel and tomato soup*
zuppa di fagioli *bean soup*
zuppa di pesce *seafood soup with many delicious regional variations*
zuppa inglese *dessert similar to trifle*
zuppa pavese *a bread soup with broth and poached eggs, topped with grated cheese*

DICTIONARY
english-italian
italian-english

A

a(n) un/una/uno *see* **GRAMMAR**
abbey l'abbazia *(f)*
to be able (to) essere capace (di)
abortion l'aborto *(m)*
abortion pill la pillola per abortire
about su ; circa
a book about... un libro su...
about ten o'clock circa le dieci
above sopra
abroad: *to go abroad* andare all'estero
abscess l'ascesso *(m)*
accelerator l'acceleratore *(m)*
accent l'accento *(m)*
to accept accettare
accident l'incidente *(m)*
accident & emergency dept il pronto soccorso
accommodation l'alloggio *(m)*
to accompany accompagnare
account *(bill)* il conto
(in bank) il conto in banca
account number il numero del conto
to ache fare male
my head aches mi fa male la testa
my stomach aches mi fa male lo stomaco
my tooth aches mi fa male il dente
acid l'acido *(m)*
actor *(m/f)* l'attore/l'attrice
adaptor *(for electrical appliance)* il riduttore
adder la vipera
address l'indirizzo *(m)*
what is the address? qual è l'indirizzo?
address book la rubrica
admission charge/fee il biglietto d'ingresso
to admit *(to hospital)* ricoverare
adult l'adulto(a)
for adults per adulti
advance: *in advance* in anticipo
advertisement la pubblicità
(in newspaper) l'annuncio
to advise consigliare
aeroplane l'aeroplano *(m)*
aerosol l'aerosol *(m)*
after dopo
after lunch dopo pranzo
afternoon il pomeriggio
this afternoon oggi pomeriggio
in the afternoon di pomeriggio
tomorrow afternoon domani pomeriggio
aftershave il dopobarba
again ancora ; di nuovo
against contro
age l'età *(f)*
agency l'agenzia *(f)*
ago fa
a week ago una settimana fa
to agree essere d'accordo
agreement l'accordo *(m)*
AIDS l'AIDS *(m)*
air-conditioning l'aria condizionata *(f)*
is there air-conditioning? c'è l'aria condizionata?
air freshener il deodorante per l'ambiente
airline la linea aerea
air mail: *by air mail* per via aerea
air mattress il materassino
airplane l'aeroplano *(m)*
airport l'aeroporto *(m)*
air ticket il biglietto d'aereo *(m)*
alarm l'allarme *(m)*
alarm clock la sveglia
alcohol l'alcool *(m)*
alcohol-free analcolico(a)
alcoholic alcolico(a)
is it alcoholic? è alcolico(a)?
all tutto(a)
allergic to allergico(a) a
I'm allergic to sono allergico(a) a...

allergy l'allergia *(f)*
to allow permettere
all right *(agreed)* va bene
are you all right? sta bene?
almond la mandorla
almost quasi
alone solo(a)
Alps le Alpi
also anche
altar l'altare *(m)*
aluminium foil la carta stagnola
always sempre
am *see* (to be) **GRAMMAR**
amber *(light)* il giallo
ambulance l'ambulanza *(f)*
America l'America *(f)*
American americano(a)
anaesthetic l'anestetico *(m)*
local anaesthetic l'anestetico locale
general anaesthetic l'anestetico generale
anchor l'ancora *(f)*
anchovy l'acciuga *(f)*
ancient antico(a)
and e
angel l'angelo *(m)*
angina l'angina pectoris *(f)*
angry arrabbiato(a)
animal l'animale *(m)*
aniseed l'anice *(m)*
ankle la caviglia
anniversary l'anniversario *(m)*
annual annuale
another un altro/un'altra
another beer un'altra birra
another coffee un altro caffè
answer la risposta
to answer rispondere
answerphone la segretaria telefonica
antacid l'antiacido *(m)*
antibiotic l'antibiotico *(m)*
antifreeze l'antigelo *(m)*
antihistamine l'antistaminico *(m)*
antique shop il negozio d'antiquariato
antiques i pezzi d'antiquariato
antiseptic l'antisettico *(m)*
any dei/delle/degli (di) *see* **GRAMMAR**
I haven't any money non ho soldi
apartment l'appartamento *(m)*
apéritif l'aperitivo *(m)*
appendicitis l'appendicite *(f)*
apple la mela
apple juice il succo di mela
appointment l'appuntamento *(m)*
I have an appointment ho un appuntamento
apricot l'albicocca *(f)*
April aprile
architect *m/f* l'architetto
architecture l'architettura *(f)*
are *see* (to be) **GRAMMAR**
arm il braccio
armbands *(swimming)* i braccioli
armchair la poltrona
aromatherapy l'aromaterapia *(f)*
to arrange sistemare
to arrest arrestare
arrivals *(plane, train)* gli arrivi
to arrive arrivare
art l'arte *(f)*
art gallery la galleria d'arte ; la pinacoteca
arthritis l'artrite *(f)*
artichoke il carciofo
artist *m/f* l'artista
ashtray il portacenere
to ask *(question)* domandare
(for something) chiedere
asleep: ***he/she is asleep*** dorme
asparagus gli asparagi
aspirin l'aspirina *(f)*
soluble aspirin l'aspirina solubile
asthma l'asma *(f)*
I have asthma ho l'asma
at a/al/alla, etc *see* **GRAMMAR**
at home a casa

at 8 o'clock alle otto
at once subito
at night di notte
Atlantic Ocean l'Atlantico *(m)*
to attack aggredire
attic il solaio
attractive attraente
aubergine la melanzana
au pair la ragazza alla pari
auction l'asta *(f)*
audience il pubblico
August agosto
aunt la zia
Australia l'Australia *(f)*
Australian australiano(a)
author *m/f* l'autore/l'autrice
automatic car la macchina con cambio automatico
auto-teller *(cash dispenser)* il Bancomat®
autumn l'autunno *(m)*
available disponibile
avalanche la valanga
avenue il viale
average medio(a)
avocado l'avocado *(m)*
to avoid evitare
awful terribile
axle *(car)* l'asse *(m)*

B

baby il/la bambino(a)
baby food gli alimenti per bambini
baby wipes le salviettine per bambini
baby's bottle il biberon
babyseat *(in car)* il sedile per bambini
babysitter il/la babysitter
babysitting service il servizio di babysitting
bachelor lo scapolo
back *(of body)* la schiena
backpack lo zaino
bacon la pancetta
bad *(food)* andato(a) a male
(weather, news, etc) brutto(a)
bag la borsa
baggage i bagagli
baggage reclaim il ritiro bagagli
bait *(for fishing)* l'esca *(m)*
baked al forno
baker's la panetteria ; il panificio
balcony il balcone
bald *(person)* calvo(a)
(tyre) liscio(a)
ball *(large: football, etc)* il pallone
(small: golf, tennis, etc) la pallina
ballet il balletto
balloon il palloncino
banana la banana
band *(musical)* la banda
bandage la benda
bank la banca
(river) la riva
bank account il conto in banca
banknote la banconota
bankrupt fallito(a)
bar il bar
barbecue il barbecue
to have a barbecue fare il barbecue
barber il barbiere
barcode il codice a barra
to bark abbaiare
barn il granaio
barrel *(wine/beer)* il barile
basement il seminterrato
basil il basilico
basket il cestino
basketball il basket
bath il bagno
to have a bath fare un bagno
bathing cap la cuffia
bathroom il bagno
with bathroom con bagno
battery *(radio, camera, etc)* la pila
(car) la batteria

bay *(along coast)* la baia
bay leaf la foglia d'alloro
to be essere (to be) *see* **GRAMMAR**
beach la spiaggia
private beach la spiaggia privata
sandy beach la spiaggia con sabbia
beach hut la cabina
bean il fagiolo
broad bean la fava
coffee bean il chicco
french/green bean il fagiolino
kidney bean il fagiolo rosso
soya bean il seme di soya
bear l'orso *(m)*
beard la barba
beautiful bello(a)
beauty salon l'istituto di bellezza *(m)*
because perché
bed il letto
double bed il letto matrimoniale
single bed il letto a una piazza
sofa bed il divano letto
twin beds i letti gemelli
bed and breakfast la pensione familiare
bedroom la camera da letto
bee l'ape *(f)*
beef il manzo
beer la birra
draught beer la birra alla spina
beetroot la barbabietola
before prima di
before breakfast prima di colazione
to begin cominciare
behind dietro di
beige beige
to believe credere
bell *(church)* la campana
(doorbell) il campanello
below sotto
belt la cintura
bend *(in road)* la curva
beside *(next to)* accanto a
beside the bank accanto alla banca
best: *the best* il/la migliore
to bet scommettere
better (than) meglio (di)
between fra
to beware of stare attento(a) a
beyond oltre
bib *(baby's)* il bavaglino
bicycle la bicicletta ; la bici
by bicycle in bicicletta
bicycle lock il lucchetto della bici
bicycle repair kit il kit per riparare la bici
bidet il bidet
big grande
bigger (than) più grande (di)
bike *(pushbike)* la bici
bikini il bikini
bilberry il mirtillo
bill *(in hotel, restaurant)* il conto
(for work done) la fattura
(gas, telephone) la bolletta
billion il miliardo
bin *(dustbin)* il bidone
bin liner la borsa della spazzatura
binoculars il binocolo
bird l'uccello *(m)*
biro la biro
birth certificate il certificato di nascita
birthday il compleanno
happy birthday! auguri! buon compleanno
my birthday is on... il mio compleanno è il...
birthday card il biglietto d'auguri di compleanno
birthday present il regalo di compleanno
biscuits i biscotti
bishop il vescovo
bit il pezzo
a bit un po'
to bite *(animal)* mordere
(insect) morsicare

b

bitten morso(a)
(by insect) morsicato(a)
bitter *(taste)* amaro(a)
black nero(a)
blackberries le more
blackcurrant il ribes nero
black ice il ghiaccio sulla strada
blanket la coperta
bleach la candeggina
to bleed sanguinare
blender il frullatore
blind *(person)* cieco(a)
blind *(for window)* l'avvolgibile *(f)*
blister la vescica
block of flats il palazzo
blocked *(pipe, sink)* ingorgato(a)
blond *(person)* biondo(a)
blood il sangue
blood group il gruppo sanguigno
blood pressure la pressione sanguigna
blood test l'analasi del sangue *(f)*
blouse la camicetta
to blow-dry asciugare con il fon
blue *(light)* azzurro(a)
dark blue blu scuro
blunt *(knife, blade)* non taglia
boar il cinghiale
boarding card/pass la carta d'imbarco
boat la barca ; il battello
(rowing) la barca a remi
boat trip la gita in battello
body il corpo
(clothing) il body
to boil bollire
boiled bollito(a)
bomb la bomba
bone l'osso *(m)*
fish bone la spina di pesce
bonnet *(car)* il cofano
book il libro
to book prenotare
booking la prenotazione
booking office *(train)* la biglietteria
book of tickets il blocchetto di biglietti
bookshop la libreria
boots *(long)* gli stivali
(ankle) gli stivaletti
border *(of country)* la frontiera
boring noioso(a)
born: *to be born* essere nato(a)
to borrow prendere in prestito
boss il capo
both tutti e due
bottle la bottiglia
a bottle of wine una bottiglia di vino
a half-bottle una mezza bottiglia
bottle opener l'apribottiglie *(m)*
bowl *(for cereal, soup)* la scodella
bow tie la cravatta a farfalla
box la scatola
box office *(theatre)* il botteghino
boxer shorts i boxer
boy *(young child)* il bambino
(teenage) il ragazzo
boyfriend il ragazzo
bra il reggiseno
bracelet il braccialetto
brain il cervello
to brake frenare
brake fluid il liquido dei freni
brake light il fanalino dello stop
brakes i freni
branch *(of tree)* il ramo
(of bank, etc) la succursale
brand *(make)* la marca
brandy il brandy
brass l'ottone *(m)*
brave coraggioso(a)
bread il pane
brown bread il pane integrale
french bread il filoncino
sliced bread il pancarré
bread roll il panino
breadcrumbs il pangrattato
to break rompere
breakable fragile

breakdown *(car)* il guasto
(nervous) l'esaurimento nervoso *(m)*
breakdown van il carro attrezzi
breakfast la (prima) colazione
breast *(of chicken)* il petto di pollo
to breathe respirare
brick il mattone
bride la sposa
bridegroom lo sposo
bridge il ponte
(game) il bridge
briefcase la cartella
to bring portare
Britain la Gran Bretagna
British britannico(a)
broccoli i broccoli
brochure l'opuscolo *(m)*
broken rotto(a)
broken down *(car, etc)* guasto(a)
bronchitis la bronchite
bronze il bronzo
brooch la spilla
broom *(brush)* la scopa
brother il fratello
brother-in-law il cognato
brown marrone
bruise il livido
brush la spazzola
Brussels sprouts i cavoletti di Bruxelles
bubble bath il bagnoschiuma
bucket il secchiello
buffet car la vagone ristorante
to build costruire
building l'edificio *(m)*
bulb *(lightbulb)* la lampadina
bull il toro
bumbag il marsupio
bumper *(on car)* il paraurti
bunch *(of flowers)* il mazzo di fiori
(of grapes) il grappolo d'uva
bungee jumping il bungee jumping
bureau de change l'agenzia di cambio *(f)*
burger l'hamburger *(m)*
burglar il/la ladro(a)
burglar alarm l'antifurto *(m)*
to burn bruciare
bus l'autobus *(m)*
bus pass la tessera dell'autobus
bus station la stazione delle autolinee
bus stop la fermata (dell'autobus)
bus ticket il biglietto d'autobus
business gli affari
on business per affari
business card il biglietto da visita
business class la business class
businessman/woman l'uomo/la donna d'affari
business trip il viaggio d'affari
busy occupato(a) ; impegnato(a)
but ma ; però
butcher's il macellaio
butter il burro
buttercup il ranuncolo
butterfly la farfalla
button il bottone
to buy comprare
by *(next to)* accanto a
(via) via
by bus in autobus
by car in macchina
by train in treno
by ship in battello
bypass *(road)* la circonvallazione

C

cab *(taxi)* il taxi
cabaret il cabaret
cabbage il cavolo
cabin *(on boat)* la cabina
cable TV la TV via cavo
cablecar la funivia
café il bar
internet café il cyber-café
cafetière la caffettiera

C

cake *(big)* la torta
(small) il pasticcino
cake shop la pasticceria
calculator la calcolatrice
calendar il calendario
calf *(young cow)* il vitello
to call chiamare
(phone) chiamare per telefono
calm calmo(a)
camcorder la videocamera
camera la macchina fotografica
camera case la custodia della macchina fotografica
to camp campeggiare
camping gas il camping gas
camping stove il fornellino da campeggio
campsite il campeggio
can il barattolo ; la scatola
to can *(to be able)* potere
I/we can posso/possiamo
I cannot/we cannot non posso/non possiamo
can I...? posso...?
can we...? possiamo...?
Canada il Canada
Canadian canadese
canal il canale
to cancel cancellare ; annullare
cancellation la cancellazione
cancer il cancro
candle la candela
canoe la canoa
to canoe andare in canoa
can opener l'apriscatole *(m)*
cap *(hat)* il berretto
(diaphragm) il diaframma
capital *(city)* la capitale
car la macchina
car alarm l'antifurto *(m)*
car ferry il traghetto
car hire l'autonoleggio *(m)*
car insurance l'assicurazione della macchina *(f)*
car keys le chiave della macchina
car park il parcheggio
car parts i pezzi di ricambio
car seat *(for children)* il sedile per bambini
car wash il lavaggio auto
carafe la caraffa
caravan la roulotte
carburettor il carburatore
card *(greetings)* il biglietto d'auguri
(business) il biglietto da visita
(playing cards) le carte da gioco
cardboard il cartone
cardigan il cardigan
careful attento(a)
to be careful fare attenzione
carnation il garofano
carpenter il falegname
carpet *(fitted)* la moquette
(rug) il tappeto
carriage *(railway)* il vagone
carrots le carote
to carry portare
carton il cartone
case *(suitcase)* la valigia
cash i contanti
to cash *(cheque)* incassare
cash desk la cassa
cash dispenser *(autoteller)* il Bancomat®
cashier il/la cassiere(a)
casino il casinò
casserole la casseruola
cassette la cassetta
cassette player il registratore
castle il castello
casualty department il pronto soccorso
cat il gatto
catacombs le catacombe
catalogue il catalogo
to catch *(bus, train, etc)* prendere
cathedral il duomo
Catholic cattolico(a)
cauliflower il cavolfiore

cave la grotta
caviar il caviale
CD il CD
CD player il lettore CD
ceiling il soffitto
celery il sedano
cellar la cantina
cemetery il cimitero
centimetre il centimetro
central centrale
central heating il riscaldamento
central locking *(car)* la chiusura centralizzata
centre il centro
century il secolo
ceramics la ceramica
certificate il certificato
chain la catena
chair la sedia
chairlift la seggiovia
chalet lo chalet
challenge la sfida
chambermaid la cameriera
Champagne lo Champagne
change il cambio
(small coins) gli spiccioli
(money returned) il resto
to change money cambiare soldi
to change clothes cambiarsi
to change train cambiare treno
changing room lo spogliatoio
Channel *(English)* la Manica
chapel la cappella
charcoal il carbone
charter flight il volo charter
cheap economico(a)
cheaper più economico(a)
cheap rate *(phone)* la tariffa economica
to check controllare
to check in *(airport)* fare il check-in
(at hotel) firmare il registro
check-in il check-in
cheek la guancia
cheers! salute! ; cin-cin!
cheese il formaggio
chef il cuoco
chemical toilet il gabinetto biologico
chemist's la farmacia
cheque l'assegno *(m)*
cheque book il libretto degli assegni
cheque card la carta assegni
cherries le ciliegie
chest *(anat)* il petto
chest of drawers il cassettone
chestnuts le castagne
chewing gum la cicca
chicken il pollo
chicken breast il petto di pollo
chickenpox la varicella
chickpeas i ceci
child il/la bambino(a)
children *(small)* i bambini
(older children) i ragazzi
for chidren per bambini
child safety seat *(car)* il seggiolino di sicurezza per bambini
chilli il peperoncino
chimney il camino
chin il mento
china la porcellana
chips *(french fries)* le patatine fritte
chives l'erba cipollina *(f)*
chocolate la cioccolata
chocolates i cioccolatini
choir il coro
choice la scelta
to choose scegliere
chop *(meat)* la costoletta
chopping board il tagliere
christening il battesimo
Christian name il nome di battesimo
Christmas il Natale
Merry Christmas! Buon Natale!
Father Christmas Babbo Natale
Christmas card il biglietto di auguri natalizi

C

Christmas Eve la vigilia di Natale
Christmas present il regalo di Natale
chrysanthemum il crisantemo
church la chiesa
cider il sidro
cigar il sigaro
cigarette la sigaretta
cigarette lighter l'accendino *(m)*
cigarette papers le cartine
cinema il cinema
circle *(theatre)* la galleria
circuit breaker il salvavita
circus il circo
cistern la cisterna
(of toilet) il serbatoio dell'acqua
citizen il/la cittadino(a)
city la città
city centre il centro città
class: ***first class*** prima classe
second class seconda classe
clean pulito(a)
to clean pulire
cleanser *(for face)* il detergente
clear chiaro(a)
client il/la cliente
cliff *(along coast)* la scogliera
(mountain) la rupe
to climb scalare
climbing l'alpinismo *(m)*
climbing boots gli scarponi da montagna
clingfilm® la pellicola per alimenti
clinic la clinica
cloakroom il guardaroba
clock l'orologio *(m)*
to close chiudere
closed *(shop, etc)* chiuso(a)
cloth il panno
clothes i vestiti
clothes peg la molletta
clothes shop il negozio d'abbigliamento
cloudy nuvoloso(a)
clove *(spice)* il chiodo di garofano
club il club
clutch *(car)* la frizione
coach il pullman
coach station la stazione dei pullman
coach trip la gita in pullman
coal il carbone
coast la costa
coastguard il guardacoste
coat il cappotto
coat hanger la gruccia
Coca Cola® la Coca Cola®
cockroach lo scarafaggio
cocktail il cocktail
cocoa il cacao
coconut la noce di cocco
code il codice
coffee *(espresso)* il caffè
black coffee il caffè americano
white coffee il caffellatte
cappuccino il cappuccino
decaffeinated coffee il decaffeinato
coil *(IUD)* la spirale
coin la moneta
Coke® la Coca®
colander lo scolapasta
cold freddo(a)
I'm cold ho freddo
it's cold fa freddo
cold *(illness)* il raffreddore
I have a cold ho il raffreddore
cold sore l'herpes *(m)*
Coliseum il Colosseo
collar il colletto
collar bone la clavicola
colleague il/la collega
to collect raccogliere
(to collect someone) andare a prendere
colour il colore
colour-blind daltonico(a)
colour film *(for camera)* la pellicola a colori
comb il pettine

to come venire
(to arrive) arrivare
to come back tornare
to come in entrare
come in! avanti!
comedy la commedia
comfortable comodo(a)
company *(firm)* la ditta
compartment lo scompartimento
compass la bussola
to complain fare un reclamo
complaint il reclamo
composer il compositore/la compositrice
compulsory obbligatorio(a)
computer il computer
computer disk *(floppy)* il dischetto
computer game il videogioco
computer program il programma di computer
computer programmer il programmatore/la programmatrice
computer software il software
concert il concerto
concert hall la sala da concerti
concession la riduzione
concussion la commozione cerebrale
condensed milk il latte condensato
conditioner il balsamo
condoms i preservativi
conductor *(on bus)* il bigliettaio
(music) il direttore d'orchestra
cone il cono
conference il congresso
to confirm confermare
congratulations le congratulazioni
connection *(train, etc)* la coincidenza
to consider considerare
constipated stitico(a)
consulate il consolato
to consult consultare
to contact mettersi in contatto con
contact lens cleaner il liquido per lenti a contatto
contact lenses le lenti a contatto
to continue continuare
contraceptive l'anticoncezionale *(m)*
contract il contratto
convenient: ***is it convenient?*** va bene?
to cook cucinare
cooked cotto(a)
cooker la cucina
cool fresco(a)
cool-box *(picnic)* la borsa termica
copper il rame
copy la copia
to copy copiare
coral il corallo
coriander il coriandolo
cork il tappo
corkscrew il cavatappi
corner l'angolo *(m)*
corridor il corridoio
cosmetics i cosmetici
to cost costare
how much does it cost? quanto costa?
costume *(swimming)* il costume da bagno
cot il lettino
cottage il cottage
cotton il cotone
cotton bud il cotton fioc®
cotton wool il cotone idrofilo
couchette la cuccetta
cough la tosse
to cough tossire
cough mixture lo sciroppo per la tosse
cough sweets le pasticche per la tosse
counter *(in shop, bar, etc)* il banco
country *(not town)* la campagna
(nation) il paese
countryside la campagna
couple *(two people)* la coppia

courgettes le zucchine
courier il corriere
course *(of meal)* il piatto
(of study) il corso
cousin il/la cugino(a)
cover charge il coperto
cow la mucca
crab il granchio
crafts l'artigianato *(m)*
craftsman/woman l'artigiano(a)
cramps i crampi
crash *(car)* lo scontro
to crash *(car)* avere un incidente
crash helmet il casco
cream *(lotion)* la crema
(dairy) la panna
soured cream la panna acida
whipped cream la panna montata
credit card la carta di credito
crime il reato
crisps le patatine
croissant la brioche
croquette la crocchetta
to cross *(road)* attraversare
cross la croce
cross-country skiing lo sci di fondo
crossing *(sea, lake)* la traversata
crossroads l'incrocio *(m)*
crossword puzzle il cruciverba
crowd la folla
crowded affollato(a)
crown la corona
cruise la crociera
crutches le grucce
to cry *(weep)* piangere
crystal *(made of)* di cristallo
cucumber il cetriolo
cufflinks i gemelli
cul-de-sac il vicolo cieco
cumin il cumino
cup la tazza
cupboard l'armadio *(m)*
curlers i bigodini
currant la sultanina
current *(electric, water)* la corrente
curtain la tenda
cushion il cuscino
custom *(tradition)* il costume
customer il/la cliente
customs *(duty)* la dogana
cut il taglio
to cut tagliare
cutlery le posate
to cycle andare in bicicletta
cycle track la pista ciclabile
cyst la cisti
cystitis la cistite

D

daddy papà
daffodil la giunchiglia
dahlia la dalia
daily *(each day)* ogni giorno ;
quotidiano(a)
dairy produce i latticini
daisy la margherita
damage il danno
damp umido(a)
dance il ballo
to dance ballare
danger il pericolo
dangerous pericoloso(a)
dark *(colour)* scuro(a)
(night) buio(a)
after dark a notte fatta
date la data
date of birth la data di nascita
daughter la figlia
daughter-in-law la nuora
dawn l'alba *(f)*
day il giorno
per day al giorno
dead morto(a)
deaf sordo(a)
dear caro(a)
decaffeinated decaffeinato(a)
have you decaffeinated coffee?
ha del decaffeinato?

December dicembre
deckchair la sedia a sdraio
to declare: ***nothing to declare*** niente da dichiarare
deep profondo(a)
deep freeze il surgelatore
deer il cervo
to defrost scongelare
to de-ice sbrinare
delay il ritardo
how long is the delay? di quant'è il ritardo?
delicatessen il negozio di specialità gastronomiche
delicious delizioso(a)
to demonstrate dimostrare
dental floss il filo interdentale
dentist il/la dentista
dentures la dentiera
deodorant il deodorante
to depart partire
department il reparto
department store il grande magazzino
departure lounge la sala partenze
departures le partenze
deposit il deposito
to describe descrivere
description la descrizione
desk la scrivania
(information, etc) il banco
dessert il dolce
details i dettagli
detergent il detersivo
detour la deviazione
to develop *(photos)* sviluppare
diabetes il diabete
diabetic diabetico(a)
I'm diabetic sono diabetico(a)
to dial fare il numero
dialect il dialetto
dialling code il prefisso telefonico
dialling tone il segnale di libero
diamond il diamante
diapers i pannolini
diarrhoea la diarrea
diary l'agenda *(f)*
dice il dado
dictionary il dizionario ; il vocabolario
to die morire
diesel il gasolio
diet la dieta
I'm on a diet sono a dieta
different diverso(a)
difficult difficile
dinghy *(rubber)* il canotto
dining room la sala da pranzo
dinner *(evening meal)* la cena
to have dinner cenare
dinner jacket lo smoking
direct *(train, etc)* diretto(a)
directions le indicazioni
directory *(telephone)* l'elenco telefonico *(m)*
directory enquiries il servizio informazioni
dirty sporco(a)
disabled *(person)* disabile ; handicappato(a)
to disagree non essere d'accordo
to disappear scomparire
disaster il disastro
disco la discoteca
discount lo sconto
to discover scoprire
disease la malattia
dishwasher la lavastoviglie
disinfectant il disinfettante
disk *(computer)* il disco
floppy disk il dischetto
hard disk l'hard disk *(m)*
to dislocate *(joint)* lussarsi
distance la distanza
distilled water l'acqua distillata *(f)*
district *(of town)* il quartiere
to dive tuffarsi
diversion la deviazione
divorced divorziato(a)
I'm divorced sono divorziato(a)

DIY fatelo da voi
DIY shop il negozio di bricolage
dizzy: ***to be dizzy*** avere il capogiro
to do fare see **GRAMMAR**
doctor il medico/la dottoressa
documents i documenti
dog il cane
dog lead il guinzaglio
doll la bambola
dollars i dollari
domestic *(flight)* nazionale
dominoes il gioco del domino
door la porta
doorbell il campanello
double doppio(a)
double bed il letto matrimoniale
double room la camera doppia
down: ***to go down*** scendere
downstairs giù ; dabbasso
draught *(of air)* la corrente (d'aria)
there's a draught c'è corrente

d

draught lager la birra alla spina
drawer il cassetto
drawing il disegno
dress il vestito
to dress *(to get dressed)* vestirsi
dressing *(for food)* il condimento
dressing gown la vestaglia
drill *(tool)* il trapano
drink *(soft)* la bibita
to drink bere
drinking water l'acqua potabile *(f)*
to drive guidare
driver *(of car)* l'autista *(m/f)*
driving licence la patente
drought la siccità
to drown affogare
drug *(medicine)* il farmaco
(narcotics) la droga

d

drunk ubriaco(a)
dry secco(a) ; asciutto(a)
to dry asciugare
dry-cleaner's la tintoria ; il lavasecco
duck l'anatra *(f)*
dummy *(for baby)* la tettarella
during durante
dust la polvere
duster lo straccio
dustpan and brush lo scopino e la paletta
duty-free esente da dogana
duty-free shop il duty free
duvet il piumino
duvet cover il copripiumone
dye la tinta
dynamo la dinamo

each ogni
eagle l'aquila *(f)*
ear l'orecchio *(m)*
earache il mal d'orecchi
earlier più presto
early presto
earphones le cuffie
earrings gli orecchini
earth la terra
earthquake il terremoto
east l'est *(m)*
Easter la Pasqua
Happy Easter! Buona Pasqua!
Easter egg l'uovo di Pasqua
easy facile
to eat mangiare
to eat out mangiare fuori
ebony l'ebano *(m)*
eel l'anguilla *(f)*
egg l'uovo *(m)*
eggs le uova
fried egg l'uovo fritto
hard-boiled egg l'uovo sodo
scrambled eggs l'uova strapazzate
soft-boiled egg l'uovo alla coque
egg white l'albume *(m)*
egg yolk il tuorlo
either: ***either one*** l'uno o l'altro
elastic band l'elastico *(m)*

elastoplast/sticking plaster il cerotto
elbow il gomito
electric elettrico(a)
electrician *m/f* l'elettricista
electricity l'elettricità *(f)*
electricity meter il contatore dell'elettricità
electric razor il rasoio elettrico
elevator l'ascensore *(m)*
e-mail la posta elettronica
to send an e-mail inviare un messaggio di posta elettronica
e-mail address l'indirizzo di posta elettronica *(m)*
embassy l'ambasciata *(f)*
emergency l'emergenza *(f)*
emergency exit l'uscita d'emergenza *(f)*
emery board la limetta per le unghie
empty vuoto(a)
end la fine
engaged *(to be married)* fidanzato(a)
(phone, toilet, etc) occupato(a)
engine il motore
England l'Inghilterra *(f)*
English inglese
(language) l'inglese *(m)*
to enjoy divertirsi
(to like) piacere
I enjoyed the trip la gita mi è piaciuta
I enjoy swimming mi piace nuotare
enough abbastanza
that's enough basta così
enquiry desk il banco informazioni
to enter entrare
entertainment il divertimento
entrance l'entrata *(f)* ; l'ingresso *(m)*
entrance fee il biglietto d'ingresso
envelope la busta
epileptic epilettico(a)
epileptic fit la crisi epilettica
equal uguale ; pari
equipment l'attrezzatura *(f)*
eraser la gomma da cancellare
error l'errore *(m)*
eruption l'eruzione *(f)*
escalator la scala mobile
escape la fuga
to escape fuggire
espadrilles le espadrilles
especially specialmente
estate agent's l'agenzia immobiliare *(f)*
Euro l'Euro *(m)*
Eurocheque l'eurocheque *(m)*
Europe l'Europa *(f)*
European Union l'Unione Europea *(f)*
eve la vigilia
Christmas Eve la vigilia di Natale
New Year's Eve l'ultimo dell'anno
even numbers i numeri pari
evening la sera
this evening stasera
tomorrow evening domani sera
in the evening la sera
evening dress l'abito da sera *(m)*
evening meal la cena
every ogni ; ciascuno ; tutti
everyone tutti
everything tutto
everywhere dappertutto
examination l'esame *(m)*
example: ***for example*** per esempio
excellent ottimo(a)
excess luggage il bagaglio in eccedenza
to exchange cambiare
exchange rate il cambio
exciting emozionante
excursion l'escursione *(f)*
excuse scusare
excuse me! *(sorry)* mi scusi!
(when passing) permesso!
exercise l'esercizio *(m)*
exercise book il quaderno

exhaust pipe il tubo di scappamento
exhibition la mostra
exit l'uscita *(f)*
expense la spesa
expensive costoso(a) ; caro(a)
expert l'esperto(a)
to expire *(ticket, etc)* scadere
to explain spiegare
explosion l'esplosione *(f)*
to export esportare
exposure *(film)* la posa
express *(train)* l'espresso *(m)*
express *(parcel, etc)* espresso(a)
extension *(electrical)* la prolunga
extra *(spare)* in più
(more) supplementare
an extra bed un letto in più
eye l'occhio *(m)*
eye shadow l'ombretto *(m)*
eyebrows le sopracciglia
eye drops il collirio
eyelashes le ciglia
eyeliner l'eye-liner *(m)*

F

fabric la stoffa
face la faccia
face cloth il guanto di spugna
facial la pulizia del viso
factory la fabbrica
to fail fallire
to faint svenire
fainted svenuto(a)
fair *(just)* giusto(a)
(blond) biondo(a)
fair *(trade)* la fiera
(funfair) il luna park
fairway il fairway
fake falso(a)
fall *(autumn)* l'autunno *(m)*
to fall cadere
he/she has fallen è caduto(a)
family la famiglia
famous famoso(a)
fan *(hand-held)* il ventaglio
(electric) il ventilatore
(football) il/la tifoso(a)
fan belt la cinghia della ventola
fancy dress in costume ; in maschera
far lontano(a)
is it far? è lontano?
fare la tariffa
farm la fattoria
farmer l'agricoltore *(m)*
farmhouse la fattoria
fashionable alla moda
fast veloce
too fast troppo veloce
to fasten *(seatbelt, etc)* allacciare
fat grasso(a)
father il padre
father-in-law il suocero
fault *(defect)* il difetto
it's not my fault non è colpa mia
favour il favore
favourite preferito(a)
fax il fax
to fax mandare un fax
by fax per fax
feather la piuma
February febbraio
to feed dare da mangiare
feeding bottle il biberon
to feel sentire ; sentirsi
I don't feel well non mi sento bene
feet i piedi
felt-tip pen il pennarello
female femmina ; femminile
fennel il finocchio
ferry il traghetto
festival la festa
to fetch *(bring)* portare
(to go and get) andare a prendere
fever la febbre
few pochi
a few alcuni

fiancé(e) il/la fidanzato(a)
field il campo
figs i fichi
to fight combattere ; lottare
file *(folder)* il raccoglitore
(computer) l'archivio *(m)*
to fill riempire
to fill in *(form)* compilare
fill it up! *(petrol)* il pieno!
fillet il filetto
filling *(in tooth)* l'otturazione *(f)*
film *(at cinema)* il film
(for camera) la pellicola
colour film la pellicola a colori
black and white film la pellicola in bianco e nero
Filofax® l'agenda *(f)*
filter il filtro
filter-tipped con filtro
to find trovare
fine *(to be paid)* la multa
finger il dito
fingers le dita
to finish finire
finished finito(a)
fir l'abete *(m)*
fire il fuoco ; l'incendio *(m)*
fire! al fuoco!
fire alarm l'allarme antincendio *(m)*
fire brigade i vigili del fuoco
fire escape la scala antincendio
fire extinguisher l'estintore *(m)*
fireplace il caminetto
fireworks i fuochi d'artificio
firm *(company)* l'azienda *(f)* ; la ditta
first primo(a)
first aid il pronto soccorso
first aid kit la cassetta di pronto soccorso
first class la prima classe
first floor il primo piano
firstly per prima cosa
first name il nome di battesimo
fish il pesce
to fish pescare
fisherman il pescatore
fishing permit la licenza di pesca
fishing rod la canna da pesca
fishmonger's la pescheria
to fit *(clothes)* andare bene
it doesn't fit me non mi va bene
fit *(seizure)* l'attacco *(m)*
to fix riparare ; sistemare
can you fix it? può ripararlo?
fizzy gassato(a)
flag la bandiera
flame la fiamma
flannel *(face cloth)* il guanto di spugna
flash *(for camera)* il flash
flashlight la pila
flask *(thermos)* il thermos
flat l'appartamento *(m)*
flat piatto(a)
flat battery la batteria scarica
flat tyre la gomma a terra
flavour il gusto
what flavour? che gusto?
fleas le pulci
fleece *(top/jacket)* la felpa
flex il filo flessibile
flight il volo
flip flops gli infradito
flippers le pinne
flood l'alluvione *(f)*
flash flood l'inondazione *(f)*
floor *(of building)* il piano
(of room) il pavimento
which floor? a che piano?
ground floor il pianterreno
floorcloth lo straccio per pavimenti
floppy disk il dischetto
Florence Firenze
florist's shop il fioraio
flour la farina
flowers i fiori
flu l'influenza *(f)*
fly la mosca
to fly volare

f

to focus *(camera)* mettere a fuoco
fog la nebbia
foggy nebbioso(a)
foil *(silver paper)* la carta stagnola
to fold ripiegare
to follow seguire
food il cibo
food poisoning l'intossicazione alimentare *(f)*
foot il piede
football il calcio ; il pallone
football match la partita di calcio
football pitch il campo di calcio
football player il calciatore
footpath il sentiero
for per
for me/us per me/noi
for him/her per lui/lei
for you per te/lei/voi
forbidden proibito(a)
forehead la fronte
foreign straniero(a)
foreigner lo/la straniero(a)
forest la foresta
forever per sempre
to forget dimenticare
to forgive perdonare
fork *(for eating)* la forchetta
(in road) il bivio
form *(document)* il modulo
fort il forte
fortnight quindici giorni
foul *(football)* il fallo
fountain la fontana
fox la volpe
fracture la frattura
frame *(picture)* la cornice
France la Francia
free *(not occupied)* libero(a)
(costing nothing) gratis
freelance freelance
freezer il congelatore
French francese
(language) il francese
french beans i fagiolini
french fries le patatine fritte
frequent frequente
fresh fresco(a)
fresh water l'acqua dolce *(f)*
Friday venerdì
fridge il frigorifero
fried fritto(a)
friend l'amico(a)
friendly amichevole
frisbee il frisbee
frog la rana
frogs' legs le cosce di rana
from da *see* **GRAMMAR**
from Scotland dalla Scozia
from England dall'Inghilterra
front davanti
in front of... di fronte a...
front door la porta d'ingresso
frost la brina
frozen *(food)* surgelato(a)
fruit la frutta
dried fruit la frutta secca
fruit juice il succo di frutta
fruit salad la macedonia
to fry friggere
frying-pan la padella
fuel *(petrol)* la benzina
fuel pump la pompa
fuel tank il serbatoio della benzina
full pieno(a)
(occupied) completo(a)
full board la pensione completa
fumes *(of car)* i gas di scarico
fun il divertimento
funeral il funerale
funfair il luna park
funny *(amusing)* divertente
fur il pelo
fur coat la pelliccia
furnished ammobiliato(a)
furniture i mobili
fuse il fusibile
fuse box la scatola dei fusibili
futon il futon
future il futuro

G

gallery la galleria
gallon = approx. 4.5 litres
game il gioco
(meat) la selvaggina
garage *(private)* il garage
(for repairs) l'autofficina *(f)*
(for petrol) la stazione di servizio
garden il giardino
gardener il giardiniere
garlic l'aglio *(m)*
gas il gas
gas cooker la cucina a gas
gas cylinder la bombola del gas
gastritis la gastrite
gate il cancello
(airport) l'uscita *(f)*
gay *(person)* gay
gear *(car)* la marcia
first gear la prima
second gear la seconda
third gear la terza
fourth gear la quarta
neutral folle
reverse la retromarcia
gearbox il cambio
generous generoso(a)
gents' *(toilet)* la toilette (per uomini)
genuine *(leather, silver)* vero(a)
(antique, picture, etc) autentico(a)
geranium il geranio
German tedesco(a)
(language) il tedesco
German measles la rosolia
Germany la Germania
to get *(obtain)* ottenere
(to receive) ricevere
(to fetch) prendere
to get in/on *(vehicle)* salire in/su
to get off *(bus, etc)* scendere da
gift il regalo
gift shop il negozio di souvenir
gin il gin
gin and tonic il gin tonic
ginger *(spice)* lo zenzero
girl *(young child)* la bambina
(teenage) la ragazza
girlfriend la ragazza
to give dare
to give back restituire
glacier il ghiacciaio
glass *(substance)* il vetro
(for drinking) il bicchiere
a glass of water un bicchiere d'acqua
a glass of wine un bicchiere di vino
glasses *(spectacles)* gli occhiali
glasses case la custodia degli occhiali
gloves i guanti
glue la colla
to go andare *see* **GRAMMAR**
I'm going to... vado a...
we're going to... andiamo a...
to go home andare a casa
to go on foot andare a piedi
to go in a car andare in macchina
to go back ritornare
to go down *(stairs, etc)* scendere
to go in entrare in
to go out *(leave)* uscire
goat la capra
God Dio
goggles gli occhialini
(for skiing) gli occhiali da sci
gold l'oro *(m)*
golf il golf
golf ball la pallina da golf
golf clubs le mazze da golf
golf course il campo di golf
good buono(a)
(pleasant) bello(a)
very good ottimo(a)
good afternoon buon giorno
(after 5pm) buona sera
goodbye arrivederci
good day buon giorno
good evening buona sera

g

good morning buon giorno
good night buona notte
goose l'oca *(f)*
gooseberry l'uva spina *(f)*
Goretex® il Goretex®
granddaughter la nipote
grandfather il nonno
grandmother la nonna
grandparents i nonni
grandson il nipote
grapefruit il pompelmo
grapefruit juice il succo di pompelmo
grapes l'uva *(f)*
grass l'erba *(f)*
grated grattugiato(a)
grater la grattugia
greasy grasso(a)
great *(big)* grande
Great Britain la Gran Bretagna
green verde
green card *(car insurance)* la carta verde
greengrocer's il fruttivendolo
greetings card il biglietto d'auguri
grey grigio(a)
grill la griglia
to grill cuocere alla griglia
grilled alla griglia
grocer's il negozio di alimentari
ground la terra
ground floor il pianterreno
on the ground floor a pianterreno
groundsheet il telone impermeabile
to grow crescere
(cultivate) coltivare
guarantee la garanzia
guard *(on train)* il capotreno
guest *(house guest)* l'ospite *(m/f)*
(in hotel) il/la cliente
guesthouse la pensione
guide *(tourist)* la guida
guidebook la guida
guided tour la visita guidata
guitar la chitarra
gun *(pistol)* la pistola
(rifle) il fucile
gym shoes le scarpe da ginnastica

H

haberdasher's la merceria
habit l'abitudine *(f)*
haemorrhoids le emorroidi
hail la grandine
hair i capelli
hairbrush la spazzola per capelli
haircut il taglio di capelli
hairdresser il parrucchiere/la parrucchiera
hair dryer il fon
hair dye la tintura per capelli
hair gel il gel per capelli
hairgrip la molletta per capelli
hair mousse la spuma
hake il nasello
half la metà
a half bottle of... una mezza bottiglia di...
half an hour mezz'ora
half board mezza pensione
half-price metà prezzo
ham *(cooked)* il prosciutto cotto
(cured) il prosciutto crudo
hamburger l'hamburger *(m)*
hammer il martello
hand la mano
handbag la borsa
handicapped disabile ; handicappato(a)
handkerchief il fazzoletto
handle il manico
handlebars il manubrio
hand luggage il bagaglio a mano
hand-made fatto a mano
handsome bello(a)
hang gliding il volo con deltaplano
hanger *(coat hanger)* la gruccia

per abiti
to happen succedere
what happened? cos'è successo?
happy felice
happy birthday! buon compleanno!
harbour il porto
hard duro(a)
(difficult) difficile
hard disk l'hard disk *(m)*
hardware shop il negozio di ferramenta
hare la lepre
harvest il raccolto ; la vendemmia
hat il cappello
to have avere *see* **GRAMMAR**
I have... ho...
I don't have... non ho...
we have... abbiamo...
we don't have... non abbiamo...
do you have...? ha...?
to have to dovere
hay fever il raffreddore da fieno
hazelnut la nocciola
he egli ; lui *see* **GRAMMAR**
head la testa
headache il mal di testa
I have a headache ho mal di testa
headlights i fari
headphones la cuffia
health food il cibo naturale
health-food shop l'erboristeria *(f)*
to hear sentire
hearing aid l'apparecchio acustico *(m)*
heart il cuore
heart attack l'infarto *(m)*
heartburn il bruciore di stomaco
to heat up *(food)* riscaldare
heater il termosifone
heating il riscaldamento
heaven il paradiso
heavy pesante
heel il tallone
height l'altezza *(f)*
helicopter l'elicottero *(m)*
hello! salve! ; ciao!
(on telephone) pronto
helmet il casco
help! aiuto!
to help aiutare
can you help me? può aiutarmi?
hem l'orlo *(m)*
hen la gallina
hepatitis l'epatite *(f)*
her il/la suo(a) *see* **GRAMMAR**
her passport il suo passaporto
her room la sua camera
herb l'erba aromatica *(f)*
herb tea la tisana
here qui
here is... ecco...
here is my passport ecco il mio passaporto
hernia l'ernia *(f)*
to hide nascondere
high *(price, number, etc)* alto(a)
(speed) forte
high blood pressure la pressione alta
high chair il seggiolone
high tide l'alta marea *(f)*
hill la collina
hill-walking il trekking
him lui ; lo ; gli
hip l'anca *(f)*
hip replacement la protesi dell'anca
hire il noleggio
car hire il noleggio auto
bike hire il noleggio bici
boat hire il noleggio barche
ski hire il noleggio sci
to hire noleggiare
hire car la macchina a noleggio
his il/la suo(a) *see* **GRAMMAR**
his passport il suo passaporto
his room la sua camera
historic storico(a)
history la storia
to hit colpire

h

to hitchhike fare l'autostop
to hold tenere
(to contain) contenere
hold-up *(traffic jam)* l'ingorgo *(m)*
hole il buco
holiday la festa
on holiday in vacanza
holly l'agrifoglio *(m)*
home la casa
at home a casa
homeopathy l'omeopatia *(f)*
homesick: *to be homesick* avere nostalgia di casa
I'm homesick ho nostalgia di casa
are you homesick? ha nostalgia di casa?
homosexual omosessuale
honest onesto(a)
honey il miele
honeymoon la luna di miele
hood *(on jacket)* il cappuccio
to hope sperare
I hope so/not spero di sì/no
hors d'œuvre l'antipasto *(m)*
horse il cavallo
horse racing l'ippica *(f)*
to horse ride andare a cavallo
hosepipe la canna dell'acqua
hospital l'ospedale *(m)*
hostel l'ostello *(m)*
hot caldo(a)
I'm hot ho caldo
it's hot *(weather)* fa caldo
hot water l'acqua calda *(f)*
hot chocolate la cioccolata calda
hot-water bottle la borsa dell'acqua calda
hotel l'albergo *(m)* ; l'hotel *(m)*
hour l'ora *(f)*
half an hour mezz'ora
house la casa
housewife la casalinga
house wine il vino della casa
hovercraft l'hovercraft *(m)*
how? *(in what way)* come?
how much? quanto(a)?
how many? quanti(e)?
how are you? come sta?
hundred cento
hungry: *to be hungry* avere fame
hunt la caccia
to hunt andare a caccia
hunting permit la licenza di caccia
hurry: *I'm in a hurry* ho fretta
to hurt fare male
that hurts fa male
husband il marito
hut *(bathing/beach)* la cabina
(mountain) la baita
hydrofoil l'aliscafo *(m)*
hypodermic needle l'ago ipodermico *(m)*

I

I io *see* **GRAMMAR**
ice il ghiaccio
with ice con ghiaccio
without ice senza ghiaccio
ice box il freezer
ice cream il gelato
iced coffee il caffè freddo
iced tea il tè freddo
ice lolly il ghiacciolo
ice rink la pista di pattinaggio su ghiaccio
to ice skate pattinare sul ghiaccio
ice skates i pattini da ghiaccio
icon l'icona *(f)*
identify identificare
identity card la carta d'identità
if se
ignition l'accensione *(f)*
ignition key la chiave dell'accensione
ill malato(a)
I'm ill sto male
immediately subito
immersion heater lo scaldabagno elettrico

immunisation l'immunizzazione *(f)*
to import importare
important importante
impossible impossibile
it's impossible è impossibile
to improve migliorare
in in *see* **GRAMMAR**
in 2 hours in due ore
in London a Londra
in front of davanti a
inch = approx. 2.5 cm
included compreso(a) ; incluso(a)
inconvenient scomodo(a)
to increase aumentare
(to increase volume) alzare il volume
indicator *(in car)* la freccia
indigestion l'indigestione *(f)*
indigestion tablets le compresse per digerire
indoors dentro
(at home) a casa
infection l'infezione *(f)*
infectious contagioso(a)
informal *(clothes)* sportivo(a)
information le informazioni
information office l'ufficio informazioni *(m)*
ingredients gli ingredienti
inhaler l'inalatore *(m)*
injection l'iniezione *(f)* ; la puntura
to injure ferire
injured ferito(a)
injury la lesione
ink l'inchiostro *(m)*
inn la locanda
inner tube la camera d'aria
insect l'insetto *(m)*
insect bite la puntura d'insetto
insect repellent l'insettifugo *(m)*
inside dentro
instant coffee il caffè solubile
instructor l'istruttore/l'istruttrice
insulin l'insulina *(f)*
insurance l'assicurazione *(f)*
insurance certificate il certificato di assicurazione
insured: ***to be insured*** essere assicurato(a)
intelligent intelligente
interesting interessante
international internazionale
internet l'Internet *(m)*
internet café il cyber-café
interpreter l'interprete *(m/f)*
interval l'intervallo *(m)*
interview l'intervista *(f)*
into in *see* **GRAMMAR**
into town in città
into the centre in centro
to introduce someone to presentare qualcuno a
invitation l'invito *(m)*
to invite invitare
invoice la fattura
Ireland l'Irlanda *(f)*
Irish irlandese
iron *(for clothes)* il ferro da stiro
(metal) il ferro
wrought iron il ferro battuto
to iron stirare
ironing board l'asse da stiro *(f)*
ironmonger's il negozio di ferramenta
is *see* (to be) **GRAMMAR**
island l'isola *(f)*
it lo/la *see* **GRAMMAR**
Italian italiano(a)
(language) l'italiano *(m)*
Italy l'Italia *(f)*
to itch prudere
itemised bill il conto dettagliato
ivory l'avorio *(m)*

J

jack *(for car)* il cric
jacket la giacca
waterproof jacket il giaccone impermeabile

j

jam *(food)* la marmellata
jammed bloccato(a)
January gennaio
jar *(honey, jam, etc)* il vasetto
jaundice l'itterizia *(f)*
jaw la mascella
jazz il jazz
jealous geloso(a) ; invidioso(a)
jeans i blue jeans
jelly *(dessert)* la gelatina
jellyfish la medusa
jet ski l'acqua-scooter *(m)*
jetty il molo
jeweller's la gioielleria
jewellery i gioielli
Jewish ebreo(a)
Jiffy bag® la busta imbottita
job il lavoro
to jog fare jogging
to join *(club)* iscriversi a
joint *(of body)* l'articolazione *(f)*
joke lo scherzo *(m)*
to joke scherzare
journalist il/la giornalista
journey il viaggio
judge il/la giudice *(m/f)*
jug la brocca
juice il succo
apple juice il succo di mela
orange juice il succo d'arancia
tomato juice il succo di pomodoro
July luglio
to jump saltare
jumper il maglione
jump leads *(for car)* i cavi per far partire la macchina
junction *(road)* l'incrocio *(m)*
June giugno
just: *just two* solamente due
I've just arrived sono appena arrivato(a)

K

karaoke il karaoke
to keep *(retain)* tenere
kennel il canile
kettle il bollitore
key la chiave
card key *(ie used in hotel)* il passe-partout
keyring il portachiavi
kid *(goat)* il capretto
kidneys *(as food)* i rognoni
to kill uccidere
kilo il chilo
a kilo of apples un chilo di mele
2 kilos due chili
kilogram il chilogrammo
kilometre il chilometro
how many kilometres? quanti chilometri?
kind *(person)* gentile
king il re
kingdom il regno
kiosk l'edicola *(f)*
kiss il bacio
to kiss baciare
kitchen la cucina
kitchen paper la carta assorbente da cucina
kite l'aquilone *(m)*
kitten il gattino
kiwi fruit il kiwi
knapsack lo zaino
knee il ginocchio
knee highs i gambaletti
knickers le mutandine
knife il coltello
to knit lavorare a maglia
to knock *(on door)* bussare
to knock down *(car)* investire
to knock over *(glass, vase)* rovesciare
knot il nodo

to know *(facts)* sapere
(to be acquainted with) conoscere
I don't know non lo so
to know how to sapere
to know how to swim saper nuotare

L

label l'etichetta *(f)*
lace il pizzo
laces *(shoe)* i lacci
ladder la scala
ladies' *(toilet)* la toilette (per signore)
lady la signora
lager la birra bionda
draught lager la birra alla spina
lake il lago
lamb l'agnello *(m)*
lame zoppo(a)
lamp la lampada
lamppost il lampione
land la terra
to land *(plane)* atterrare
landlady la padrona di casa
landlord il padrone di casa
landslide la frana
lane la stradina
(of motorway) la corsia
langoustines gli scampi
language la lingua
lap *(sport)* il giro
laptop il laptop
large grande
last ultimo(a) ; scorso(a)
the last bus l'ultimo autobus
the last train l'ultimo treno
last night ieri notte
last week la settimana scorsa
last year l'anno scorso
late tardi
the train's late il treno è in ritardo
sorry we're late scusi il ritardo
later più tardi
to laugh ridere
launderette la lavanderia automatica
laundry il bucato
lavatory il gabinetto ; la toilette
lavender la lavanda
law la legge
lawyer l'avvocato/l'avvocatessa
laxative il lassativo
lazy pigro(a)
lead *(electric)* il filo
lead *(metal)* il piombo
lead-free senza piombo
leaf la foglia
leak *(of gas, liquid)* la perdita
(in roof) il buco
it's leaking perde
to learn imparare
lease *(rental)* l'affitto *(m)*
leather il cuoio ; la pelle
to leave *(leave behind)* lasciare
(train, bus, etc) partire
when does the bus leave? a che ora parte l'autobus?
when does the train leave? a che ora parte il treno?
leeks i porri
left la sinistra
on/to the left a sinistra
left-luggage il deposito bagagli
leg la gamba
leggings i fuseaux
lemon il limone
lemonade la limonata
to lend prestare
length la lunghezza
lens *(camera)* l'obiettivo *(m)*
(contact lens) la lente a contatto
lenses le lenti
lentils le lenticchie
lesbian lesbica
less meno
lesson la lezione
to let *(allow)* permettere
(to hire out) affittare

letter la lettera
letterbox la cassetta delle lettere
lettuce la lattuga
level crossing il passaggio a livello
library la biblioteca
licence il permesso
(driving) la patente
lid il coperchio
lie *(untruth)* la bugia
life belt il salvagente
lifeboat la scialuppa di salvataggio
lifeguard il bagnino
life insurance l'assicurazione sulla vita *(f)*
life jacket il giubbotto salvagente
life raft la zattera di salvataggio
lift *(elevator)* l'ascensore *(m)*
(in car) il passaggio
lift pass *(on ski slopes)* lo skipass
light *(not heavy)* leggero(a)
(colour) chiaro(a)
light la luce
have you got a light? ha da accendere?
light bulb la lampadina
lighter l'accendino *(m)*
lighthouse il faro
lightning il fulmine
to like piacere
I like coffee mi piace il caffè
I don't like... non mi piace...
I'd/we'd like... vorrei/vorremmo...
lilo il materassino
lily il giglio
lime *(fruit)* la limetta
line *(row, queue)* la fila
(telephone) la linea
linen il lino
lingerie la biancheria intima da donna
lion il leone
lip reading la labiolettura
lips le labbra
lip salve il burro di cacao
lipstick il rossetto
liqueur il liquore
list l'elenco *(m)* ; la lista
to listen (to) ascoltare
litre il litro
a litre of milk un litro di latte
litter *(rubbish)* i rifiuti
little *(small)* piccolino(a)
a little... un po' di...
live *(TV, etc)* in diretta
to live vivere ; abitare
I live in London vivo a Londra
he lives in a flat abita in un appartamento
liver il fegato
living room il salotto
loaf of bread la pagnotta
lobster l'aragosta *(f)*
local locale
to lock chiudere a chiave
lock la serratura
the lock is broken la serratura è rotta
locker l'armadietto *(m)*
log book *(car)* il libretto di circolazione
logs i ceppi
lollipop il lecca lecca
London Londra
in/to London a Londra
long lungo(a)
for a long time molto tempo
long sighted ipermetrope
to look at guardare
to look after prendersi cura di
to look for cercare
loose *(not fastened)* slegato(a)
lorry il camion
to lose perdere
lost *(object)* perso(a)
I've lost my... ho perso il/la...
I've lost my wallet ho perso il portafoglio
I'm lost mi sono smarrito(a)
we're lost ci siamo smarriti(e)
lost property office l'ufficio oggetti smarriti *(m)*

lot: *a lot* molto
lottery la lotteria
loud forte
lounge *(in hotel)* il salone
(in house) la sala
(in airport) la sala d'attesa
love l'amore *(m)*
to love *(person)* amare
I love you ti amo
lovely bellissimo(a)
low basso(a)
(standard, quality) scadente
lower *(volume)* abbassare
low-fat magro(a)
low tide la bassa marea
lucky fortunato(a)
luggage i bagagli
luggage rack il portabagagli
luggage tag l'etichetta *(f)*
luggage trolley il carrello
lump *(swelling)* il gonfiore
lunch il pranzo ; la colazione
lung il polmone
luxury di lusso

M

machine la macchina
mad *(insane)* matto(a)
(angry) arrabbiato(a)
magazine la rivista
maggot il baco
magnet la calamita
magnifying glass la lente d'ingrandimento
magpie la gazza
magnolia la magnolia
maid *(in hotel)* la cameriera
maiden name il nome da ragazza
mail la posta
main principale
main course *(meal)* il secondo
to make *(generally)* fare see **GRAMMAR**
(meal) preparare
make-up il trucco
male maschio ; maschile
mallet la mazza
man l'uomo *(m)*
to manage *(be in charge of)* dirigere
managing director il direttore/la direttrice
man-made fibre la fibra sintetica
manual *(gear change)* manuale
many molti(e)
map *(of country)* la carta geografica
(city) la piantina
marathon la maratona
marble il marmo
March marzo
margarine la margarina
marina il porticciolo
marinated marinato(a)
marjoram la maggiorana
mark *(stain)* la macchia ; il segno
(brand) la marca
market il mercato
where is the market? dov'è il mercato?
when is the market? quando c'è il mercato?
marmalade la marmellata d'arance
married sposato(a)
I'm married sono sposato(a)
are you married? è sposato(a)?
marrow la zucca
marry: ***to get married*** sposarsi
marsh la palude
mascara il mascara
masher *(potato)* il passapatate
mass *(in church)* la messa
mast l'albero *(m)*
masterpiece il capolavoro
match *(game)* la partita
matches i fiammiferi
material il materiale
(cloth) il tessuto

m

to matter importare
it doesn't matter non importa
what's the matter? cosa c'è?
mattress il materasso
May maggio
mayonnaise la maionese
mayor il/la sindaco(a)
maximum il massimo
me me ; mi
meal il pasto
to mean *(signify)* voler dire
what does it mean? cosa vuol dire?
measure la misura
to measure misurare
meat la carne
mechanic il/la meccanico(a)
medicine la medicina
medieval medievale
Mediterranean il Mediterraneo
medium rare *(steak)* poco cotto(a)
to meet incontrare
pleased to meet you! piacere!
meeting la riunione
(by chance) l'incontro *(m)*
melon il melone
watermelon l'anguria *(f)*
to melt sciogliere
member *(of club, etc)* il/la socio(a)
men gli uomini
to mend riparare
meningitis la meningite
menu il menù
set menu il menù a prezzo fisso ; il menù turistico
à la carte menu il menù alla carta
meringue la meringa
merit il valore
message il messaggio
metal il metallo
meter il contatore
metre il metro
metro *(underground)* la metropolitana
microwave oven il forno a microonde
midday il mezzogiorno
at midday a mezzogiorno
middle il mezzo
middle-aged di mezz'età
midge il moscerino
midnight la mezzanotte
at midnight a mezzanotte
migraine l'emicrania *(f)*
I have a migraine ho l'emicrania
Milan Milano
mild dolce ; mite
mile 8 km = approx. 5 miles
milk il latte
fresh milk il latte fresco
hot milk il latte caldo
long-life milk il latte a lunga conservazione
powdered milk il latte in polvere
semi-skimmed milk il latte parzialmente scremato
soya milk il latte di soia
with milk col latte
milkshake il frappé
millimetre il millimetro
million il milione
mince *(meat)* la carne macinata
mind: *do you mind?* le dà fastidio?
I don't mind non mi dà fastidio
mineral water l'acqua minerale *(f)*
minimum il minimo
minister *(church)* il sacerdote
(political) il ministro
mink il visone
mint *(herb)* la menta
mint tea il tè alla menta
minute il minuto
mirror lo specchio
to misbehave comportarsi male
miscarriage l'aborto spontaneo *(m)*
to miss *(train, etc)* perdere
Miss Signorina
missing *(thing)* smarrito(a)
(person) scomparso(a)
mistake l'errore *(m)*
misunderstanding il malinteso

to mix mescolare
mobile phone il telefonino
modem il modem
modern moderno(a)
moisturizer l'idratante *(m)*
moment: ***just a moment*** un momento
monastery il monastero
Monday lunedì
money i soldi
I have no money non ho soldi
money belt il marsupio
money order il vaglia
month il mese
this month questo mese
last month il mese scorso
next month il mese prossimo
monthly mensilmente
monument il monumento
moon la luna
mooring l'ormeggio *(m)*
moped il motorino
more (than) più (di)
more than 3 più di tre
more bread dell'altro pane
more wine ancora un po' di vino
morning la mattina
in the morning di mattina
this morning stamattina
tomorrow morning domani mattina
mosque la moschea
mosquito la zanzara
mosquito net la zanzariera
most il/la più ; il massimo
moth *(clothes)* la tarma
mother la madre
mother-in-law la suocera
motor il motore
motorbike la moto
motor boat il motoscafo
motorway l'autostrada *(f)*
mould la muffa
mountain la montagna
mountain bike la mountain bike
mountain rescue il soccorso alpino
mountaineering l'alpinismo *(m)*
mouse il topo
(computer) il mouse
mousse la spuma
moustache i baffi
mouth la bocca
mouthwash il colluttorio
move: ***it isn't moving*** non si muove
Mr Signor
Mrs Signora
Ms Signora
much molto
too much troppo
mud il fango
mugging lo scippo
mummy mamma
mumps gli orecchioni
muscle il muscolo
museum il museo
mushrooms i funghi
music la musica
musical il musical
mussels le cozze
must *(to have to)* dovere
see **GRAMMAR**
mustard la senape
mutton il montone
my il/la mio(a)
my passport il mio passaporto
my room la mia camera

N

nail *(metal)* il chiodo
(fingernail) l'unghia *(f)*
nailbrush lo spazzolino per le unghie
nail clipper il tagliaunghie
nail file la limetta per le unghie
nail polish/varnish lo smalto per le unghie
nail polish remover l'acetone *(m)*

n

nail scissors le forbicine
name il nome
my name is... mi chiamo...
what is your name? come si chiama?
nanny la bambinaia
napkin il tovagliolo
Naples Napoli
nappies i pannolini per bambini
narrow stretto(a)
national nazionale
national park il parco nazionale
nationality la nazionalità
natural naturale
nature la natura
nature reserve la riserva naturale
navy blue blu marino
near to vicino(a) a
is it near? è vicino?
near the bank vicino alla banca
necessary necessario(a)
neck il collo
necklace la collana
nectarine la nocepesca
to need avere bisogno di...
I need... ho bisogno di...
we need... abbiamo bisogno di...
needle l'ago *(m)*
a needle and thread un ago e filo
negative *(photo)* il negativo
neighbour il/la vicino(a)
nephew il nipote
nest il nido
net la rete
nettle l'ortica *(f)*
never mai
I never drink wine non bevo mai il vino
new nuovo(a)
news le notizie
(on television) il telegiornale
newsagent's il giornalaio
newspaper il giornale
newsstand l'edicola *(f)*
New Year il Capodanno
happy New Year! buon Anno!
New Year's Eve la notte di San Silvestro ; l'ultimo dell'anno *(m)*
New Zealand la Nuova Zelanda
next prossimo(a)
next week la settimana prossima
the next bus il prossimo autobus
the next train il prossimo treno
the next stop la prossima fermata
next to accanto a
nice piacevole
(person) simpatico(a)
niece la nipote
night la notte
at night di notte
last night ieri notte
per night a notte
tomorrow night domani sera
tonight stasera
night porter il portiere notturno
nightclub il nightclub
nightdress la camicia da notte
no no
no entry vietato l'ingresso
no smoking vietato fumare
no thanks no, grazie
(without) senza
no sugar senza zucchero
no ice senza ghiaccio
nobody nessuno
noise il rumore
noisy rumoroso(a)
it's very noisy è molto rumoroso(a)
non-alcoholic analcolico(a)
none nessuno(a)
non-smoking per non-fumatori
noodles i taglierini
north il nord
North Sea il Mare del Nord
Northern Ireland l'Irlanda del Nord *(f)*
nose il naso
note *(bank note)* la banconota
(letter) il biglietto

note pad il bloc-notes
nothing niente
nothing else nient'altro
notice l'avviso *(m)*
notice board la bacheca
novel il romanzo
November novembre
now adesso
nowhere da nessuna parte
nuclear nucleare
nudist beach la spiaggia nudista
number il numero
number plate *(car)* la targa
nurse l'infermiera/l'infermiere *(f/m)*
nursery school la scuola materna
nursery slope la pista per principianti
nut *(to eat)* la noce
(for bolt) il dado

O

oak la quercia
oars i remi
to obtain ottenere
occasionally ogni tanto
occupation *(work)* il lavoro
ocean l'oceano *(m)*
October ottobre
octopus il polpo
odd numbers i numeri dispari
of di *see* **GRAMMAR**
a bottle of wine una bottiglia di vino
a glass of water un bicchiere d'acqua
made of... fatto di...
off *(machine, etc)* spento(a)
(milk, food) andato(a) a male
this meat is off questa carne è andata a male
office l'ufficio *(m)*
often spesso
how often? ogni quanto?
oil l'olio *(m)*
oil filter il filtro dell'olio
oil gauge l'indicatore del livello dell'olio *(m)*
ointment la pomata
OK! va bene!
old vecchio(a)
how old are you? quanti anni ha?
I'm ... years old ho ... anni
old age pensioner il/la pensionato(a)
olive oil l'olio d'oliva *(m)*
olives le olive
omelette l'omelette *(f)* ; la frittata
on *(light, engine)* acceso(a)
(tap) aperto(a)
on the table sulla tavola
on time in orario
once una volta
at once subito
one uno
one-way *(street)* a senso unico
onions le cipolle
only solo(a)
open aperto(a)
to open aprire
opera l'opera *(f)*
operation *(surgical)* l'operazione *(f)*
operator *(telephone)* il/la centralinista
opposite di fronte a
opposite the hotel di fronte all'albergo
optician's l'ottico *(m)*
or o
tea or coffee tè o caffè
orange *(colour)* arancione
orange *(fruit)* l'arancia *(f)*
orange juice il succo d'arancia
orange squash l'aranciata *(f)*
orchard il frutteto
orchestra l'orchestra *(f)*
order *(in restaurant)* l'ordine *(f)*
out of order fuori servizio
to order *(in restaurant)* ordinare
oregano l'origano *(m)*

O

organic biologico(a)
to organize organizzare
other l'altro(a)
the other one l'altro
have you any others? ce ne sono altri?
ounce = approx. 30 grams
our il/la nostro(a)
our car la nostra macchina
our hotel il nostro albergo
out *(light)* spento(a)
he/she's out è fuori
he's gone out è uscito
outdoor *(pool, etc)* all'aperto
outside: ***it's outside*** è fuori
oven il forno
oven glove il guanto da forno
ovenproof dish la pirofila
over *(on top of)* sopra
to overcharge far pagare troppo
overcoat il cappotto
overdone *(food)* troppo cotto(a)
overdose l'overdose *(f)*
to overheat surriscaldare
to overtake *(in car)* sorpassare
to owe dovere
I owe you... le devo...
owl la civetta ; il gufo
owner il/la proprietario(a)
oxygen l'ossigeno *(m)*
oyster l'ostrica *(f)*

P

pace il passo
pacemaker il pacemaker
to pack *(suitcase)* fare la valigia
package il pacco
package tour il viaggio organizzato
packet il pacchetto
padded envelope la busta imbottita
paddling pool la piscina per bambini
padlock il lucchetto
Padua Padova
page la pagina
paid pagato(a)
I've paid ho pagato
pain il dolore
painful doloroso(a)
painkiller l'analgesico *(m)*
paint la vernice
to paint *(wall, house)* verniciare *(picture)* dipingere
painting *(picture)* il quadro
pair il paio
palace il palazzo
pale pallido(a)
pan *(saucepan)* la pentola *(frying pan)* la padella
pancake la crêpe
panniers *(bike)* le borse per la bici
panties le mutandine
pants le mutande
panty liner il proteggislip
paper la carta
paper napkins i tovaglioli di carta
paracetamol® il paracetamolo
paraffin il cherosene
parcel il pacco
pardon? scusi?
I beg your pardon mi scusi
parents i genitori
park il parco
to park parcheggiare
parking disk il disco orario
parking meter il parchimetro
parking ticket *(fine)* la multa per sosta vietata
parmesan il parmigiano
grated parmesan il parmigiano grattugiato
parsley il prezzemolo
partner *(business)* il/la socio(a) *(boy/girlfriend)* il/la compagno(a)
party *(celebration)* la festa *(political)* il partito

O

p

pass *(mountain)* il valico
(bus, train) la tessera
passenger il/la passeggero(a)
passport il passaporto
passport control il controllo passaporti
pasta la pasta
pastry la pasta
(fancy cake) il pasticcino
pâté il pâté
path il sentiero
patience *(cardgame)* il solitario
patient *(in hospital)* il/la paziente
pavement il marciapiede
to pay pagare
I want to pay vorrei pagare
payment il pagamento
payphone il telefono pubblico
peace la pace
peaches le pesche
peak rate la tariffa ore di punta
peanuts le arachidi
peanut butter il burro d'arachidi
pearls le perle
pears le pere
peas i piselli
pedal il pedale
pedal boat/pedalo il pedalò
pedestrian il/la pedone(a)
pedestrian crossing il passaggio pedonale
to peel *(fruit)* sbucciare
peg *(for clothes)* la molletta
(for tent) il picchetto
pen la penna
penalty *(football)* il rigore
pencil la matita
penicillin la penicillina
peninsula la penisola
penis il pene
penknife il temperino
pension la pensione
pensioner il/la pensionato(a)
pepper *(spice)* il pepe
(vegetable) il peperone
per per
per day al giorno
per hour all'ora
per week alla settimana
per person a persona
100 km per hour 100 km all'ora
perch *(fish)* il pesce persico
perfect perfetto(a)
performance la rappresentazione
perfume il profumo
perhaps forse
period *(menstrual)* le mestruazioni
perm la permanente
permit il permesso
person la persona
per person a persona
personal organizer l'agenda elettronica *(f)*
personal stereo il walkman®
to persuade convincere
pet l'animale domestico *(m)*
petrol la benzina
4-star petrol il super
unleaded petrol la benzina senza piombo
petrol cap il tappo del serbatoio
petrol pump la pompa della benzina
petrol station la stazione di servizio
pharmacy la farmacia
pheasant il fagiano
phone il telefono
by phone per telefono
to phone telefonare
phonebook l'elenco telefonico *(m)*
phonebox la cabina telefonica
phonecard la scheda telefonica
photocopy la fotocopia
I need a photocopy mi serve una fotocopia
to photocopy fotocopiare
photograph la foto
to take a photo fare una foto
phrase book il manuale di conversazione

p

piano il pianoforte
to pick *(fruit, flowers)* cogliere
(to choose) scegliere
pickpocket il borseggiatore
pickle i sottaceti
picnic il picnic
picnic rug il plaid
picnic table il tavolo da picnic
picture *(painting)* il quadro
(photo) la foto
picture frame la cornice
pie *(sweet)* la torta
(savoury) il pasticcio
piece il pezzo
pier il pontile
pig il maiale
pill la pillola
to be on the Pill prendere la pillola
pillow il guanciale ; il cuscino
pillowcase la federa
pilot il pilota
pin lo spillo
pine il pino
pine nut il pinolo
pineapple l'ananas *(m)*
pink rosa
pint = approx. 0.5 litre
pipe *(water, etc)* il tubo
(smoker's) la pipa
pistachio il pistacchio
pity: ***what a pity!*** che peccato!
pizza la pizza
place il luogo
plain *(obvious)* chiaro(a) ; evidente
(unflavoured) naturale
plait la treccia
plan il piano
to plan progettare
plane l'aereo *(m)*
plant la pianta
plaster *(sticking)* il cerotto
(for broken limb) l'ingessatura *(f)*
plastic *(made of)* di plastica
plastic bag il sacchetto di plastica
plate il piatto
platform *(railway)* il binario
from which platform? da quale binario?
play *(theatre)* la commedia
to play *(games)* giocare
playground il parco giochi
playroom la stanza dei giochi
pleasant piacevole
please per favore
pleased: ***pleased to meet you*** piacere
plenty l'abbondanza *(f)*
pliers le pinze
plug *(electrical)* la spina
(for sink) il tappo
plum la prugna ; la susina
plumber l'idraulico *(m)*
plumbing l'impianto idraulico *(m)*
plunger *(to clear sink)* lo sturalavandini
poached *(egg)* in camicia
(fish) bollito(a)
pocket la tasca
points le puntine
poison il veleno
poisonous velenoso(a)
police la polizia
policeman/woman il poliziotto/la donna poliziotto
police station il commissariato ; la questura
polish *(for shoes)* il lucido
(for furniture) la cera
polluted inquinato(a)
pony il pony
pool *(swimming)* la piscina
poor povero(a)
pope il papa
poppy il papavero
popular popolare
pork la carne di maiale
port *(seaport, wine)* il porto
porter il portiere
(for luggage) il facchino

portion la porzione
Portugal il Portogallo
Portuguese portoghese
post: ***by post*** per posta
to post *(letters, etc)* imbucare
postbox la buca delle lettere
postcard la cartolina
postcode il codice postale
poster il poster
postman/woman il/la postino(a)
post office la posta ; l'ufficio postale *(m)*
to postpone rimandare
potato la patata
baked potato la patata al forno
boiled potatoes le patate lesse
fried potatoes le patate fritte
mashed potatoes il purè di patate
roast potatoes le patate arrosto
potato masher lo schiacciapatate
potato peeler il pelapatate
potato salad l'insalata di patate *(f)*
pothole la buca
pottery la terracotta
pound *(weight)* = approx. 0.5 kilo *(money)* la sterlina
to pour versare
powder: ***in powder form*** in polvere
powdered milk il latte in polvere
pram la carrozzina
prawn il gambero
to pray pregare
to prefer preferire
pregnant incinta
I'm pregnant sono incinta
to prepare preparare
to prescribe ordinare
prescription la ricetta
present *(gift)* il regalo
pressure: ***tyre pressure*** la pressione dei pneumatici
blood pressure la pressione del sangue
pretty carino(a)
price il prezzo
price list il listino prezzi
priest il prete
prince il principe
princess la principessa
print *(photo)* la foto
prison il carcere ; la prigione
private privato(a)
prize il premio
probably probabilmente
problem il problema
professor il professore/la professoressa
programme il programma
prohibited proibito(a)
to promise promettere
to pronounce pronunciare
how's it pronounced? come si pronuncia?
Protestant protestante
prunes le prugne secche
public pubblico(a)
public holiday la festa nazionale
pudding il dessert
to pull tirare
pullover il pullover
pump la pompa
puncture la gomma a terra
puppet il burattino
puppet show lo spettacolo di burattini
purple viola
purpose: ***on purpose*** apposta
purse il borsellino
to push spingere
pushchair il passeggino
to put *(to place)* mettere
to put back rimettere
pyjamas il pigiama

Q

quail la quaglia
quality la qualità
quarantine la quarantena

q

to quarrel litigare
quarter: ***a quarter*** un quarto
quay il molo
queen la regina
question la domanda
queue la coda
to queue fare la coda
quiche la torta salata
quick veloce
quickly velocemente
quiet *(place)* tranquillo(a)
  a quiet room una stanza tranquilla
quilt la trapunta
quiz show il gioco a quiz

R

rabbit il coniglio
rabies la rabbia
race *(sport)* la gara
race course l'ippodromo *(m)*
rack *(luggage)* la rete portabagagli
racket *(tennis, etc)* la racchetta
radiator *(car)* il radiatore
  (heater) il termosifone
radio la radio
radishes i ravanelli
rag lo straccio
railway station la stazione ferroviaria
rain la pioggia
to rain piovere
  it's raining piove
raincoat l'impermeabile *(m)*
raisin l'uvetta *(f)*
rake il rastrello
rape lo stupro
raped violentata
  mi hanno violentata I've been raped
rapid rapido(a)
rare *(unique)* raro(a)
  (steak) al sangue
rash *(skin)* l'orticaria *(f)*
raspberries i lamponi
rate *(cost)* la tariffa
rate of exchange il cambio
raw crudo(a)
razor il rasoio
razor blades le lamette
to read leggere
ready pronto(a)
real vero(a)
to realize rendersi conto di
rearview mirror lo specchietto retrovisore
receipt la ricevuta
receiver *(phone)* il ricevitore
recently recentemente
reception *(desk)* la reception
receptionist il/la receptionist
to recharge *(battery)* ricaricare
recipe la ricetta
to recognize riconoscere
to recommend raccomandare
record *(disk)* il disco
to recover *(from illness)* rimettersi
to recycle riciclare
red rosso(a)
redcurrants il ribes rosso
to reduce ridurre
reduction la riduzione
to refer to *(for information)* rivolgersi a
refill *(pen)* il ricambio
  (lighter) la bomboletta di gas
refund il rimborso
to refuse rifiutare
regarding riguardo a
region la regione
register il registro
  to sign the register firmare il registro
registered letter la lettera raccomandata
registration form il modulo d'iscrizione
to reimburse rimborsare

r

r

relation *(family)* il/la parente
to remain restare ; rimanere
to remember ricordare
I don't remember non mi ricordo
remote control il telecomando
to remove togliere
rent l'affitto *(m)*
to rent *(house)* affittare
(car) noleggiare
rental *(house)* l'affitto *(m)*
(car) il nolo
repair la riparazione
to repair riparare
to repeat ripetere
to reply rispondere
report il resoconto
to report *(crime)* denunciare
request la richiesta
to require richiedere
to rescue salvare
reservation la prenotazione
to reserve prenotare
reserved prenotato(a)
resident residente
resort la località di vacanza
rest *(repose)* il riposo
the rest of the wine il resto del vino
to rest riposarsi
restaurant il ristorante
restaurant car il vagone ristorante
retail price il prezzo al dettaglio
retired: *I'm retired* sono in pensione
to return *(go back)* ritornare
(to give back) restituire
return ticket il biglietto di andata e ritorno
to reverse fare marcia indietro
reverse charge call la chiamata a carico del destinatario
reverse gear la retromarcia
rheumatism il reumatismo
rhubarb il rabarbaro
rice il riso
rich ricco(a)
ride *(in a car)* il giro in macchina
to ride a horse andare a cavallo
right *(correct)* giusto(a)
right la destra
at/to the right a destra
on the right sulla destra
to ring *(bell)* suonare
(phone) squillare
ring l'anello *(m)*
ring road la circonvallazione
ripe maturo(a)
river il fiume
road la strada
road map la carta stradale
roadworks i lavori stradali
roast arrosto(a)
roll *(bread)* il panino
rollerblades i pattini in linea
rolling pin il matterello
romance *(novel)* il romanzo (rosa)
Romanesque romanico(a)
roof il tetto
roof-rack il portabagagli
room *(hotel)* la camera
(space) lo spazio
double room la camera doppia
family room la camera per famiglia
single room la camera singola
room number il numero di camera
room service il servizio in camera
rope la corda
rose la rosa
rosé wine il vino rosato
rosemary il rosmarino
rotten *(food)* marcio(a)
rough *(sea)* mosso(a)
round rotondo(a)
roundabout la rotatoria
row *(in theatre, etc)* la fila
to row *(boat)* remare
rowing boat la barca a remi
royal reale

r

rubber *(eraser)* la gomma da cancellare
(material) la gomma
rubber band l'elastico *(m)*
rubber gloves i guanti di gomma
rubbish la spazzatura
rubella la rosolia
rucksack lo zaino
rudder il timone
rug *(carpet)* il tappeto
ruins le rovine
ruler *(for measuring)* il righello
rum il rum
to run correre
rush hour l'ora di punta *(f)*
rust la ruggine
rusty arrugginito(a)

S

saccharin la saccarina
sad triste
saddle la sella
safe *(for valuables)* la cassaforte
safe *(medicine, etc)* senza pericolo
safety la sicurezza
safetybelt la cintura di sicurezza
safety pin la spilla di sicurezza
to sail viaggiare per mare
sailboard la tavola da windsurf
sailing boat la barca a vela
saint il/la santo(a)
salad l'insalata *(f)*
green salad l'insalata verde
mixed salad l'insalata mista
potato salad l'insalata di patate
tomato salad l'insalata di pomodori
salad dressing il condimento per l'insalata
salami il salame
sales *(reductions)* i saldi
salesman/woman il/la commesso(a)
sales rep il/la rappresentante
salmon il salmone
smoked salmon il salmone affumicato
salt il sale
salt water l'acqua salata
salty salato(a)
same stesso(a)
sample il campione
sand la sabbia
sandals i sandali
sandwich il panino ; il tramezzino
toasted sandwich il toast
sanitary towels gli assorbenti
sardine la sardina
Sardinia la Sardegna
satellite dish l'antenna parabolica *(f)*
satellite TV la televisione via satellite
Saturday sabato
sauce la salsa
tomato sauce la salsa di pomodoro
saucepan la pentola
saucer il piattino
sauerkraut i crauti
sauna la sauna
sausage la salsiccia
to save *(life)* salvare
(money) risparmiare
savoury *(not sweet)* salato(a)
to say dire
scales *(weighing)* la bilancia
scallop la cappasanta
scarf la sciarpa
(headscarf) il foulard
scenery il paesaggio
school la scuola
secondary school il liceo
scissors le forbici
score il punteggio
to score *(goal)* segnare
Scotland la Scozia
Scottish scozzese
scouring pad la paglietta

screen *(computer, TV)* lo schermo
screen wash il liquido lavavetri
screw la vite
screwdriver il cacciavite
phillips screwdriver il cacciavite a stella
scrunchie la girella
scuba diving le immersioni subacquee
sculptor lo scultore/la scultrice
sculpture la scultura
sea il mare
seacat il catamarano
seafood i frutti di mare
seam *(of dress)* la cucitura
sea sickness il mal di mare
seaside: ***at the seaside*** al mare
season *(of year)* la stagione
in season di stagione
seasoning il condimento
season ticket l'abbonamento *(m)*
seat *(chair)* la sedia
(in theatre, plane, etc) il posto
seatbelt la cintura di sicurezza
seaweed le alghe
second *(time)* il secondo
second secondo(a)
second class la seconda classe
second-hand di seconda mano
secretary la segretaria
security guard la guardia giurata
to see vedere
seed il seme
to seize afferrare
self-catering con uso di cucina
self-employed autonomo(a)
self-service self-service
to sell vendere
do you sell...? vende...?
sell-by date la data di scadenza
Sellotape® lo Scotch®
semi-skimmed milk il latte parzialmente scremato
to send mandare ; spedire ; inviare
senior citizen l'anziano(a)
sensible pratico(a)
separated separato(a)
separately: ***to pay separately*** pagare separatamente
September settembre
septic tank la fossa settica
sequel *(film, book, etc)* il seguito
serious grave
(not funny) serio(a)
to serve servire
service *(in church)* la funzione
(in restaurant) il servizio
is service included? il servizio è incluso?
service charge il servizio
service station la stazione di servizio
serviette la salvietta
set menu il menù turistico
to sew cucire
sewerage la fognatura
sex il sesso
shade l'ombra *(f)*
in the shade all'ombra
to shake *(bottle)* agitare
shallow basso(a)
shampoo lo shampoo
shampoo and set lo shampoo e messa in piega
to share dividere
sharp *(razor, blade)* affilato(a)
to shave farsi la barba
shaving cream la crema da barba
shawl lo scialle
she ella ; lei *see* **GRAMMAR**
sheep la pecora
sheet *(bed)* il lenzuolo
shelf la mensola
shell *(seashell)* la conchiglia
shellfish i frutti di mare
sheltered riparato(a)
to shine brillare
shingles *(illness)* il fuoco di sant'Antonio

S

ship la nave
shirt la camicia
shock *(electric)* la scossa
shock absorber l'ammortizzatore *(m)*
shoe la scarpa
shoelaces i lacci delle scarpe
shoe mender's il calzolaio
shoe polish il lucido per scarpe
shoe shop il negozio di calzature
shop il negozio
shop assistant il/la commesso(a)
shop window la vetrina
shopping: ***to go shopping*** fare compere ; fare la spesa
shopping centre il centro commerciale
shore la riva
short corto(a)
(person) basso(a)
short cut la scorciatoia
shorts i calzoncini corti
short-sighted miope
shoulder la spalla
to shout gridare
show *(at theatre)* lo spettacolo
to show mostrare
shower la doccia
to take a shower fare la doccia
shower cap la cuffia da doccia
shower curtain la tenda della doccia
shrimp il gamberetto
to shrink restringersi
shrub l'arbusto *(m)*
shut *(closed)* chiuso(a)
shutter l'imposta *(f)*
Sicily la Sicilia
sick *(ill)* malato(a)
(nauseous) nauseato(a)
I feel sick mi sento male
side dish il contorno
sidelight la luce di posizione
sidewalk il marciapiede
sieve il setaccio
to sightsee fare un giro turistico
sightseeing tour il giro turistico
to sign firmare
signature la firma
signpost il segnale
silk la seta
silver l'argento *(m)*
silver foil la carta stagnola
similar to simile a
to sing cantare
single *(unmarried)* non sposato(a)
(not double) singolo(a)
(ticket) di (sola) andata
single bed il letto a una piazza
single room la camera singola
sink il lavandino
sir Signore
sister la sorella
sister-in-law la cognata
to sit sedersi
please, sit down prego, si accomodi
size *(of clothes)* la taglia
(of shoes) il numero
to skate *(on ice)* pattinare sul ghiaccio
skates *(ice)* i pattini da ghiaccio
(roller) i pattini a rotelle
to ski sciare
ski lo sci
skis gli sci
ski boots gli scarponi da sci
ski instructor il/la maestro(a) di sci
ski jump il trampolino
ski lift lo ski-lift
ski suit la tuta da sci
ski pass lo skipass
ski pole/stick la racchetta da sci
ski run la pista
skimmed milk il latte scremato
skin la pelle
skirt la gonna
sky il cielo
slang il gergo
sledge la slitta
to sleep dormire

sleeper *(on train)* la cuccetta
sleeping bag il sacco a pelo
sleeping car il vagone letto
sleeping pill il sonnifero
slice *(piece of)* la fetta
sliced bread il pancarrè
slide *(photo)* la diapositiva
to slip scivolare
slippers le pantofole
slow lento(a)
slowly lentamente
small piccolo(a)
smaller (than) più piccolo (di)
smell l'odore (m)
bad smell il puzzo
nice smell il profumo
smile il sorriso
to smile sorridere
smoke il fumo
to smoke fumare
I don't smoke non fumo
can I smoke? posso fumare?
smoke alarm l'allarme antincendio *(m)*
smoked *(food)* affumicato(a)
smokers *(sign)* fumatori
smooth liscio(a)
snack lo spuntino *(m)*
to have a snack fare lo spuntino
snail la lumaca
snake il serpente
(grass) la biscia
snake bite il morso di vipera
to sneeze starnutire
to snore russare
snorkel il boccaglio
snow la neve
to snow: *it's snowing* nevica
snowboard lo snowboard
snow chains le catene da neve
snow tyres i pneumatici da neve
soap il sapone
soap powder il detersivo in polvere
sober sobrio(a)
socket *(electric)* la presa
socks i calzini
soda water l'acqua di selz *(f)*
sofa il divano
sofa bed il divano letto
soft soffice ; morbido(a)
soft drink la bibita
soldier il soldato
sole *(fish)* la sogliola
(of foot, shoe) la suola
soluble solubile
some di (del/della) *see* **GRAMMAR**
(a few) alcuni/alcune
someone qualcuno
something qualcosa
sometimes qualche volta
son il figlio
son-in-law il genero
song la canzone
soon presto
as soon as possible il più presto possibile
sore throat il mal di gola
sorry: *I'm sorry!* mi scusi!
sound il suono
soup la minestra
sour aspro(a) ; agro(a)
soured cream la panna acida
south il sud
souvenir il souvenir
spa la stazione termale
spade il badile
Spain la Spagna
Spanish spagnolo(a)
spanner la chiave inglese
spare parts i pezzi di ricambio
spare wheel la ruota di scorta
sparkling frizzante
sparkling water l'acqua gassata
sparkling wine il vino frizzante
spark plugs le candele
to speak parlare
do you speak English? parla inglese?
special speciale

S

specialist lo/la specialista
speciality la specialità
speech il discorso
speed la velocità
speed limit il limite di velocità
to exceed the speed limit superare il limite di velocità
speedboat il motoscafo
speedometer il tachimetro
to spell scrivere
how is it spelt? come si scrive?
to spend spendere
spice le spezie *(fpl)*
spicy piccante
spinach gli spinaci *(mpl)*
spine la spina dorsale
to spill rovesciare
spirits *(alcohol)* i liquori
splinter la scheggia
sponge la spugna
spoon il cucchiaio
sport lo sport
sports shop il negozio di articoli sportivi
sprain la slogatura
spring *(season)* la primavera
spring onion il cipollotto
square *(in town)* la piazza
squash *(game)* lo squash
to squeeze premere ; stringere
squid il calamaro
stadium lo stadio
staff il personale
stage *(theatre)* il palcoscenico
stain la macchia
stained glass il vetro colorato
stairs le scale
stale *(bread)* raffermo(a)
stalls *(in theatre)* la platea
stamp il francobollo
to stand stare in piedi
star la stella
starfish la stella marina
to start cominciare
starter *(in meal)* l'antipasto *(m)*
(in car) il motorino d'avviamento
station la stazione
stationer's la cartoleria
statue la statua
to stay *(remain)* rimanere
I'm staying at the Grand Hotel sono al Grand Hotel
steak la bistecca
medium steak la bistecca poco cotta
rare steak la bistecca al sangue
well-done steak la bistecca ben cotta
to steal rubare
steamed al vapore
to steam cuocere a vapore
steel l'acciaio *(m)*
steep: *is it steep?* è in salita?
steering wheel il volante
stem il gambo
stepfather il patrigno
stepmother la matrigna
stereo lo stereo
personal stereo il walkman®
sterling la sterlina
stew lo stufato
steward lo steward
stewardess la hostess
sticking plaster il cerotto
still *(motionless)* fermo(a)
(water) naturale
sting la puntura
to sting pungere
stitches i punti
stock cubes i dadi da brodo
stockings le calze
stomach lo stomaco ; la pancia
stomachache il mal di pancia
stone la pietra
to stop *(come to a halt)* fermarsi
(stop doing something) smettere
stopover la sosta
store *(shop)* il negozio
storey il piano
storm la tempesta ; il temporale

story il racconto
straight *(drink)* liscio(a)
straightaway subito
straight on diritto
strange strano(a)
straw *(for drinking)* la cannuccia
strawberries le fragole
stream il ruscello
street la strada
street map la piantina
stress lo stress
strike *(of workers)* lo sciopero
string lo spago
striped a strisce
stroke *(medical)* l'infarto *(m)*
strong forte
strong coffee il caffè ristretto
strong tea il tè forte
stuck bloccato(a)
student lo studente/la studentessa
student discount lo sconto per studenti
stuffed farcito(a)
stung punto(a)
stupid stupido(a)
subscription l'abbonamento *(m)*
subtitles i sottotitoli
suddenly all'improvviso
suede il camoscio
sugar lo zucchero
icing sugar lo zucchero a velo
sugar-free senza zucchero
to suggest proporre
suit *(man's)* l'abito *(m)*
(woman's) il tailleur
suitcase la valigia
summer l'estate *(f)*
summer holidays le vacanze estive
summit il vertice
sun il sole
to sunbathe prendere il sole
sunblock la protezione solare totale
sunburn la scottatura solare
Sunday domenica
sunflower il girasole
sunflower oil l'olio di girasole *(m)*
sunglasses gli occhiali da sole
sunny: ***it's sunny*** c'è il sole
sunroof *(car)* il tettuccio apribile
sunshade l'ombrellone *(m)*
sunstroke l'insolazione *(f)*
suntan lotion la crema abbronzante
supermarket il supermercato
supper *(dinner)* la cena
supplement il supplemento
sure sicuro(a) ; certo(a)
I'm sure sono sicuro(a)
surf il surf
to surf fare il surf
surfboard la tavola da surf
surgery *(surgical treatment)* la chirurgia
surname il cognome
my surname is... di cognome mi chiamo...
surprise la sorpresa
to survive sopravvivere
to swallow inghiottire
swan il cigno
to swear *(bad language)* dire le parolacce
to sweat sudare
sweater il maglione
sweatshirt la felpa
sweet *(not savoury)* dolce
sweetener il dolcificante
sweets le caramelle
to swim nuotare
swimming pool la piscina
swimsuit il costume da bagno
swing *(for children)* l'altalena *(f)*
Swiss svizzero(a)
switch l'interruttore *(m)*
to switch off spegnere
to switch on accendere
Switzerland la Svizzera

swollen gonfio(a)
swordfish il pescespada
synagogue la sinagoga
syringe la siringa

T

table la tavola
tablecloth la tovaglia
tablespoon il cucchiaio
tablet *(pill)* la pastiglia
table tennis il ping pong
table wine il vino da tavola
tailor il sarto
to take *(carry)* portare
(to grab, seize) prendere
(to take someone to) portare a
how long does it take? quanto tempo ci vuole?
take-away *(food)* da asporto
to take-off decollare
to take out *(of bag)* tirar fuori
talc il borotalco
talent il talento
to talk parlare
tall alto(a)
tampons gli assorbenti interni
tangerine il mandarino
tank la cisterna
(car) il serbatoio
(fish) l'acquario *(m)*
tap il rubinetto
tape il nastro
tape measure il metro a nastro
tape recorder il registratore
target lo scopo
tarragon il dragoncello
tart la crostata
tartar sauce la salsa tartara
taste il sapore
to taste assaggiare ; provare
can I taste some? ne posso assaggiare un po'?
tax la tassa ; l'imposta *(f)*
taxi il taxi
taxi driver il/la tassista
taxi rank il posteggio dei taxi
tea il tè
herbal tea la tisana
fruit tea il tè alla frutta
lemon tea il tè al limone
tea with milk il tè al latte
strong tea il tè forte
tea bag la bustina di tè
to teach insegnare
teacher l'insegnante *(m/f)*
(university) il/la docente
team la squadra
teapot la teiera
tear *(in material)* lo strappo
teaspoon il cucchiaino
tea towel lo strofinaccio per i piatti
tee il tee
teeshirt la maglietta
teeth i denti
telegram il telegramma
telephone il telefono
to telephone telefonare
telephone box la cabina telefonica
telephone call la telefonata
telephone card la scheda telefonica
telephone directory l'elenco telefonico *(m)*
telephone number il numero di telefono
television la televisione
telex il telex
to tell dire
temperature la temperatura
to have a temperature avere la febbre
temple il tempio
temporary provvisorio(a)
tendon il tendine
tennis il tennis
tennis ball la pallina da tennis
tennis court il campo da tennis
tennis racket la racchetta da tennis

tent la tenda
tent peg il picchetto
term *(school)* il trimestre
terminal *(airport)* il terminal
terrace la terrazza
terracotta la terracotta
terrorist il/la terrorista
to test *(try out)* provare
testicles i testicoli
to thank ringraziare
thank you grazie
 thanks very much molte grazie
that quel/quella/quello
 that one quello là
the *(sing)* il/lo/la
 (plural) i/gli/le
theatre il teatro
theft il furto
their il/la loro
them loro ; li ; le
there *(over there)* lì
there is/there are c'è/ci sono
thermometer il termometro
these questi/queste
 these ones questi qui
they loro ; essi/esse *see* **GRAMMAR**
thick spesso(a)
thief il/la ladro(a)
thigh la coscia
thin sottile
 (person) magro(a)
thing la cosa
 my things la mia roba
to think pensare
thirsty: ***to be thirsty*** avere sete
this questo/questa
those quei/quelle/quegli
thousand mille
thread il filo
thriller il thriller
throat la gola
through attraverso
to throw away buttare via
thrush *(candida)* la candida
thumb il pollice
thunder il tuono
thunderstorm il temporale
Thursday giovedì
thyme il timo
ticket *(bus, train, etc)* il biglietto
 (entry fee) il biglietto d'ingresso
 a single ticket un biglietto di (sola) andata
 a return ticket un biglietto di andata e ritorno
 tourist ticket il biglietto turistico
 book of tickets il blocchetto di biglietti
ticket collector il controllore
ticket office la biglietteria
tide *(sea)* la marea
 high tide l'alta marea
 low tide la bassa marea
tidy ordinato(a)
tie la cravatta
tight stretto(a)
tights i collant ; la calzamaglia
tile *(floor)* la piastrella
till *(cash desk)* la cassa
till *(until)* fino a
 till 2 o'clock fino alle due
 till 6 o'clock fino alle sei
time il tempo
 (of day) l'ora *(f)*
 this time questa volta
 what time is it? che ore sono?
 do you have the time? ha l'ora?
timetable l'orario *(m)*
tin *(can)* la scatola ; la lattina
tinfoil la carta stagnola
tin-opener l'apriscatole *(m)*
tiny minuscolo(a)
tip *(to waiter, etc)* la mancia
to tip *(waiter, etc)* dare la mancia
Tippex® il liquido correttore
tired stanco(a)
tissues i fazzoletti di carta
to a *see* **GRAMMAR**
 to London a Londra
 to Spain in Spagna
 to the airport all'aeroporto

t

toast *(to eat)* il pane tostato
(raising glass) il brindisi
tobacco il tabacco
tobacconist's il tabaccaio
today oggi
toe il dito del piede
together insieme
toilet la toilette
toilet for disabled la toilette per i disabili
toilet brush lo spazzolino del gabinetto
toilet paper la carta igienica
toiletries gli articoli per l'igiene
token *(for phone)* il gettone
toll *(motorway)* il pedaggio
tomato il pomodoro
tinned tomatoes i pelati
tomato juice il succo di pomodoro
tomato purée il concentrato di pomodoro
tomato sauce la salsa di pomodoro
tomorrow domani
tomorrow morning domani mattina
tomorrow afternoon domani pomeriggio
tomorrow evening domani sera
tongue la lingua
tonic water l'acqua tonica *(f)*
tonight stasera
too *(also)* anche
too big troppo grande
too small troppo piccolo(a)
too hot troppo caldo(a)
too noisy troppo rumoroso(a)
tool l'attrezzo *(m)*
toolkit gli attrezzi
tooth il dente
toothache il mal di denti
toothbrush lo spazzolino da denti
toothpaste il dentifricio
toothpick lo stuzzicadenti
top: ***the top floor*** l'ultimo piano *(m)*
top la cima
on top of sopra di
topless topless
torch *(flashlight)* la pila
torn strappato(a)
total il totale
to touch toccare
tough *(meat)* duro(a)
tour il giro
guided tour la visita guidata
tour guide la guida turistica *(m/f)*
tour operator l'operatore turistico *(m)*
tourist il/la turista
tourist information le informazioni turistiche
tourist office l'ufficio di turismo *(m)*
tourist route l'itinerario turistico *(m)*
tourist ticket il biglietto turistico
tournament il torneo
to tow rimorchiare
tow rope il cavo da rimorchio
towel l'asciugamano *(m)*
tower la torre
town la città
town centre il centro città
town hall il municipio
town plan la piantina
toxic tossico(a)
toy il giocattolo
toy shop il negozio di giocattoli
tracksuit la tuta sportiva
traditional tradizionale
traffic il traffico
traffic jam l'ingorgo *(m)*
traffic lights il semaforo
trailer il rimorchio
train il treno
the next train il prossimo treno
the first train il primo treno
the last train l'ultimo treno
trainers le scarpe da ginnastica
tram il tram
tranquilliser il tranquillante

to transfer trasferire
to translate tradurre
translation la traduzione
to travel viaggiare
travel agent's l'agenzia di viaggi *(f)*
travel documents i documenti di viaggio
travel guide la guida
travel sickness *(sea)* il mal di mare
(air) il mal d'aria
(car) il mal d'auto
traveller's cheques i traveller's (cheque)
tray il vassoio
tree l'albero *(m)*
trip la gita ; il viaggio
trolley il carrello
trousers i pantaloni
trout la trota
truck il camion
true vero(a)
trunk *(luggage)* il baule
trunks *(swimming)* i calzoncini da bagno
truth la verità
to try provare
to try on *(clothes, shoes)* provare
t-shirt la maglietta
Tuesday martedì
tulip il tulipano
tumble dryer l'asciugatrice *(f)*
tuna il tonno
tunnel la galleria
Turin Torino
turkey *(bird)* il tacchino
to turn *(handle, wheel)* girare
to turn around girarsi
to turn off *(light, etc)* spegnere
(tap) chiudere
to turn on *(light, etc)* accendere
(tap) aprire
turnip la rapa
turquoise *(colour)* turchese
tweezers le pinzette
twice due volte ; il doppio
twin beds i letti gemelli
twins i gemelli
to type battere a macchina
tyre la gomma ; il pneumatico
tyre pressure la pressione delle gomme

U

ugly brutto(a)
ulcer *(stomach)* l'ulcera *(f)*
(mouth) l'afta *(f)*
umbrella l'ombrello *(m)*
(sunshade) l'ombrellone *(m)*
uncle lo zio
uncomfortable scomodo(a)
unconscious svenuto(a)
under sotto
underground *(metro)* la metropolitana
underpants le mutande
underpass il sottopassaggio
to understand capire
I don't understand non capisco
do you understand? capisce?
underwater sott'acqua
underwear la biancheria intima
unemployed disoccupato(a)
to unfasten slacciare
United States gli Stati Uniti
university l'università *(f)*
unleaded petrol la benzina senza piombo ; la benzina verde
unlikely improbabile
to unlock aprire
to unpack disfare la valigia
I must unpack devo disfare le valigie
to unscrew svitare
until fino a
up: ***to get up*** alzarsi
upside down sottosopra
upstairs di sopra
urgent urgente

urine l'orina *(f)*
U-turn l'inversione a U *(f)*
us ci ; noi
to use usare
useful utile
usually di solito

V

vacancy *(in hotel)* la camera libera
vacant libero(a)
vaccination la vaccinazione
vacuum cleaner l'aspirapolvere *(m)*
vagina la vagina
valid valido(a)
valley la valle
valuable di valore
value il valore
valve la valvola
van il furgone
vanilla la vaniglia
vase il vaso
VAT l'IVA *(f)*
veal il vitello
vegan vegetaliano(a)
vegetables le verdure
vegetarian vegetariano(a)
I'm vegetarian sono vegetariano
vehicle il veicolo
vein la vena
Velcro® il velcro®
venereal disease la malattia venerea
Venice Venezia
venison la carne di cervo
very molto
vest la canottiera
vet il/la veterinario(a)
to video *(from TV)* registrare su videocassetta
video il video
video camera la videocamera
video cassette/tape la videocassetta
video game il videogioco
video recorder il videoregistratore
view la vista
villa la villa
village il paese
vinaigrette la vinaigrette
vinegar l'aceto *(m)*
vineyard la vigna
violet *(flower)* la viola
viper la vipera
virus il virus
visa il visto
to visit visitare
visiting hours l'orario delle visite *(m)*
visitor il visitatore/la visitatrice
vitamin la vitamina
vodka la vodka
voice la voce
volcano il vulcano
volleyball la pallavolo
voltage il voltaggio
to vomit vomitare
voucher il buono

W

wage il salario
waist la vita
waistcoat il gilè
waistline la vita
to wait (for) aspettare
waiter/waitress il cameriere/la cameriera
waiting room la sala d'aspetto
to wake up svegliare
Wales il Galles
walk la passeggiata
to walk andare a piedi
walking boots gli scarponcini
walking stick il bastone
Walkman® il walkman®
wall il muro ; la parete
wallet il portafoglio
walnut la noce

to want volere
I want... voglio...
we want... vogliamo...
war la guerra
ward *(hospital)* il reparto
wardrobe l'armadio *(m)*
warm caldo(a)
it's warm fa caldo
warning triangle il triangolo d'emergenza
to wash lavare
(to wash oneself) lavarsi
wash and blow dry lo shampoo e messa in piega
washing machine la lavatrice
washing powder il detersivo in polvere
washing-up bowl la bacinella
washing-up liquid il detersivo per i piatti
wasp la vespa
waste bin il bidone della spazzatura
watch l'orologio *(m)*
to watch guardare
watchstrap il cinturino dell'orologio
water l'acqua *(f)*
drinking water l'acqua potabile
mineral water l'acqua minerale
sparkling water l'acqua gassata
still water l'acqua naturale
watercress il crescione
waterfall la cascata
water heater lo scaldabagno
watermelon l'anguria *(f)*
waterproof impermeabile
to water-ski fare lo sci nautico
waterwings i braccioli salvagente
waves *(on sea)* le onde
waxing *(hair removal)* la ceretta
way in *(entrance)* l'entrata *(f)* ; l'ingresso *(m)*
way out *(exit)* l'uscita *(f)*
we noi *see* **GRAMMAR**
weak *(person)* debole
(tea, coffee, etc) leggero(a)
to wear portare
weather il tempo
weather forecast le previsioni del tempo
website il sito web
wedding il matrimonio
wedding anniversary l'anniversario di matrimonio *(m)*
wedding cake la torta nuziale
wedding dress l'abito da sposa *(m)*
wedding present il regalo di matrimonio
wedding ring la fede
Wednesday mercoledì
week la settimana
last week la settimana scorsa
next week la prossima settimana
per week alla settimana
this week questa settimana
weekday il giorno feriale
weekend il fine settimana
next weekend il prossimo fine settimana
this weekend questo fine settimana
weekly settimanale
to weigh pesare
weight il peso
welcome benvenuto
well bene
well-done *(steak)* ben cotto(a)
Welsh gallese
west ovest
wet bagnato(a)
wetsuit la muta
what cosa?
what is it? cos'è?
wheel la ruota
wheelchair la sedia a rotelle
wheel clamp il ceppo bloccaruote
when? quando?
where? dove?
which qual/quale

W

while mentre
in a while fra poco
whipped cream la panna montata
whisky l'whisky *(m)*
white bianco(a)
who? chi?
whole tutto
wholemeal bread il pane integrale
whose: ***whose is it?*** di chi è?
why? perché?
wide largo(a) ; ampio(a)
widow la vedova
widower il vedovo
width la larghezza
wife la moglie
wildlife la natura
wig la parrucca
to win vincere
wind il vento
windbreak *(camping)* il frangivento
windmill il mulino a vento
window la finestra
(shop) la vetrina
(car) il finestrino
windscreen il parabrezza
windscreen wiper il tergicristallo
to windsurf fare il windsurf
windy: ***it's windy*** c'è vento
wine il vino
red wine il vino rosso
white wine il vino bianco
dry wine il vino secco
sweet wine il vino dolce
rosé wine il vino rosato
sparkling wine il vino frizzante
house wine il vino della casa
wine list la lista dei vini
wing mirror lo specchietto laterale
winter l'inverno *(m)*
wire il filo
with con
with ice col ghiaccio
with milk col latte
with sugar con lo zucchero
without senza
without ice senza ghiaccio
without milk senza latte
without sugar senza zucchero
witness il/la testimone
wolf il lupo
woman la donna
wonderful meraviglioso(a)
wood *(material)* il legno
(forest) il bosco
wool la lana
word la parola
work il lavoro
to work *(person)* lavorare
(machine, car, etc) funzionare
it doesn't work non funziona
world il mondo
worried preoccupato(a)
worse peggio
worth *(value)* il valore
it's worth £5 vale cinque sterline
to wrap up *(parcel)* incartare
wrinkles le rughe ; le grinze
to write scrivere
please write it down lo scriva per favore
writing paper la carta da lettere
wrong sbagliato(a)
what's wrong? cosa c'è che non va?
wrought iron il ferro battuto

X

x-ray la radiografia

Y

yacht lo yacht
year l'anno *(m)*
this year quest'anno
next year l'anno prossimo
last year l'anno scorso
yellow giallo(a)
Yellow Pages le pagine gialle®

yes sì
yesterday ieri
yet: ***not yet*** non ancora
yoga lo yoga
yoghurt lo yogurt
plain yoghurt lo yogurt naturale
yolk il tuorlo
you lei ; tu ; voi *see* **GRAMMAR**
young giovane
your il/la suo(a) ; il/la tuo(a) ; il/la vostro(a)
your passport il suo passaporto
your room la sua camera
youth hostel l'ostello della gioventù *(m)*

Z

zero lo zero
zip la cerniera
zone la zona
zoo lo zoo

a at ; in ; to *see* **GRAMMAR**
abbaglianti *mpl* full-beam headlights
abbiamo... we have...
non abbiamo... we don't have...
abbigliamento *m* clothes
abbonamento *m* subscription ; season ticket
abbronzatura *f* suntan
abito *m* dress ; man's suit
aborto *m* abortion
aborto spontaneo miscarriage
abuso *m* misuse
a.C. = B.C.
accamparsi to camp
accanto (a) beside ; next (to)
acceleratore *m* accelerator
accendere to turn on ; to light
accendere i fari switch on your headlights
accendino *m* cigarette lighter
accensione *f* ignition
accento *m* accent *(pronunciation)*
acceso(a) on *(light, engine)*
accesso *m* access

DIVIETO DI ACCESSO no access

accettazione *f* reception

ACCETTAZIONE BAGAGLI check-in

accomodarsi to make oneself comfortable
si accomodi do take a seat
accompagnare to accompany
accordo *m* agreement
acetone *m* nail polish remover
ACI *m* = Automobile Association
acqua *f* water
acqua calda hot water
acqua corrente running water
acqua distillata distilled water
acqua gassata sparkling water
acqua minerale mineral water
acqua naturale still water
acqua potabile drinking water
acquisto *m* purchase
addetto(a) authorized
adesso now
adulto(a) adult
aereo *m* plane ; aircraft
aeroplano *m* airplane
aeroporto *m* airport
affari *mpl* business
per affari on business
affittare to rent ; to let

AFFITASI for rent

affitto *m* lease ; rent
affogare to drown
agenda *f* diary
agenzia *f* agency
agenzia di viaggi travel agent
agenzia immobiliare estate agent
aggredire to attack
aglio *m* garlic
ago *m* needle
ago ipodermico hypodermic needle

AGOSTO August

AIDS *m* AIDS
aiutare to help
aiuto! help!
alba *f* dawn
albergo *m* hotel
albero *m* tree ; mast
albicocca *f* apricot
alcolici *mpl* alcoholic drinks
alcolico(a) alcoholic
alcool *m* alcohol
alcuni(e) some ; a few
alcuno(a) any ; some
alimentari *mpl* groceries
allacciare to fasten *(seatbelt, etc)*
allarme *m* alarm
allarme antincendio fire alarm
allergia *f* allergy
allergico(a) a allergic to

a

alloggio *m* accommodation
alluvione *f* flood
Alpi *fpl* Alps
alpinismo *m* climbing

ALT stop

altezza *f* height
alto(a) high ; tall
alta stagione high season
alta marea high tide
altro(a) other
altri passaporti other passports
alzarsi to get up ; to stand up
amabile sweet *(wine)*
amare to love *(person)*
amarena *f* bitter cherry
amaro(a) bitter *(taste)*
ambasciata *f* embassy
ambiente *m* environment
ambulanza *f* ambulance
ambulatorio *m* surgery ; out-patients
America *f* America
americano(a) American
amico(a) *m/f* friend
ammalato(a) ill
amministratore delegato *m* managing director
ammontare *m* total amount
ammortizzatore *m* shock absorber
amo *m* bait
amore *m* love
analasi del sangue *f* blood test
analcolico *m* soft drink
analcolico(a) non-alcoholic
analgesico *m* painkiller
ananas *m* pineapple
anatra *f* duck
anca *f* hip
anche too ; also ; even
ancora still ; yet ; again
ancora un po'? a little more?
non ancora not yet
ancora *f* anchor
andare to go *see* **GRAMMAR**
andare a cavallo to ride a horse
andare a piedi to go on foot
andare bene to fit *(clothes)*
andare in macchina to go by car
andata e ritorno return *(ticket)*
di (sola) andata single *(ticket)*
andiamo! let's go!
andiamo a... we're going to...
anestetico *m* anaesthetic
angina pectoris *f* angina
anguria *f* watermelon
anice *m* aniseed
animale *m* animal
animale domestico pet
annata *f* vintage ; year
vino d'annata vintage wine
anniversario *m* anniversary
anno *m* year
buon anno! happy New Year!
annuale annual
annullamento *m* cancellation
annullare to cancel
annuncio *m* announcement ; advert
antibiotico *m* antibiotic
anticipo *m* advance *(loan)*
in anticipo in advance ; early
anticoncezionale *m* contraceptive
antifurto *m* burglar alarm
antigelo *m* antifreeze ; de-icer
antipasto *m* starter ; hors d'œuvre
antisettico *m* antiseptic
antistaminico *m* anihistamine
anziano(a) *m/f* senior citizen
ape *f* bee
aperitivo *m* apéritif

APERTO open

all'aperto open-air
appartamento *m* flat ; apartment
appendicite *f* appendicitis
appuntamento *m* appointment ; date
apribottiglie *m* bottle opener

APRILE April

aprire to open ; to turn on *(tap)*
apriscatole *m* tin-opener
arachide *f* peanut
arancia *f* orange
aranciata *f* orange squash
arancione orange *(colour)*
area *f* area
area di servizio service area
argento *m* silver
aria condizionata *f* air-conditioning
armadio *m* cupboard ; wardrobe
arrabbiato(a) angry
arredato(a) furnished
arrestare to arrest
arrivare to arrive
arrivederci goodbye

ARRIVI arrivals

arrivi nazionali domestic arrivals
arrivi internazionali international arrivals
arrosto *m* roast
arte *f* art ; craft
articolo *m* article
articoli da dichiarare goods to declare
articoli da regalo gifts
artigiano(a) *m/f* craftsperson
artista *m/f* artist
artrite *f* arthritis

ASCENSORE lift/elevator

ascesso *m* abscess
asciugamano *m* towel
asciugare to dry
asciugatrice *f* tumble dryer
ascoltare to listen (to)
asma *f* asthma
aspettare to wait (for) ; to expect
aspirapolvere *m* vacuum cleaner
aspirina *f* aspirin
assaggiare to taste
asse *m* axle *(car)*
asse da stiro ironing board
assegno *m* cheque
assicurato(a) insured
assicurazione *f* insurance
assistente *m/f* assistant
assistenza *f* assistance ; aid
associazione *f* society
assorbenti *mpl* sanitary towels
assorbenti interni tampons
ATM public transport service
attaccare to attach ; to attack ; to fasten
attacco *m* fit *(seizure)*
attacco cardiaco heart attack
attendere to wait for

ATTENTI AL CANE beware of dog

attento(a) careful
attenzione *f* caution
fare attenzione to be careful
atterraggio *m* landing *(of plane)*
atterrare to land *(plane)*
attestare to declare
attore *m* actor
attracco *m* mooring ; berth
attraente attractive
attraversare to cross
attraverso through
attrazione *f* attraction
attrezzatura *f* equipment
attrezzo *m* tool
attrice *f* actress
auguri! happy birthday! ; best wishes
aumentare to increase
Australia *f* Australia
australiano(a) Australian
austriaco(a) Austrian
autentico(a) genuine
autista *m/f* driver
auto *f* car
autobus *m* bus
autofficina *f* garage *(for repairs)*
autoforniture *fpl* car parts and accessories
autonoleggio *m* car hire
autore *m* author

a

autorimessa *f* garage
autorizzazione *f* authorization
autostop *m* hitchhiking

AUTOSTRADA motorway

autunno *m* autumn
avanti in front ; forward(s)
avanti! come in!
avere to have *see* **GRAMMAR**
avere bisogno di to need
avere fame to be hungry
avere sete to be thirsty
avvertire to warn
avvisare to inform ; to warn
avviso *m* notice ; advertisement
azienda *f* business ; firm
azienda di soggiorno local tourist board
azzardo *m* risk ; hazard
azzurro(a) light blue

B

b

babbo *m* daddy
Babbo Natale Father Christmas
baciare to kiss
bacinella *f* washing-up bowl
bacio *m* kiss
baci! love and kisses *(in letter)*
baffi *mpl* moustache
bagagli *mpl* luggage
bagagliaio *m* boot *(of car)*
bagaglio *m* luggage
bagaglio a mano hand luggage
bagnarsi to bathe; to get wet
bagnino *m* lifeguard
bagno *m* bath ; bathroom
balcone *m* balcony
ballare to dance
balletto *m* ballet
ballo *m* dance
balneazione *f* bathing

DIVIETO DI BALNEAZIONE
no swimming

balsamo *m* hair conditioner
bambino(a) *m/f* child ; baby
bambini *mpl* chidren
per bambini for chidren
bambola *f* doll
banana *f* banana
banca *f* bank
bancarella *f* stall ; stand
banchina *f* platform ; quay
banco *m* counter ; desk
banco informazioni enquiry desk
Bancomat® *m* cash dispenser
banconota *f* banknote
bandiera *f* flag
bar *m* bar ; café
barattolo *m* tin ; jar
barba *f* beard
barbiere *m* barber
barca *f* boat
barista *m/f* barman/barmaid
basso(a) low ; short
bassa marea low tide
basta that's enough
battello *m* boat
batteria *f* battery *(car)*
batteria scarica flat battery
baule *m* trunk *(luggage)*
bavaglino *m* bib
bello(a) beautiful ; fine ; lovely
benda *f* bandage
bene well ; all right ; OK
benvenuto welcome
benzina *f* petrol
fare benzina to get petrol
bere to drink
bevanda *f* drink
biancheria *f* linen *(for beds, table)*
biancheria intima underwear
bianco(a) white ; blank
lasciate in bianco leave blank
biberon *m* baby's bottle
bibita *f* soft drink

BIBITE soft drinks

bicchiere *m* glass *(for drinking)*

b

bici *f* bike *(pushbike)*
bicicletta *f* bicycle
bidet *m* bidet
bidone *m* bin ; dustbin ; can

BIGLIETTERIA ticket office

biglietto *m* ticket ; note ; card
  biglietto d'auguri greetings card
  biglietto da visita business card
bin. abbrev. of **binario**

BINARIO platform

biologico(a) organic
biondo(a) blond *(person)*
biro *f* Biro
birra *f* beer
  birra alla spina draught beer
  birra bionda lager
  birra chiara lager
birreria *f* bar ; pub
biscotto *m* biscuit
bisogno *m* need
  avere bisogno di to need
bistecca *f* steak
bloccare to block
  bloccare un assegno to stop a cheque
blocchetto di biglietti *m* book of tickets
blocco *m* block ; notepad
blu blue
blue jeans *mpl* jeans
boa *f* buoy
bocca *f* mouth
boccaglio *m* snorkel
bocce *fpl* bowls *(game)*
bolletta *f* bill
bollire to boil
bollitore *m* kettle
bomba *f* bomb
bombola del gas *f* gas cylinder
bombolone *m* doughnut
borotalco *m* talc
borsa *f* bag ; handbag ; briefcase
  borsa della spazzatura bin liner
  borsa termica cool-box *(for picnic)*
borseggiatore *m* pickpocket
borsellino *m* purse
bosco *m* wood ; *forest*
bottega *f* shop
botteghino *m* box office
bottiglia *f* bottle
bottone *m* button
boxer *mpl* boxer shorts
braccialetto *m* bracelet
braccio *m* arm
braccioli *mpl* armbands *(swimming)*
braciola *f* steak ; chop
brindisi *m* toast *(raising glass)*
brioche *f* croissant
britannico(a) *f* British
bronchite *f* bronchitis
bruciare to burn
bruciore di stomaco *m* heartburn
brutto(a) bad *(weather, news)*; ugly
buca delle lettere *f* postbox
bucato *m* washing ; laundry
  bucato in lavatrice machine wash
  bucato a mano hand washing
buco *m* hole ; leak
buono(a) good
  buon appetito! enjoy your meal!
  buon compleanno! happy birthday!
  buon giorno good morning/ afternoon
  buona notte good night
  buona sera good afternoon/ evening
  a buon mercato cheap
buono *m* voucher ; coupon ; token
burattino *m* puppet
burrasca *f* storm
burro *m* butter
burro di cacao *m* lip salve
bussare to knock *(on door)*
busta *f* envelope
bustina di tè *f* tea bag
buttare via to throw away

C

cabina *f* beach hut ; cabin
  cabina telefonica phonebox
cacciavite *m* screwdriver
cadere to fall

CADUTA MASSI danger rockfalls

caffè *m* coffee *(espresso)*
  caffè corretto espresso with spirit such as grappa
  caffè macchiato espresso with a little warm milk
  caffè solubile instant coffee
  caffellatte milky coffee
caffettiera *f* espresso-maker
calamita *f* magnet
calciatore *m* football player
calcio *m* football ; kick
calcolatrice *f* calculator

CALDO hot

calendario *m* calendar
calle *f* street *(in Venice dialect)*
callo *m* corn *(on foot)*
calmante *m* painkiller
calmo(a) calm
calpestare to tread on
calvo(a) bald
calza *f* stocking ; sock
calzamaglia *f* tights
calzature *fpl* shoeshop
calze *fpl* stockings
calzini *mpl* socks
calzolaio *m* shoe mender's
calzoleria *f* shoeshop
calzoncini corti *mpl* shorts
  calzoncini da bagno swimming trunks
cambiamento *m* change
cambiare to change
  cambiare autobus/treno to change bus/train
  cambiare soldi to change money
  cambiarsi to change one's clothes

CAMBIO bureau de change

camera *f* room *(in house, hotel)*
  camera da letto bedroom
  camera doppia double room
  camera libera vacancy *(in hotel)*
  camera per famiglia family room
  camera singola single room

CAMERE vacancies

cameriera *f* chambermaid
cameriere *m* waiter
camiceria *f* shirt shop
camicetta *f* blouse
camicia *f* shirt
  camicia da notte nightdress
camion *m* lorry
camminare to walk
camoscio *m* suede
campagna *f* countryside ; campaign
campanello *m* bell
campeggiare to camp
campeggio *m* camping ; campsite
  campeggio libero free campsite
camping gas *m* camping gas
campione *m* sample ; champion
campo *m* field ; court
  campo da tennis tennis court
  campo di calcio football pitch
  campo di golf golf course
  campo sportivo sports ground
camposanto *m* cemetery
Canada *m* Canada
canadese Canadian
canale *m* canal ; channel
cancellare to erase ; to cancel
cancellazione *f* cancellation
cancro *m* cancer
candeggina *f* bleach
candela *f* candle ; spark plug
candida *f* thrush *(candida)*
cane *m* dog
canile *m* kennel
canna da pesca *f* fishing rod
cannuccia *f* straw *(for drinking)*
canoa *f* canoe

canottaggio *m* rowing
canottiera *f* vest
canotto *m* dinghy *(rubber)*
cantante *m/f* singer
cantare to sing
cantiere *m* building site
cantina *f* cellar ; wine cellar
canzone *f* song
capelli *mpl* hair
capire to understand
capisce? do you understand?
non capisco I don't understand
capitale *f* capital *(city)*
capitolo *m* chapter
capo *m* head ; leader ; boss
Capodanno *m* New Year's day
capogruppo *m* group leader
capolavoro *m* masterpiece
capolinea *m* terminus
capoluogo *m* county town
capotreno *m* guard *(on train)*
cappella *f* chapel
cappello *m* hat
cappotto *m* overcoat
cappuccino *m* frothy white coffee
capra *f* goat
carabiniere *m* policeman
caraffa *f* carafe
caramelle *fpl* sweets
carbone *m* coal ; charcoal
carburante *m* fuel
carburatore *m* carburettor
carcere *m* prison
caricare to charge *(battery)*
carico *m* load ; shipment ; cargo
carino(a) pretty ; lovely ; nice
carne *f* meat
carnevale *m* carnival
caro(a) dear ; expensive
carote *fpl* carrots
carrello *m* trolley
carriera *f* career
carro *m* cart
carro attrezzi breakdown van
carrozza *f* carriage
carrozze cuccette couchettes
carrozza letto sleeper
carrozzeria *f* bodywork
carrozzina *f* pram
carta *f* paper ; card ; map
carta assegni cheque card
alla carta à la carte
carta d'argento senior citizen's rail card
carta di credito credit card
carta famiglia family rail card
carta d'identità identity card
carta igienica toilet paper
carta d'imbarco boarding card
carta stradale road map
carta verde green card
carte da gioco *fpl* playing-cards
cartella *f* briefcase ; folder
cartello *m* sign ; signpost
cartine *fpl* cigarette papers
cartoccio *m* paper bag
cartoleria *f* stationer's
cartolina *f* postcard
casa *f* house ; home
a casa at home
casalinga *f* housewife
casalinghi *mpl* household articles
cascata *f* waterfall
casco *m* helmet
casella postale *f* post-office box
casinò *m* casino
caso: in caso di in case of

CASSA cash desk

cassa chiusa position closed
cassaforte *f* safe *(for valuables)*
cassetta *f* cassette
cassetta delle lettere letterbox
cassetto *m* drawer
cassiere(a) *m/f* cashier ; teller
castello *m* castle
catena *f* chain ; mountain range
catene (da neve) snow chains
cattedrale *f* cathedral
cattivo(a) bad ; nasty ; naughty
cattolico(a) Catholic

causa *f* cause ; case *(lawsuit)*
a causa di because of
cavalcare to ride *(horse)*
cavallo *m* horse
cavatappi *m* corkscrew
cavo *m* cable
cavo da rimorchio tow rope
cavolfiore *m* cauliflower
CD *m* CD
c'è there is
cedro *m* cedar ; lime *(fruit)*
CE *f* EC
celibe single *(not married)*
cellulare *m* mobile phone
cena *f* dinner *(evening meal)*
cenare to have dinner
cenone *m* New Year's Eve dinner
centimetro *m* centimetre
cento hundred
centrale central
centralino *m* switchboard

CENTRO centre

centro città city centre
centro commerciale shopping centre
centro storico old town
ceppo bloccaruote *m* wheel clamp
cera *f* wax *(for furniture)*
ceramica *f* ceramics ; pottery
cercare to look for
ceretta *f* waxing *(hair removal)*
cerini *mpl* matches
cerniera *f* zip
cerotto *m* sticking plaster
certificato *m* certificate
certificato di nascita birth certificate
cervello *m* brain
cestino *m* basket ; waste paper bin
che what ; who ; which
che gusto? what flavour?
che ore sono? what time is it?
cherosene *m* paraffin
chi? who?
di chi è? whose is it?
chiamare to call
chiamare per telefono to phone
chiamarsi to be called *(name)*
come si chiama? what's your name?
chiamata *f* call *(telephone)*
chiave *f* key
chiave inglese spanner
chiedere to ask ; to ask for
chiesa *f* church
chilo *m* kilo
chilogrammo *m* kilogram
chilometraggio *m* mileage *(in km)*
chilometro *m* kilometre
chiodo *m* nail *(metal)*
chirurgia *f* surgery *(operations)*
chitarra *f* guitar
chiudere to close ; to turn off *(tap)*
chiudere a chiave to lock

CHIUSO closed
CHIUSO PER TURNO closed for weekly day off
CHIUSO PER FERIE closed for holidays

chiusura centralizzata *f* central locking *(car)*
ciabatta *f* flat bread ; slipper
ciao! hi! ; bye!
cibo *m* food
cielo *m* sky
ciliegia *f* cherry
cinghia della ventola *f* fan belt
cintura *f* belt
cintura di sicurezza seatbelt
cinturino dell'orologio *m* watch-strap
cioccolato *m* chocolate
cipolla *f* onion
circo *m* circus
circolare to move *(traffic)*
circolazione *f* traffic
circonvallazione *f* ring road
cisterna *f* cistern ; tank

cisti *f* cyst
cistite *f* cystitis
CIT *f* Italian Tourist Agency
citofono *m* intercom
città *f* city ; town

CITTADINI UE EU citizens

classe *f* class
clavicola *f* collar bone
cliente *m/f* customer
climatizzato(a) air-conditioned
clinica *f* clinic
cocco *m* coconut
cocomero *m* watermelon
coda *f* tail ; queue
codice *m* code
  codice a barra barcode
  codice postale postcode
cofano *m* bonnet *(car)*
cognata *f* sister-in-law
cognato *m* brother-in-law
cognome *m* surname
  di cognome mi chiamo... my surname is...
coincidenza *f* connection *(train, etc)*
colazione *f* breakfast ; lunch
collana *f* necklace
collant *mpl* tights
collega *m/f* colleague
colletto *m* collar
collina *f* hill
collo *m* neck ; package
colluttorio *m* mouthwash
colomba *f* dove ; Easter cake
colore *m* colour
Colosseo *m* Coliseum
colpa *f* fault
  non è colpa mia it's not my fault
coltello *m* knife
combustibile *m* fuel
come like ; as ; how
  come? how? *(in what way)*
  come si chiama? what's your name?
  come si pronuncia? how's it pronounced?
  come si scrive? how is it spelt?
  come sta? how are you?
cominciare to begin
commesso(a) *m/f* assistant ; clerk
commissariato *m* police station
commozione cerebrale *f* concussion
comodo(a) comfortable
compagnia *f* company
  compagnia aerea airline
compilare to fill in *(form)*
compleanno *m* birthday

COMPLETO no vacancies

comporre to dial *(number)*
comprare to buy
compreso(a) included
compressa *f* tablet
computer *m* computer
comune *m* town hall ; commune
con with
  con bagno with bathroom
  con filtro filter-tipped
  con ghiaccio with ice
concerto *m* concert
conchiglia *f* seashell
condimento *m* seasoning ; dressing *(for food)*
conducente *m/f* driver *(taxi, bus)*
confermare to confirm
confine *m* boundary ; border
congelatore *m* freezer
congratulazioni! congratulations!
congresso *m* conference
cono *m* cone
  cono gelato ice-cream cone
conoscere to know *(to be acquainted with)*
consegna *f* consignment ; delivery
conservante *m* preservative
consigliare to advise
consiglio *m* advice
consumare to use up
  da consumarsi entro best before

C

consumazione *f* drink
contanti *mpl* cash
pagare in contanti to pay cash
contatore *m* electricity meter
contento(a) happy
continuare to continue
conto *m* account ; bill
conto dettagliato itemised bill
conto in banca bank account
contorno *m* vegetable side dish
contrabando *m* smuggling
contratto *m* contract
contravvenzione *f* fine
contro against ; versus
controllare to check
controllo *m* check ; control
controllo passaporti passport control
controllore *m* ticket collector

CONVALIDA date stamp

convalidare to validate *(ticket)*
convincere to persuade
coperta *f* blanket
coperto *m* place setting ; cover charge
copertura *f* cover *(insurance)*
coppa gelato *f* ice cream served in goblet/tub
coppia *f* couple *(two people)*
copriletto *m* bedspread
coraggioso(a) brave
corda *f* rope
cornetto *m* ice cream cone
corpo *m* body
corrente *f* current *(electric, water)*
corrente d'aria draught
correre to run
corridoio *m* corridor
corriere *m* courier
corsa *f* race ; journey
corsa semplice single fare
corsia *f* lane ; hospital ward ; route
corsia di emergenza hard shoulder
corsia di sorpasso outside lane
corso *m* course ; avenue
corso dei cambi exchange rates
corso intensivo crash course
cortile *m* courtyard
corto(a) short
cos'è? what is it?
cos'è successo? what happened?
cosa *f* thing
cosa? what?
coscia *f* thigh
così so ; thus *(in this way)*
cosmetici *mpl* cosmetics
costa *f* coast
Costa Azzurra French Riviera
costare to cost
costoletta *f* chop
costoso(a) expensive
costruire to build
costume *m* custom ; costume
costume da bagno swimsuit
cotone *m* cotton
cotone idrofilo cotton wool
cotto(a) cooked
poco cotto(a) medium rare *(steak)*
cotton fioc® *m* cotton bud
crampi *mpl* cramps
cravatta *f* tie
credere to believe
credito *m* credit
non si fa credito no credit given
crema *f* cream ; custard
crema da barba shaving cream
crescere to grow
crespella *f* fried pastry twist
cric *m* jack *(for car)*
crisi epilettica *f* epileptic fit
cristallo *m* crystal
di cristallo made of crystal
croccante *f* crisp
croce *f* cross
crocevia *m* crossroads
crociera *f* cruise
crollo *m* collapse
cronaca *f* news

cruciverba *m* crossword puzzle
crudo(a) raw
cuccetta *f* couchette ; sleeper
cucchiaino *m* teaspoon
cucchiaio *m* spoon ; tablespoon
cucina *f* cooker ; kitchen ; cooking
  cucina a gas gas cooker
cucinare to cook
cucire to sew
cuffia *f* bathing cap
cuffie *fpl* earphones
cugino(a) *m/f* cousin
culla *f* cradle
cuocere to cook
  cuocere a vapore to steam
  cuocere alla griglia to grill
cuoco *m* chef
cuoio *m* leather
cuore *m* heart
cupola *f* dome
curva *f* bend ; corner
cuscino *m* cushion
custode *m* caretaker
custodia *f* case; holder
cyber-café *m* internet cafe

D

da from ; by ; with *see* **GRAMMAR**
  da asporto take away (food)
  dall'Inghilterra from England
  dalla Scozia from Scotland
danneggiare to spoil ; to damage
danno *m* damage
dappertutto everywhere
dare to give
  dare su to overlook ; to give onto
  dare la precedenza give way
  dare da mangiare to feed
  dare la mancia to tip *(waiter, etc)*
data *f* date
  data di nascita date of birth
  data di scadenza sell-by date
dati *mpl* data
dattero *m* date *(fruit)*
davanti a in front of ; opposite
dazio *m* customs duty
d.C. = A.D.
debito *m* debt
decaffeinato(a) decaffeinated
decollare to take-off
decollo *m* takeoff
delizioso(a) delicious
dente *m* tooth
dentiera *f* dentures
dentifricio *m* toothpaste
dentro in ; indoors ; inside
deodorante *m* deodorant
  deodorante per ambienti air freshener

DEPOSITO BAGAGLI left-luggage

descrivere to describe
descrizione *f* description
desiderare to want ; to desire
destinazione *f* destination
destra *f* right
detergente *m* cleanser
detersivo *m* detergent
  detersivo in polvere soap powder
  detersivo per i piatti washing-up liquid
detrazione *f* deduction
dettagli *mpl* details
deviazione *f* detour ; diversion
di of ; some *see* **GRAMMAR**
  di cristallo/plastica made of crystal/plastic
  di lusso luxury *(hotel, etc)*
  di mattina/pomeriggio/di notte in the morning/afternoon/at night
  di stagione in season
  di valore of value ; valuable
diabete *m* diabetes
diabetico(a) diabetic
diaframma *m* cap *(diaphragm)*
dialetto *m* dialect
diamante *m* diamond
diapositiva *f* slide *(photo)*
diarrea *f* diarrhoea

d

DICEMBRE December

dichiarare to declare
dichiarazione *f* declaration
dieta *f* diet
essere a dieta to be on a diet
dietro behind ; after
dietro di behind
difetto *m* fault
difficile difficult
diga *f* dam ; dyke
digerire to digest
digestivo *m* after-dinner liqueur
dimenticare to forget
Dio *m* God
dipinto(a) painted
diramazione *f* fork *(in road)*
dire to say ; to tell
diretto(a) direct
treno diretto through train
direttore *m* manager ; director
direzione *f* management ; direction
dirigere to manage *(be in charge of)*
diritto(a) straight
sempre diritto straight on
disabile disabled *(person)*
disastro *m* disaster
dischetto *m* floppy disk ; diskette
disco *m* disk ; record
disco orario parking disk
discoteca *f* disco
disdire to cancel
disegno *m* drawing
disfare la valigia to unpack
disinfettante *m* disinfectant
disoccupato(a) unemployed
dispiacere: mi dispiace I'm sorry
disponibile available
distaccare to detach ; to unplug
distante far ; distant
distanza *f* distance
distorsione *f* sprain
distributore *m* dispenser
distributore di benzina petrol station
disturbare to disturb
disturbo *m* trouble
dito *m* finger
dito del piede toe
ditta *f* firm ; company
diurno(a) day(time)
divano *m* sofa ; divan
divano letto sofa bed
diversi(e) several ; various
diverso(a) different
divertente funny *(amusing)*
divertimento *m* entertainment ; fun
divertirsi to enjoy oneself
dividere to share

DIVIETO forbidden/no...

divieto di sorpasso no overtaking
divieto di sosta no parking
divisa *f* uniform
divorziato(a) divorced
dizionario *m* dictionary
DOC abbrev. of denominazione di origine controllata *(guarantee of wine quality)*
doccia *f* shower
docente *m/f* lecturer
DOCG abbrev. of denominazione di origine controllata e garantita
documenti *mpl* papers *(passport)*
dogana *f* customs
dolce sweet *(not savoury)* ; mild
dolce *m* sweet ; dessert ; cake
dolcelatte *m* creamy blue cheese
dolcificante *m* sweetener
dolciumi *mpl* sweets
dollari *mpl* dollars
dolore *m* pain ; grief
doloroso(a) painful
domanda *f* question
domandare to ask *(a question)*
domani tomorrow
domani mattina tomorrow morning
domani pomeriggio tomorrow afternoon

domani sera tomorrow evening/ night
domattina tomorrow morning

DOMENICA Sunday

donna *f* woman

DONNE Ladies

dopo after ; afterward(s)
dopobarba *m* aftershave
doppio(a) double
dormire to sleep
dove? where?
dovere to have to *see* **GRAMMAR**
droga *f* drugs *(narcotics)*
drogheria *f* grocery shop
duepezzi *m* bikini
duomo *m* cathedral
durante during
durare to last
duro(a) hard ; tough ; harsh

E

e and
E east *(abbrev.)*
è is (to be) *see* **GRAMMAR**
ebreo(a) Jewish
ecc. etc.
eccedenza *f* excess ; surplus
eccesso *m* excess
eccesso di velocità speeding
eccezionale exceptional
eccezione *f* exception
ecco here is/are
economico(a) cheap
edicola *f* newsstand ; kiosk
edificio *m* building
effetto *m* effect
effetti personali belongings
egregio(a) dear *(in formal letter)*
elastico *m* rubber band
elenco *m* list
elenco telefonico phone directory
elettricista *m/f* electrician
elettricità *f* electricity
elettrico(a) electric(al)
elettrodomestici *mpl* electrical goods
emergenza *f* emergency
emicrania *f* migraine
emorroidi *fpl* haemorrhoids
enoteca *f* stock of vintage wines
ente *m* corporation ; body
entrambi(e) both
entrare to come/go in ; to enter

ENTRATA entrance

entrata abbonati season ticket holders' entrance
entrata libera free admission
epatite *f* hepatitis
epilessia *f* epilepsy
epilettico(a) epileptic
equitazione *f* horse-riding
erba *f* grass
ernia *f* hernia
errore *m* mistake
esame *m* examination
esatto(a) exact ; accurate
esaurimento nervoso *m* nervous breakdown
esaurito(a) exhausted ; out of print

TUTTO ESAURITO sold out

esca *m* fishing bait
escluso(a) excluding
escursione *f* excursion
esente exempt
esente da dogana duty-free
esempio example
per esempio for example
esercizio *m* exercise ; business
esigenza *f* requirement
esperto(a) expert ; experienced
esplosione *f* explosion
esportare to export
esposto(a) exposed
esposto(a) a nord north-facing

espresso *m* express train ; coffee
espresso(a) express *(parcel, etc)*
essere to be *see* **GRAMMAR**
  essere assicurato(a) to be insured
  essere capace (di) to be able (to)
  essere d'accordo to agree
  essere nato(a) to be born
est *m* east
estate *f* summer
esterno(a) outside ; external
estero(a) foreign
  all'estero abroad
estintore *m* fire extinguisher

ESTIVO summer

età *f* age
etichetta *f* luggage tag ; label
eurocheque *m* Eurocheque
Europa *f* Europe
eventuale possible
evitare to avoid

F

fa ago
fabbrica *f* factory
fabbricare to manufacture
facchino *m* porter *(for luggage)*
faccia *f* face
facile easy
fagiano *m* pheasant
fallire to fail
fallito(a) bankrupt
fallo *m* foul *(football)*
falso(a) fake
fame *f* hunger
  avere fame to be hungry
famiglia *f* family
familiare family ; familiar
famoso(a) famous
fanale *m* light
fanalino dello stop *m* brake light
fango *m* mud
farcito(a) stuffed ; filled
fare to do ; to make *see* **GRAMMAR**
  fare attenzione to be careful
  fare la spesa to go shopping
farfalla *f* butterfly
fari *mpl* headlights
farina *f* flour
farmacia *f* chemist's ; pharmacy
  farmacie di turno duty chemists
farmaco *m* drug *(medicine)*
faro *m* headlight ; lighthouse
fascia *f* band ; bandage
fastidio: non mi dà fastidio I don't mind
fatelo da voi *m* DIY
fatto a mano hand-made
fatto di ... made of ...
fattoria *f* farm ; farmhouse
fattura *f* invoice
favore *m* favour
  per favore please
fax *m* fax
fazzoletto *m* handkerchief
  fazzoletto di carta tissue

FEBBRAIO February

febbre *f* fever
  avere la febbre to have a temperature
  febbre da fieno hay fever
fede *f* wedding ring
federa *f* pillowcase
fegato *m* liver
felice happy
felpa *f* sweatshirt
femmina *f* female

FERIALE workday/mon-sat

ferie *fpl* holiday(s)
  essere in ferie to be on holiday
ferire to injure
ferita *f* wound ; injury ; cut
ferito(a) injured
fermare to stop
fermata *f* stop
  fermata dell'autobus bus stop

fermata a richiesta request stop
fermo(a) still ; off *(machine)*
stare fermo to stay still
ferro da stiro *m* iron *(for clothes)*
ferrovia *f* railway
festa *f* festival ; holiday ; party
festa nazionale public holiday

FESTIVO sundays/public holiday

fetta *f* slice
FF SS Italian State Railways
fiamma *f* flame
fiammifero *m* match
fico *m* fig
fidanzato(a) engaged *(to marry)*
fieno *m* hay
fiera *f* fair *(trade)*
figlia *f* daughter
figlio *m* son
fila *f* line *(row, queue)*
fare la fila to queue
filiale *f* branch ; subsidiary
film *m* film *(at cinema)*
filo *m* thread ; wire
filo interdentale dental floss
filtro *m* filter
filtro dell'olio oil filter
finanza *f* finance
Guardia di finanza Customs and Excise
fine *f* end
fine settimana weekend
fine stagione end of season
finestra *f* window
finestrino *m* window *(car, train)*
finire to finish
finito(a) finished
fino(a) fine ; elegant
fino a until ; as far as
fino alle due till 2 o'clock
fioraio *m* florist's shop
fior di lattte *m* cream *(ice cream flavour)*
fiori *mpl* flowers
fiorista *m/f* florist
Firenze Florence
firma *f* signature
firmare to sign
firmare il registro to sign register
fiume *m* river
focaccia *f* flat salted bread
foglia *f* leaf *(of tree, etc)*
fogna *f* sewer ; drain
folla *f* crowd
folle mad
in folle in neutral *(car)*
fon *m* hairdryer
fondo *m* back *(of room)* ; bottom
fontana *f* fountain
fonte *f* source
foratura *f* puncture
forbici *fpl* scissors
forbicine nail scissors
forchetta *f* fork *(for eating)*
foresta *f* forest
forfora *f* dandruff
formaggio *m* cheese
fornaio *m* baker
fornello *m* stove ; hotplate
fornitore *m* supplier
forno *m* oven
forno a microonde microwave
forse perhaps
forte strong ; loud ; high *(speed)*
fortunato(a) lucky
forza *f* strength ; force
foto *f* photo
fotocopia *f* photocopy
fotocopiare to photocopy
fototessera *f* passport-type photo
foulard *m* headscarf
fra between ; among(st)
fra 2 giorni in 2 days
fra poco in a while
fragile breakable
fragola *f* strawberry
frana *f* landslide
francese French
francese *m* French *(language)*
Francia *f* France

f

francobollo *m* stamp
frappé *m* milk shake
fratello *m* brother
frattura *f* fracture
frazione *f* village
freccia *f* indicator *(car)* ; arrow

FREDDO cold

frenare to brake
freno *m* brake
freno a mano handbrake
frequente frequent
fretta *f* hurry
avere fretta to be in a hurry
friggere to fry
frigorifero *m* refrigerator
frittata *f* omelette
fritto(a) fried
frizione *f* clutch *(car)*
frizzante fizzy ; sparkling
fronte *f* forehead ; front
di fronte a facing ; opposite
frontiera *f* frontier ; border
frullato *m* milkshake
frutta *f* fruit
frutta secca dried fruit
frutti di mare *mpl* seafood
fruttivendolo *m* greengrocer
FS Italian State Railways
fuga *f* escape ; leak *(gas)*
fuggire to escape
fulmine *m* lightning
fumare to smoke
non fumo I don't smoke

FUMATORI smokers

fumo *m* smoke
funerale *m* funeral
funghi *mpl* mushrooms
funghi porcini boletus mushrooms
funghi secchi dried mushrooms
funicolare *f* funicular railway
funzionare to work *(mechanism)*
non funziona it doesn't work
fuoco *m* fire ; focus
fuochi d'artificio fireworks
fuori outside ; out

FUORI SERVIZIO out of order

furgone *m* van
furto *m* theft
fuseaux *mpl* leggings
fusibile *m* fuse
futuro *m* future

G

gabinetto *m* lavatory
gabinetto biologico chemical toilet
gabinetto medico doctor's surgery
galleria *f* tunnel ; gallery ; arcade ; circle *(theatre)*
galleria d'arte art gallery
Galles *m* Wales
gallese Welsh
gamba *f* leg
gara *f* race *(sport)*
garanzia *f* guarantee ; warranty
gas *m* gas
gasolio *m* diesel
gassato(a) fizzy
gassosa *f* lemonade
gastrite *f* gastritis
gatto *m* cat
gay gay *(person)*
gel per capelli *m* hair gel
gelateria *f* ice-cream shop
gelatina *f* jelly
gelato *m* ice cream
gelo *m* frost
geloso(a) jealous
gemelli *mpl* twins ; cufflinks
genere *m* kind *(type)* ; gender
genero *m* son-in-law
genitori *mpl* parents

GENNAIO January

Genova *f* Genoa
gentile kind *(person)*
Germania *f* Germany
gesso *m* chalk ; plaster *(for limb)*
gettare to throw
non gettare rifiuti no dumping
gettone *m* token *(for phone)*
ghiaccio *m* ice
ghiacciolo *m* ice lolly
giacca *f* jacket
giallo *m* thriller *(book or film)*
giallo(a) yellow ; amber *(light)*
giardiniere *m* gardener
giardino *m* garden
gilè *m* waistcoat
gin *m* gin
gin tonic gin and tonic
ginocchio *m* knee
giocare to play ; to gamble
giocattolo *m* toy
gioco *m* game
gioco a quiz quiz show
gioielleria *f* jeweller's
gioielli *mpl* jewellery
gioielliere *m* jeweller
giornalaio *m* newsagent
giornale *m* newspaper
giornalista *m/f* journalist
giornata *f* day
giorno *m* day

GIORNI FERIALI Mon-Sat
GIORNI FESTIVI Sun/holidays

giovane young

GIOVEDÌ Thursday

girare to turn ; to spin
girarsi to turn around
girasole *m* sunflower
girella *f* scrunchie
giro *m* tour ; turn
fare un giro a piedi to go for a stroll
giro turistico sightseeing tour
gita *f* trip ; excursion
gita in barca boat trip
gita in pullman coach trip
giù down ; downstairs
giubbotto salvagente *m* life jacket
giudice *m* judge

GIUGNO June

giusto(a) fair ; right *(correct)*
gli the ; to him/it
globale inclusive *(costs)*
goccia *f* drop *(of liquid)* ; drip
gola *f* throat ; gorge
golfo *m* gulf
gomito *m* elbow
gomma *f* rubber ; tyre
gomma a terra flat tyre
gomma da cancellare eraser
gommone *m* dinghy *(inflatable)*
gonfiare to inflate
gonfio(a) swollen
gonfiore *m* lump *(swelling)*
gonna *f* skirt
gradazione *f* content *(of alcohol)*
gradevole pleasant
gradino *m* step ; stair
Gran Bretagna *f* (Great) Britain
grana *f* parmesan cheese
granaio *m* barn
granchio *m* crab
grande large ; great ; big
grande magazzino *m* department store
grandine *f* hail
granita *f* water ice *(flavoured)*
grappa *f* strong spirit *(often drunk with coffee)*
grasso(a) fat ; greasy
gratis free of charge
grattacielo *m* skyscraper
grattugia *f* grater
grattugiato(a) grated
gratuito(a) free of charge
il servizio è gratuito service included

g

grave serious
grazie thank you
gridare to shout
grigio(a) grey
griglia *f* grill
  alla griglia grilled
grissini *mpl* breadsticks
grosso(a) big ; thick
grucce *fpl* crutches
gruccia *f* coat hanger
gruppo *m* group
  gruppo sanguigno blood group
guadagnare to earn
guanciale *m* pillow
guanto *m* glove
  guanto da forno oven glove
  guanto di spugna facecloth
  guanti di gomma rubber gloves
guardacoste *m* coastguard
guardare to look (at) ; to watch
guardaroba *m* cloakroom
guardia *f* guard
  Guardia di finanza Customs and Excise

GUASTO out of order

guerra *f* war
guida *f* guide *(person or book)* ; directory
  guida a sinistra left-hand drive
  guida telefonica telephone directory
  guida turistica tour guide
guidare to drive ; to steer
guidatore *m* driver
guinzaglio *m* lead *(for dog)*
gustare to taste ; to enjoy
gusto *m* flavour

H

ha...? do you have...?
  ha l'ora? do you have the time?
hamburger *m* burger
herpes *m* cold sore ; herpes
ho... I have...
  ho ... anni I'm ... years old
  ho bisogno di... I need...
  ho fame I'm hungry
  ho fretta I'm in a hurry
  ho sete I'm thirsty
hostess *f* stewardess

I

i the
identificare to identify
idratante *m* moisturizer
idraulico *m* plumber
ieri yesterday
il the
imbarcarsi to embark
imbarcazione *f* boat
imbarco *m* boarding
  carta d'imbarco boarding card
imbottigliato(a) bottled
imbucare to post *(letters, etc)*
immediatamente at once
immergere to dip *(into liquid)*
immersioni subacquee *fpl* scuba diving
immondizie *fpl* rubbish
immunizzazione *f* immunisation
impanato coated in breadcrumbs
imparare to learn
impasto *m* mixture
imperatore *m* emperor
impermeabile *m* raincoat
impero *m* empire
impiego *m* use ; employment
impiegato(a) *m/f* employee ; white-collar worker
importante important
importare to import ; to matter
  non importa it doesn't matter
importo *m* (total) amount
impossibile impossible
imposta *f* tax *(on income)* ; shutter
  imposta sul valore aggiunto (IVA) value-added tax (VAT)

improbabile unlikely
in in ; to *see* **GRAMMAR**
  in Spagna to Spain
  in vacanza on holiday
inalatore *m* inhaler
inadempienza *f* negligence
incantevole charming
incaricarsi di to take charge of
incartare to wrap up *(parcel)*
incassare to cash *(cheque)*
incendio *m* fire
inchiostro *m* ink
incidente *m* accident
incinta pregnant
incluso(a) included ; enclosed
incontrare to meet
incontro *m* meeting *(by chance)*
incrocio *m* crossroads ; junction
indicatore *m* indicator ; gauge
  indicatore del livello dell'olio oil gauge
indicazioni *fpl* directions
indice *m* index ; contents
indietro backwards ; behind
indirizzo *m* address
infarto *m* heart attack
infatti in fact ; actually
infermeria *f* infirmary
infermiera *f* nurse
infezione infection
infiammabile inflammable
infiammazione *f* inflammation
influenza *f* flu
informare to inform
  informarsi (di) to inquire (about)
informazioni *fpl* information
ingessatura *f* plaster cast
Inghilterra *f* England
inghiottire to swallow
inglese English
ingorgato(a) blocked *(pipe, sink)*
ingorgo *m* blockage ; hold-up
  ingorgo stradale traffic jam

INGRESSO entry/entrance
  ingresso gratuito free entry

iniezione *f* injection
inizio *m* start
innocuo(a) harmless
inondazione *m* flood
inoltre besides
inquinato(a) polluted
insalata *f* salad
  insalata di patate potato salad
  insalata di pomodori tomato salad
  insalata mista mixed salad
  insalata verde green salad
insegnante *m/f* teacher
insegnare to teach
inserire to insert
  inserire le banconote una per volta insert banknotes one at a time
insettifugo *m* insect repellent
insetto *m* insect
insieme together
insieme *m* outfit
insolazione *f* sunstroke
insulina *f* insulin
intelligenza *f* intelligence
interessante interesting
internazionale international
Internet *m* Internet
interno *m* inside ; extension *(phone)*
intero(a) whole
interpretazione *f* interpretation
interprete *m/f* interpreter
interruttore *m* switch
intervallo *m* half-time ; interval
intervento *m* operation
inversione *f* U-turn
intervista *f* interview
intestato(a) a registered in the name of
intimi donna *mpl* ladies' underwear
intorno around
intossicazione alimentare *f* food-poisoning
introdurre to introduce

i

inutile unnecessary ; useless
invalido(a) disabled ; invalid
invece di instead of

invernale winter

inverno *m* winter
investire to knock down *(car)*
inviare to send
invitare to invite
invito *m* invitation
io I
ipermercato *m* hypermarket
ipermetrope long-sighted
Irlanda *f* Ireland
  Irlanda del Nord Northern Ireland
irlandese Irish
iscritto *m* member
  per iscritto in writing
iscriversi a to join *(club)*
iscrizione *f* inscription ; enrolment
isola *f* island
istituto *m* institute
istruttore(trice) *m/f* instructor
istruzioni *fpl* instructions
Italia *f* Italy
italiano Italian
itinerario *m* route
  itinerario turistico scenic route
itterizia *f* jaundice
IVA *f* VAT

J

jolly *m* joker *(cards)*

L

l' the; him ; her ; it ; you
la the ; her ; it ; you
là there
  per di là that way
labbra *fpl* lips
lacca *f* lacquer ; hair spray
ladro *m* thief
lago *m* lake
lamette *fpl* razor blades
lampada *f* lamp
lampadina *f* lightbulb
lampone *m* raspberry
lana *f* wool
largo(a) wide ; broad
lasciare to leave ; to let *(allow)*
lassativo *m* laxative
lassù up there
latte *m* milk
  latte a lunga conservazione long-life milk
  latte di soia soya milk
  latte fresco fresh milk
  latte in polvere powdered milk
  latte intero full-cream milk
  latte scremato skimmed milk
  latte parzialmente scremato semi-skimmed milk
lattuga *f* lettuce
lavabile washable
lavaggio *m* washing
  lavaggio auto *m* car wash
  per lavaggi frequenti for frequent use
lavanderia *f* laundry *(place)*
  lavanderia automatica launderette
lavandino *m* sink
lavare to wash
  lavare a secco to dry-clean
lavarsi to wash *(oneself)*
lavasecco *m* dry-cleaner's
lavastoviglie *f* dishwasher
lavatrice *f* washing machine
lavorare to work *(person)*
lavoro *m* job ; occupation ; work
  lavori stradali road works
  lavori in corso road works
le the ; them ; to her/it ; to you
legge *f* law
leggere to read
leggero(a) light (not heavy) ; weak
legno *m* wood *(material)*
lei she ; her ; you

lentamente slowly
lente *f* lens *(of glasses)*
lente d'ingrandimento magnifying glass
lenti a contatto contact lenses

LENTO slow

lenzuolo *m* sheet *(bed)*
lesbica lesbian
lesione *f* injury
lettera *f* letter
lettera raccomandata registered letter
lettino *m* cot
letto *m* bed
letto a una piazza single bed
letto matrimoniale double bed
letti gemelli twin beds
letti a castello bunk beds
lettore CD *m* CD player
lì there *(over there)*

LIBERO free/vacant

libreria *f* bookshop
libretto *m* booklet
libretto degli assegni cheque book
libro *m* book
licenza *f* licence ; permit
licenza di caccia hunting permit
licenza di pesca fishing permit
limetta per le unghie *f* nail file
limite *m* limit ; boundary
limite di velocità speed limit
limone *m* lemon
linea *f* line ; route
linea aerea airline
lingua *f* language ; tongue
lino *m* linen
liquido *m* liquid
liquido dei freni brake fluid
liquido lavavetri screen wash
liquido per lenti a contatto contact lens solution
liquore *m* liqueur
liquori *mpl* spirits *(alcohol)*
liscio(a) straight ; smooth
lista *f* list
lista dei vini wine list
listino prezzi *m* price list
litro *m* litre
livello *m* level
lo him ; it
locale local
locale *m* room ; place ; local train
locale notturno nightclub
località di vacanza *f* resort
locanda *f* inn
Londra *f* London
lontano(a) far
lozione *f* lotion
lozione solare suntan lotion
lucchetto *m* padlock
lucchetto della bici bike lock
luce *f* light
lucertola *f* lizard

LUGLIO July

lui him
lumaca *f* snail
luna *f* moon
luna di miele honeymoon
luna park *m* funfair

LUNEDÌ Monday

lunghezza *f* length
lungo(a) long
lungo la strada along the street
a lungo for a long time
lungomare *m* promenade ; seafront
luogo *m* place
luogo di nascita place of birth
lupo *m* wolf
lusso *m* luxury
di lusso luxury *(hotel, etc)*

M

ma but
macchia *f* stain ; mark
macchina *f* car ; machine

m

macchina a noleggio hire car
macchina fotografica camera
macchina sportiva sports car
macedonia *f* fruit salad
macellaio *m* butcher's
macinato(a) ground *(coffee, meat)*
madre *f* mother
magazzino *m* warehouse

MAGGIO May

maggiore larger ; greater ; largest ; older ; oldest
maglietta *f* tee-shirt
maglione *m* jumper ; sweater
magro(a) thin *(person)* ; low-fat ; lean *(meat)*
mai never ; ever
maiale *m* pig ; pork
mal *see* **male**
malato(a) ill ; sick
malattia *f* disease
malattia venerea venereal disease
male badly *(not well)*
male *m* pain ; ache
mal d'aria air sickness
mal d'auto car sickness
mal d'orecchi earache
mal di denti toothache
mal di gola sore throat
mal di mare sea sickness
mal di pancia stomachache
mal di testa headache
maltempo *m* bad weather
mamma *f* mum(my)
mancia *f* tip *(to waiter, etc)*
mandare to send
mandare per fax to fax
mangiare to eat
mangiare fuori to eat out
manica *f* sleeve
la Manica the English Channel
mano *f* hand
fatto(a) a mano handmade

MANTENERE LA DESTRA keep right

Mantova *f* Mantua
manuale di conversazione *m* phrase book
manzo *m* beef
marca *f* brand *(make)*
marcia *f* gear *(car)* ; march
marciapiede *m* pavement
mare *m* sea ; seaside
Mare del Nord North Sea
margarina *f* margarine
margherita *f* daisy
marina *f* navy
marito *m* husband
marmellata *f* jam
marmellata d'arance marmalade
marrone *m* brown ; chestnut
marsupio *m* bumbag ; money belt

MARTEDÌ Tuesday

martedì grasso Shrove Tuesday
martello *m* hammer

MARZO March

maschera *f* mask ; fancy dress
maschile masculine ; male
massimo(a) maximum
masticare to chew
materassino *m* airbed ; lilo
materasso *m* mattress
materiale *m* material
matrigna *f* stepmother
matrimonio *m* wedding
mattina *f* morning
di mattina in the morning
matto(a) mad
mazza *f* mallet
mazze da golf golf clubs
meccanico *m* mechanic ; repair shop
medicina *f* medicine
medico *m* doctor
Mediterraneo *m* Mediterranean
medusa *f* jellyfish
meglio better ; best
meglio di better than

mela *f* apple
melanzana *f* aubergine ; eggplant
melone *m* melon
membro *m* member
meningite *f* meningitis
meno less ; minus
mensa *f* canteen
mensile monthly
mensilmente monthly
mensola *f* shelf
menta *f* mint
mento *m* chin
mentre while ; whereas
menù *m* menu
  menù alla carta à la carte menu
  menù a prezzo fisso set-price menu
  menù turistico set menu
meraviglioso(a) wonderful
mercatino dell'usato *m* flea market
mercato *m* market
merce *f* goods
merci *fpl* freight ; goods

MERCOLEDÌ Wednesday

merenda *f* snack
meridionale southern
mese *m* month
messa *f* mass *(in church)*
messaggio *m* message
mestruazioni *fpl* period *(menstrual)*
metà *f* half
  metà prezzo half-price
metro *m* metre
  metro a nastro tape measure
metropolitana *f* underground ; metro
mettere to put ; to put on *(clothes)*
  mettersi in contatto con to contact
mezzanotte *f* midnight
mezzi *mpl* means ; transport
mezzo *m* middle
mezzo(a) half
  mezza pensione half board
mezzogiorno *m* midday ; noon
  il Mezzogiorno the south of Italy
mezz'ora *f* half an hour
mi me ; to me ; myself
mia my
miele *m* honey
migliorare to improve
migliore better ; best
Milano Milan
miliardo *m* billion
milione *m* million
mille thousand
millimetro *m* millimetre
minestra *f* soup
minimo *m* minimum
ministro *m* minister *(political)*
minorenne underage
minori *mpl* minors
minuto *m* minute
mio my
miscela *f* blend
misto(a) mixed
mittente *m/f* sender
MM metro ; underground
mobili *mpl* furniture
moda *f* fashion
moderno(a) modern
modo *m* way ; manner
modulo *m* form *(document)*
  modulo d'iscrizione registration form
moglie *f* wife
molletta *f* clothes peg
  molletta per capelli hairgrip
molo *m* jetty ; quay ; pier
molti(e) many
  molte grazie thanks very much
molto much ; a lot ; very
  molto tempo for a long time
  molta gente lots of people
monastero *m* monastery
moneta *f* coin ; currency
montagna *f* mountain
monumento *m* monument
mordere to bite *(animal)*

m

morire to die
morsicare to bite *(insect)*
morsicato(a) bite *(from insect)*
morso(a) bitten
morto(a) dead
mosca *f* fly
moscerino *m* midge ; gnat
moschea *f* mosque
mosso(a) rough *(sea)* ; ruffled
mostra *f* exhibition
mostrare to show
moto *f* motorbike
motore *m* engine ; motor
motorino *m* moped
motorino d'avviamento *m* starter motor
multa *f* fine *(to be paid)*
municipio *m* town hall
muro *m* wall
museo *m* museum
musica *f* music
muta *f* wetsuit
mutande *fpl* underpants
mutandine *fpl* knickers ; panties

N

N north *(abbrev.)*
nafta *f* diesel
Napoli Naples
nascita *f* birth
naso *m* nose
nastro *m* tape ; ribbon
nato(a) born
nauseato(a) nauseous
nave *f* ship
nave-traghetto *f* ferry
nazionale national ; domestic *(flight)*
nazionalità *f* nationality
nazione *f* nation
né ... né neither ... nor
nebbia *f* fog
necessario(a) necessary
negativo *m* negative *(photo)*
negozio *m* shop
nero(a) black
nessuno(a) no ; nobody ; none
netto m net
  al netto di IVA net of VAT
neve *f* snow
nevicare to snow
niente nothing
  niente da dichiarare nothing to declare
nipote *f* granddaughter ; niece
nipote *m* grandson ; nephew
noce *f* walnut
nocivo(a) harmful
nodo *m* knot ; bow
  nodo ferroviario junction *(railway)*
noi we
noleggiare to hire
noleggio *m* hire
  noleggio auto car hire
  noleggio barche boat hire
  noleggio bici bike hire
  noleggio sci ski hire
nolo *m* hire
nome *m* name ; first name ;
  nome da ragazza maiden name
non not
  non ancora not yet
  non funziona it doesn't work
  non capisco I don't understand
  non pericoloso(a) safe
non-fumatore *m/f* non-smoker
nonna *f* grandmother
nonno *m* grandfather
nord *m* north
nostro(a) our
notare to notice
notizie *fpl* news
notte *f* night
  notte di San Silvestro New Year's Eve
  di notte at night

NOVEMBRE November

nubile single *(woman)*
nulla nothing ; anything

nullo(a) void *(contract)*
numero *m* number ; size *(of shoe)*
numero di camera room number
numero del conto account number
numero di telefono phone number
nuora *f* daughter-in-law
nuotare to swim
Nuova Zelanda *f* New Zealand
nuovo(a) new
di nuovo again
nuvoloso(a) cloudy

O

o or
O west (*abbrev. for* **ovest**)
obbligatorio(a) compulsory
oceano *m* ocean
occasione *f* opportunity ; bargain
occhiali *mpl* glasses
occhiali da sci skiing goggles
occhiali da sole sunglasses
occhio *m* eye

OCCUPATO busy/engaged

odore m smell
offerta *f* offer
officina *f* workshop ; repair shop
oggetto *m* object
oggi today
ogni each ; every
ogni giorno every day ; daily
ogni quanto? how often?
ogni tanto occasionally
olio *m* oil
olio solare suntan oil
olio di girasole sunflower oil
olio d'oliva olive oil
olive *fpl* olives
oltre beyond ; besides
ombra *f* shade
all'ombra in the shade
ombrello *m* umbrella
ombrellone *m* sun umbrella
ombretto *m* eye shadow
omogemeizzati *mpl* baby food
omosessuale homosexual
onde *fpl* waves
onesto(a) honest
opera *f* opera
operatore turistico *m* tour operator
operazione *f* operation *(surgical)*
opuscolo *m* brochure
ora now
ora *f* hour
ora di punta rush hour
che ore sono? what's the time?

ORARIO timetable

in orario on time
orario di apertura opening hours
orario di cassa banking hours
orario visite visiting hours
ordinare to order ; to prescribe
ordine *f* order *(in restaurant)*
orecchini *mpl* earrings
orecchio *m* ear
orecchioni *mpl* mumps
oreficeria *f* jeweller's
orina *f* urine
ormeggiare to moor
ormeggio *m* mooring
oro *m* gold
placcato oro gold-plated
orologeria *m* watchmaker's
orologio *m* clock ; watch
orticaria *f* rash *(skin)*

OSPEDALE hospital

ospite *m/f* guest ; host/hostess
osso *m* bone
ostello *m* hostel
ostello della gioventù youth hostel
ottenere to get ; obtain
ottenere la linea to get through *(on phone)*
ottimo(a) excellent

OTTOBRE October

otturazione *f* filling *(in tooth)*
ovest west

P

pacchetto *m* packet
pacco *m* package ; parcel
padella *f* frying-pan
Padova Padua
padre *m* father
padrone(a) *m/f* owner
paesaggio *m* scenery ; countryside
paese *m* country *(nation)* ; village
pagare to pay ; to pay for
pagato(a) paid
pagina *f* page
paio *m* pair
palazzo *m* building ; block of flats ; palace
palestra *f* gym
palla *f* ball
pallina *f* ball *(small)*
 pallina da golf golf ball
 pallina da tennis tennis ball
pallone *m* football
pandoro *m* Italian Christmas cake
pane *m* bread ; loaf
 pane integrale wholemeal bread
 pane carré sandwich bread
 pane e coperto cover charge
 pane di segale rye bread
pannettone *m* Italian Christmas cake
panetteria *f* baker's
pangrattato *m* breadcrumbs
panificio *m* bakery

PANINI sandwiches

panino *m* bread roll
 panino imbottito sandwich
paninoteca *f* sandwich bar
panna *f* cream
panno *m* cloth ; fabric
pannolini *mpl* nappies
pantaloni *mpl* trousers
 pantaloni corti shorts
pantofole *fpl* slippers
papa *m* pope
papà *m* daddy
parabrezza *m* windscreen
paraurti *m* bumper *(on car)*
parcheggiare to park
parcheggio *m* car park
 parcheggio custodito supervised car-park
 parcheggio libero free parking
 parcheggio sotterraneo underground car park
parchimetro *m* parking meter
parco *m* park
 parco nazionale national park
parente *m/f* relation ; relative
Parigi *f* Paris
parlare to speak ; to talk
parmigiano *m* parmesan
 parmigiano grattugiato grated parmesan
parola *f* word
parolaccia *f* swear word
parrucchiere(a) *m/f* hairdresser
parte *f* share ; part ; side

PARTENZE departures

 partenze internazionali international departures
 partenze nazionali domestic departures
partire to depart ; to leave
partita *f* match ; game
 partita di calcio football match
passaggio *m* passage ; lift *(in car)*
 dare un passaggio to give a lift
passaporto *m* passport
passeggiata *f* walk ; stroll
passeggino *m* pushchair
passo *m* pace ; pass *(mountain)*
 passo carrabile keep clear
 passo chiuso pass closed
pasticcino *m* cake *(small, fancy)*

pastiglia *f* tablet *(pill)*
pasto *m* meal
pastorizzato pasteurised
patata *f* potato
patatine *fpl* crisps
  patatine frite chips
patente *f* permit ; driving licence
patrigno *m* stepfather
pavimento *m* floor
paziente *m/f* patient
pecora *f* sheep
pedaggio *m* toll *(motorway)*
pedale *m* pedal
pedalò *m* pedalboat
pedicure *m* chiropodist
pedoni *mpl* pedestrians
peggio worse
pelati *mpl* tinned tomatoes
pelle *f* skin ; hide ; leather
pellegrino *m* pilgrim
pelletterie *fpl* leather goods
pellicola *f* film *(for camera)*
  pellicola a colori colour film
  pellicola in bianco e nero black and white film
pelo *m* fur
pene *m* penis
penicillina *f* penicillin
penisola *f* peninsula
penna *f* pen
pensare to think

PENSIONE guesthouse

  pensione completa full board
  mezza pensione half board
  pensione familiare bed and breakfast
pentola *f* saucepan
pepe *m* pepper *(spice)*
per for ; per ; in order to
  per esempio for example
  per favore please
  per via aerea air mail
pera *f* pear
perché why ; because ; so that
percorso *m* walk ; journey ; route
  percorso panoramico scenic route
perdere to lose ; to miss *(train, etc)*
perdita *f* leak *(of gas, liquid)*
pericolante unsafe
pericolo *m* danger
pericoloso(a) dangerous
  non pericoloso(a) safe
periferia *f* outskirts ; suburbs
permanente continua parking restrictions still apply
permanenza *f* stay ; residency
permesso *m* licence ; permit
  permesso! excuse me! *(to get by)*
  permesso di soggiorno residence permit
permettere to allow
perso(a) lost *(object)* ; missed *(train, plane, etc)*
persona *f* person
personale *m* staff
pesante heavy
pesare to weigh
pesca *f* angling ; fishing ; peach
  divieto di pesca no fishing
pescare to fish
pesce *m* fish
pescivendolo *m* fishmonger's
peso *m* weight
pettine *m* comb
petto *m* chest ; breast
  petto di pollo chicken breast
pezzo *m* piece ; bit ; cut *(of meat)*
piacere to please
  le piace? do you like it?
  piacere! pleased to meet you!
piangere to cry *(weep)*
piano slowly ; quietly
piano *m* floor *(of building)* ; plan
pianta *f* map ; plan ; plant

PIANTERRENO ground floor

piantina *f* street map
piatto *m* dish ; course ; plate
  primo piatto first course

piazza *f* square *(in town)*
piazzale *m* large square
piazzola (di sosta) *f* lay-by
piccante spicy ; hot
picchetto *m* tent peg
piccolo(a) little ; small
piede *m* foot
  a piedi on foot
pieno(a) full
pietra *f* stone
pigiama *m* pyjamas
pigro(a) lazy
pila *f* battery ; torch
pillola *f* pill
pinne *fpl* flippers
pino *m* pine
pinze *fpl* pliers
pinzette *fpl* tweezers
pioggia *f* rain
piombo *m* lead *(metal)*
piovere to rain
piscina *f* swimming pool
  piscina per bambini paddling pool
pista *f* track ; race track
  pista da ballo dance floor
  pista da sci ski run
più more ; most ; plus
  più di more than
  più economico(a) cheaper
  più tardi later
piumino *m* duvet
pizzeria *m* pizza restaurant
pizzico *m* pinch ; sting
pizzo *m* lace
plastica *f* plastic
  di plastica made of plastic
pneumatico *m* tyre
po' a little *(shortened form of* **poco***)*
pochi(e) few
poco(a) little ; not much
  un po' a little
poi then

POLIZIA police

  polizia stradale traffic police
poliziotto *m* policeman
polizza *f* policy
pollo *m* chicken
polmone *m* lung
poltrona *f* armchair ; seat in stalls
pomata *f* ointment
pomeriggio *m* afternoon
  di pomeriggio in the afternoon
pomodoro *m* tomato
pompa *f* pump
pompelmo *m* grapefruit
ponte *m* bridge ; deck
  ponte macchine car deck
pontile *m* jetty ; pier
porcellana *f* china
porta *f* door ; gate ; goal
  porta di sicurezza emergency exit
portabagagli *m* luggage rack ; porter *(at airport, station, etc)*
portacenere *m* ashtray
portafoglio *m* wallet
portare to carry/bring ; to wear
portiere *m* porter *(doorkeeper)* ; goalkeeper
portineria *f* caretaker's lodge
porto *m* port ; harbour
  porto di scalo port of call
Portogallo *m* Portugal
porzione *f* portion ; helping
posate *fpl* cutlery
posologia *f* dosage
possiamo we can
  non possiamo we cannot
posso I can
  non posso I cannot
posta *f* post office ; mail
  posta elettronica e-mail
  posta raccomandata registered mail
posteggio *m* car park
  posteggio taxi taxi rank
posto *m* place ; job ; seat
  posti in piedi standing room
  posti a sedere seating capacity

posti prenotati reserved seats

POTABILE ok to drink

potere to be able
pranzo *m* lunch
pré-maman *m* maternity dress
preavviso *m* advance notice
precotto(a) ready-cooked
predeterminare l'importo desiderato select required amount
preferire to prefer
preferito(a) favourite
prefisso *m* prefix ; area code
prefisso telefonico dialling code
pregare to pray
si prega... please...
prego don't mention it!
prelievo *m* collection ; sample
premere to push ; to press
premio *m* prize
prendere to take ; to catch *(bus, etc)*
prendere il sole to sunbathe
prendere in prestito to borrow
prenome *m* first name
prenotare to book ; to reserve
prenotato(a) reserved
prenotazione *f* reservation
preoccupato(a) worried
preparare to prepare ; to get ready
presa *f* socket *(electric)*
preservativo *m* condom
pressione del sangue *f* blood pressure
prestare to lend
presto early ; soon
prete *m* priest
previsione *f* forecast
previsioni del tempo weather forecast
previsto(a) scheduled ; expected
come previsto as expected
prezzo *m* price
prezzo al dettaglio retail price
prezzo fisso set price
prezzo di catalogo list price
prezzo al minuto retail price
prezzo d'ingresso entrance fee
prima di before
primavera *f* spring *(season)*
primo(a) first ; top ; early
primo piano first floor
primo piatto first course
principale main
principiante *m/f* beginner
privato(a) private
problema *m* problem
professione *f* profession
professore *m/f* teacher ; professor
profondità *f* depth
profondo(a) deep
profumeria *f* perfume shop
progettare to plan
programma *m* programme ; syllabus ; schedule
proibire to ban ; to prohibit
proibito(a) forbidden ; prohibited
prolunga *f* extension *(electrical)*
promettere to promise
pronto(a) ready
pronto! hello! *(on telephone)*

PRONTO SOCCORSO casualty

proprietario(a) *m/f* owner
proprio(a) own
prossimamente coming soon
prossimo(a) next
proteggislip *m* panty liner
protesi dell'anca *f* hip replacement
protestante Protestant
provare to try ; to test *(try out)* ; to try on *(clothes)*
provvisorio(a) temporary
prugna *f* plum
PTP *abbrev. of* Posto Telefonico Pubblico
pubblicità *f* advertisement
pubblico *m* audience ; public
pulce *f* flea
pulito(a) clean
pulizia *f* cleaning

p

pulizia del viso facial
pullman *m* coach
pulmino *m* minibus
punteggio *m* score
puntine *fpl* points
punto *m* point ; stitch ; full stop
punto d'incontro meeting place
puntura *f* bite ; sting ; injection
puzzo *m* bad smell

Q

qua here
quaderno *m* exercise book
quadro *m* picture ; painting
qual(e) what ; which ; which one
qualche some
qualche volta sometimes
qualcosa something ; anything
qualcuno someone ; somebody
qualificato(a) qualified
qualità *f* quality
qualsiasi any
qualunque any
quando? when?
quanto(a)? how much?
quanti(e)? how many?
quartiere *m* district
quarto *m* quarter
quarto d'ora quarter of an hour
quattro four
quei those ; those ones
quel(la) that ; that one
quelli(e) those ; those ones
quello(a) that ; that one
questi(e) these ; these ones
questo(a) this ; this one
questura *f* police station
qui here
quindi then ; therefore
quindici giorni fortnight
quotidiano *m* daily (paper)
quotidiano(a) daily

q

q

R

rabarbaro *m* rhubarb
rabbia *f* anger ; rabies
racchetta *f* racket ; bat
racchetta da neve snowshoe
racchetta da sci ski pole
raccomandare to recommend
racconto *m* story
radiatore *m* radiator
radio *f* radio
radiografia *f* x-ray
raffreddore *m* cold *(illness)*
raffreddore da fieno hay fever
ragazza *f* girl ; girlfriend
ragazza alla pari au pair
ragazzo *m* boy ; boyfriend
RAI *f* Italian State Broadcasting

RALLENTARE slow down

rapido *m* express train
rapido(a) high-speed ; quick
rasoio *m* razor
rasoio elettrico electric razor
reato *m* crime
recarsi alla cassa pay at cash desk
recentemente recently
reclamo *m* complaint
recupero monete returned coins
regalo *m* present ; gift
reggiseno *m* bra
regione *f* region ; district ; area
registrare to record
registratore *m* cassette player
registro *m* register
Regno Unito *m* United Kingdom
regolamento *m* regulation
regolare regular ; steady
remare to row *(boat)*
rendersi conto di to realize
rene *m* kidney
reparto *m* department ; ward
restare to stay ; to remain
restituire to return ; to give back

restituzione *f* return ; repayment
resto *m* remainder ; change *(money returned)*
restringersi to shrink
rete *f* net ; goal
rete portabagagli rack *(luggage)*
retro *m* back
vedi retro please turn over
retromarcia *f* reverse gear
reumatismo *m* rheumatism
ricambio *m* spare part ; refill
ricaricare to recharge *(battery)*
ricetta *f* prescription ; recipe
ricevere to receive ; to welcome
ricevitore *m* receiver *(phone)*
ricevuta *f* receipt
richiedere to require
richiesta *f* request
riciclare to recycle
riconoscere to recognize
riconoscimento *m* identification
ricordare to remember
non mi ricordo I don't remember
ricordo *m* souvenir ; memory
ricorrere a to resort to
ricoverare to admit *(to hospital)*
ridere to laugh
ridurre to reduce
riduttore *m* adaptor
riduzione *f* reduction
riempire to fill
rientro *m* return ; return home
rifare to do again ; to repair
rifiutare to refuse
rifiuti *mpl* rubbish ; waste
rifugio *m* mountain inn ; shelter
righello *m* ruler *(for measuring)*
rigore *m* penalty *(football)*
riguardo *m* care ; respect
riguardo a... regarding...
rilasciato(a) a issued at
rimandare to postpone
rimanere to stay ; to remain
rimborsare to reimburse
rimborso *m* refund
rimessa *f* remittance ; garage
rimettere to put back
rimettersi to recover *(from illness)*
rimorchiare to tow
rimorchio *m* trailer
a rimorchio on tow
rimozione *f* removal ; towing away
Rinascimento *m* Renaissance
rinfreschi *mpl* refreshments
ringraziare to thank
rinnovare to renew
rinunciare to give up
riparare to repair
riparato(a) sheltered
riparazione *f* repair
ripetere to repeat
ripido(a) abrupt ; steep
ripiegare to fold
ripieno *m* stuffing
riposarsi to rest
riposo *m* rest *(repose)*
risalita *f* reascent
risarcimento *m* compensation
riscaldamento *m* heating
riscaldare to heat up *(food)*
rischio *m* risk
risciacquare to rinse
riscuotere to collect ; to cash
riserva *f* reserve ; reservation
riserva di caccia private hunting
riserva naturale nature reserve
riservare to reserve
riservato(a) reserved
riso *m* rice ; laugh
risotto *m* rice cooked in stock
risparmiare to save *(money)*
rispondere to answer ; to reply
risposta *f* answer
ristorante *m* restaurant
ritardo *m* delay
ritirare to withdraw
ritiro *m* retirement ; withdrawal

RITIRO BAGAGLI baggage reclaim

ritornare to return *(go back)*

r r r

r

ritorno *m* return
riunione *f* meeting
riuscita *f* result ; outcome
riva *f* bank ; shore
riviera *f* riviera
rivista *f* magazine ; revue
rivolgersi a to refer to *(for info)*
roba *f* stuff ; belongings
roccia *f* rock
rognoni *mpl* kidneys
romanico(a) Romanesque
romanzo *m* novel
  romanzo rosa *m* romantic novel
rompere to break
rondine *f* swallow *(bird)*
rosa pink
rosa *f* rose
rosmarino *m* rosemary
rosolia *f* German measles ; rubella
rossetto *m* lipstick
rosso(a) red
rosticceria *f* shop selling cooked food
rotonda *f* roundabout
rotondo(a) round
rotto(a) broken
roulotte *f* caravan
rovesciare to spill ; to knock over
rovine *fpl* ruins

RTD delay

rubare to steal
rubinetto *m* tap
rubrica *f* address book
ruggine *f* rust
rughe *fpl* wrinkles
rullino *m* roll of film
rum *m* rum
rumore *m* noise
rumoroso(a) noisy
ruota *f* wheel
  ruota di scorta spare wheel
rupe *f* mountain cliff
ruscello *m* stream
russare to snore

S

S south *(abbrev for* **sud***)*

SABATO Saturday

sabbia *f* sand
saccarina *f* saccharin
sacchetto *m* small bag
  sacchetto di carta paper bag
  sacchetto di plastica plastic bag
sacco a pelo *m* sleeping bag
sacerdote *m* priest
sagra *f* local food festival
sala *f* hall ; auditorium
  sala da pranzo dining room
  sala d'aspetto waiting room
  sala partenze departure lounge
salame *m* salami
salario *m* wage
salato(a) salted ; savoury
saldare to settle *(bill)* ; to weld

SALDI sale

saldo *m* payment ; balance
sale *m* salt
salire to rise ; to go up
  salire in to get in *(vehicle)*
salita *f* climb ; slope
  in salita uphill
salmone *m* salmon
  salmone affumicato smoked salmon
salone *m* lounge ; salon
salotto *m* living room ; lounge
salsa *f* sauce
salsiccia *f* sausage
saltare to jump
saltato(a) sautéed
salumeria *f* delicatessen
salumi *mpl* cured pork meats
salute *f* health
  salute! cheers!
saluto *m* greeting
salvagente *m* life belt
salvare to rescue ; to save *(life)*

salvavita *m* circuit breaker
salve! hello!
salvia *f* sage *(herb)*
salvietta *f* serviette
salviettine per bambini *fpl* baby wipes
salvo except ; unless
sandali *mpl* sandals
sangue *m* blood
 al sangue rare *(steak)*
sanguinare to bleed
sapere to know
sapone *m* soap
sapore *m* flavour ; taste
saporito(a) tasty
Sardegna *f* Sardinia
sarto *m* tailor
sartoria *f* tailor's ; dressmaker's
sasso *m* stone
sauna *f* sauna
sbagliato(a) wrong
sbaglio *m* mistake
sbarco *m* landing *(boat)*
sbrigare to hurry
scadente low *(standard, quality)*
scadenza *f* expiry
scadere to expire *(ticket, etc)*
scaduto(a) out-of-date ; expired
scala *f* scale ; ladder ; staircase
 scala anticendio fire escape
 scala mobile escalator
scalare to climb
scaldabagno *m* water heater
scaldare to heat up
scale *fpl* stairs
scalino *m* step
scalo *m* stopover
scaloppina *f* veal escalope
scarico(a) flat *(battery)*
scarpa *f* shoe
 scarpe da ginnastica trainers
scarponcini *mpl* walking boots
scarponi da sci *mpl* ski boots
scatola *f* box ; tin
scegliere to choose
scelta *f* range ; selection ; choice
scendere to go down
 scendere da to get off *(bus, etc)*
scheda *f* slip *(of paper)* ; card
 scheda telefonica phonecard
schiena *f* back *(of body)*
sci *m* ski ; skiing
 sci di fondo cross-country skiing
 sci nautico water-skiing
scialuppa di salvataggio *f* lifeboat
sciare to ski
sciarpa *f* scarf
sciogliere to melt
sciopero *m* strike
sciovia *f* ski-lift
scivolare to slip
scomodo(a) inconvenient ; uncomfortable
scomparire to disappear
scompartimento *m* compartment
scongelare to defrost
sconto *m* discount

SCONTI reductions

scontrino *m* ticket ; receipt ; chit
scopa *f* broom *(brush)*
scorso(a) last
scossa *f* shock *(electric)*
scottatura *f* burn
 scottatura solare sunburn
Scozia *f* Scotland
scozzese Scottish
scrivania *f* desk
scrivere to write ; to spell
scultura *f* sculpture
scuola *f* school
 scuola di sci ski school
 scuola materna nursery school
scuro(a) dark *(colour)*
scusare to excuse ; to forgive
scusarsi to apologise
scusi? pardon?
se if ; whether
sé oneself
seconda *f* second gear

S

secondo *m* second *(time)* ; main course *(meal)*
secondo(a) second ; according to
  seconda classe second class
  di seconda mano secondhand
sede *f* seat ; head office
sedersi to sit down
sedia *f* chair
  sedia a rotelle wheelchair
  sedia a sdraio deckchair
sedile per bambini *m* babyseat *(car)*
seggiolone *m* highchair
seggiovia *f* chair-lift
segnale *m* signal ; road sign
segnare to score *(goal)*
segreteria telefonica *f* answering machine
seguente following
seguire to follow ; to continue
sella *f* saddle
selvatico(a) wild
semaforo *m* traffic lights
semifreddo *m* dessert made with ice cream

SEMINTERRATO basement

semplice plain ; simple
sempre always ; ever

SENSO UNICO one-way street
SENSO VIETATO no entry

sentiero *m* path ; footpath
sentire to hear
sentirsi to feel
senza without
separato(a) separated
sera *f* evening
serbatoio *m* tank *(car)*
  serbatoio dell'acqua cistern
serio serious (not funny)
serpente *m* snake
serratura *f* lock
servire to serve
servizio *m* service ; report *(in press)*
  servizio al tavolo waiter service

SERVIZIO COMPRESO service included

servizi *mpl* facilities ; bathroom
sesso *m* sex
seta *f* silk
sete *f* thirst
  avere sete to be thirsty

SETTEMBRE September

settentrionale northern
settimana *f* week
  settimana bianca week's skiing holiday
settimanale weekly
sfida *f* challenge
sfuso(a) loose ; on tap *(wine)*
sganciare to lift receiver
sì yes
Sicilia *f* Sicily
sicurezza *f* safety ; security
sicuro(a) sure
sidro *m* cider
Sig. Mr *abbrev. for* **Signor**
Sig.a Mrs/Ms *abbrev. for* **Signora**
sigaretta *f* cigarette
sigaro *m* cigar
Sig.na Miss *abbrev. for* **Signorina**
Signor: il Signor Grandi Mr Grandi
signora *f* lady ; madam ; Mrs ; Ms

SIGNORE ladies

signore *m* gentleman ; sir

SIGNORI gents

signorina *f* young woman ; Miss
silenzio *m* silence
simile a similar to
simpatico(a) pleasant ; nice
sindaco *m* mayor
singolo(a) single
sinistra *f* left
sistemare to arrange
sito *m* site
  sito web website

skipass *m* skipass
slacciare to unfasten ; to undo
slavina *f* snowslide ; landslide
slegato(a) loose *(not fastened)*
slogatura *f* sprain
smarrito(a) missing *(thing)*
smettere to stop doing something
soccorso *m* assistance ; help
 soccorso alpino mountain rescue
socio *m* associate ; member
soggiorno *m* stay ; sitting room
soldi *mpl* money
sole *m* sun ; sunshine
solito: di solito usually
sollevare to raise ; to relieve
sollievo *m* relief
solo(a) alone ; only
solubile soluble
 caffè solubile instant coffee
sonnifero *m* sleeping pill
sono I am (to be) *see* **GRAMMAR**
sopra on ; above ; over
 di sopra upstairs
sopracciglia *fpl* eyebrows
sopravvivere to survive
sorella *f* sister
sorpassare to overtake *(in car)*
sorpresa *f* surprise
sorridere to smile
sorriso *m* smile
sospeso(a) suspended ; postponed
sosta *f* stop
 divieto di sosta no parking
sott'acqua underwater
sotterraneo(a) underground
sotto underneath ; under ; below
Spagna *f* Spain
spagnolo(a) Spanish
spalla *f* shoulder
sparire to disappear
spazzatura *f* rubbish
spazzola *f* **brush**
 spazzola per capelli hairbrush
 spazzolino da denti toothbrush
speciale special
specialità *f* speciality
specialmente especially
spedire to send ; to dispatch
spegnere to turn off ; to put out
spendere to spend *(money)*
spento(a) turned off ; out *(light, etc)*
sperare to hope
spese *fpl* shopping ; expenses
spesso often
spettacolo *m* show ; performance
spezzatino *m* stew
spiaggia *f* beach ; shore
 spiaggia privata private beach
spiccioli *mpl* small coins ; change
 non ho spiccioli I've no change
spiegare to explain
spina *f* bone *(of fish)* ; plug *(electric)*

SPINGERE push

spirale *f* coil *(IUD)*
spogliatoio *m* dressing room
sporco(a) dirty
sportello *m* counter ; window
sportivo(a) informal *(clothes)*
sposarsi to get married
sposato(a) married
 non sposato(a) single
spugna *f* sponge
spuma *f* hair mousse
spumante *m* sparkling wine
spuntino *m* snack
squadra *f* team
squillare to ring *(phone)*
Srl Ltd
stabilimento *m* factory
stadio *m* stadium
stagione *f* season
 di stagione in season
stalla *f* stable
stampatello *m* block letters
stanco(a) tired
stanza *f* room
 stanza da bagno bathroom
 stanza dei giochi playroom
stare to be

S

stare attento(a) a... beware of..
stare in piedi to stand
stasera tonight ; this evening
Stati Uniti *mpl* United States
stazione *f* station ; resort
stazione balneare seaside resort
stazione dell'autobus bus station
stazione di servizio petrol station
stazione ferroviaria train station
stella *f* star
sterlina *f* sterling ; pound
stesso(a) same
stirare to iron
stitichezza *f* constipation
stitico(a) constipated
stivali *mpl* boots
storia *f* history
storico(a) historic(al)

CENTRO STORICO old town

strada *f* road ; street
strada chiusa road closed
strada panoramica scenic route
strada sbarrata road closed
strada statale main road
strada senza uscita no through road
stradina *f* lane
straniero(a) foreign ; foreigner
strano(a) strange
stupido(a) stupid
su on ; onto ; over ; about ; up
sua his ; her(s) ; its ; your(s)
subito at once ; immediately
succedere to happen
succo *m* juice
succo d'arancia orange juice
succo di frutta fruit juice
succo di mela apple juice
succo di pomodoro tomato juice
succursale *m* branch *(of bank, etc)*
sud *m* south
sue his ; her(s) ; its ; your(s)
suo(i) his ; her(s) ; its ; your(s)
suocera *f* mother-in-law
suocero *m* father-in-law
suola *f* sole *(of foot, shoe)*
suonare to ring ; to play
suono *m* sound
superare to exceed ; to overtake
supermercato *m* supermarket
supplemento *m* supplement
supposta *f* suppository
surf *m* surf
surgelato(a) frozen
sveglia *f* alarm clock
svegliare to wake up
svenire to faint
sviluppare to develop *(photos)*
Svizzera *f* Switzerland
svizzero(a) Swiss
svolta *f* turn

T

tabaccaio *m* tobacconist's
tacco *m* heel
tachimetro *m* speedometer
taglia *f* size *(of clothes)*
tagliare to cut
tailleur *m* women's suit
tallone *m* heel
tangenziale *f* by-pass
tanti(e) so many
tanto(a) so much ; so
tappo *m* cork ; plug ; cap
tappo del serbatoio petrol cap
tardi late
targa *f* numberplate *(car)*
tariffa *f* tariff ; rate
tariffa economica cheap rate
tariffa festiva rate on holidays
tariffa ore di punta peak rate
tartuffo *m* truffle
tasca *f* pocket
tassa *f* tax
tasso *m* rate
tasso di cambio exchange rate
tavola *f* table ; plank ; board
tavola calda hot snacks
tavola da surf surfboard

tavola a vela windsurfing board
taxi *m* taxi
tazza *f* cup
tè *m* tea
tè al latte tea with milk
tè al limone lemon tea
tè freddo iced tea
teatro *m* theatre ; drama
tedesco(a) German
telecomando *m* remote control
telefonare to (tele)phone
telefonata *f* phone call
telefonino *m* mobile phone
telefono *m* telephone
telefono pubblico payphone
televisione *f* television
telone impermeabile *m* groundsheet
temperatura *f* temperature
temperino *m* penknife
tempesta *f* storm
tempio *m* temple
tempo *m* weather ; time
temporale *m* thunderstorm
tenda *f* curtain ; tent
tendine *m* tendon
tenere to keep ; to hold
tenore *m* tenor *(singer)*
tenore alcolico *m* alcohol content
tergicristallo *m* windscreen wiper
terminal *m* terminal *(airport)*
termometro *m* thermometer
termosifone *m* heater
terra *f* earth ; ground
terrazza *f* terrace
terremoto *m* earthquake
terza *f* third gear
terzi *mpl* third party
terzo(a) third
tessera *f* pass ; season ticket
tesserino *m* pass *(bus, train)*
tessuto *m* fabric
testa *f* head
testicoli *mpl* testicles
tettarella *f* dummy *(for baby)*
tetto *m* roof
tettuccio apribile *m* sunroof *(car)*
Tevere *m* Tiber
thermos *m* thermos flask
thriller *m* thriller
timone *m* rudder

TIRARE pull

toccare to touch ; to feel

NON TOCCARE do not touch

togliere to remove ; to take away
toilette *f* toilet
tonno *m* tuna
topo *m* mouse
Torino *f* Turin
tornare to return ; to come/go back
torneo *m* tournament
toro *m* bull
torre *f* tower
torrone *m* nougat
torta *f* cake ; tart ; pie
Toscana *f* Tuscany
tosse *f* cough
tossico(a) toxic
tossire to cough
totale *m* total *(amount)*
tovaglia *f* tablecloth
tovagliolo *m* napkin
tra between ; among(st) ; in
tradizionale traditional
tradurre to translate
traduzione *f* translation
traffico *m* traffic
traghetto *m* ferry

TRAMEZZINI sandwiches

trampolino *m* diving board ; ski jump
tranquillante *m* tranquillizer
tranquillo(a) quiet *(place)*
trasferire to transfer
trasporto *m* transport
trattoria *f* restaurant

traveller's cheque *mpl* traveller's cheque
traversata *f* crossing ; flight
treno *m* train
  treno merci goods train
triangolo d'emergenza *m* warning triangle
tribuna *f* stand (stadium)
tribunale *m* law court
trimestre *m* term *(school)*
triste sad
tritare to mince ; to chop
troppi(e) too many
troppo too much ; too
trovare to find
trucco *m* make-up
tu you *(familiar)*
tubo *m* pipe ; tube
  tubo di scappamento exhaust
tuffarsi to dive
turno *m* turn ; shift
  di turno on duty
tuta sportiva *f* tracksuit
tutti (e) all ; everybody

TUTTE LE DIREZIONI all routes

tutto everything ; all

U

ubriaco(a) drunk
uccello *m* bird
uccidere to kill
UE European Union
ufficio *m* office ; church service
  ufficio informazioni information bureau

  UFFICIO OGGETTI SMARRITI lost property office

  ufficio postale post office
  ufficio turistico tourist office
uguale equal ; even
ulcera *f* ulcer
ultimo(a) last
un a ; an ; one
unghia *f* nail *(finger, toe)*
unione *f* union
  Unione Europea European Union
Unità Sanitaria Locale local health centre
università *f* university
uno(a) a ; an ; one
uomo *m* man

UOMINI gents

uova *mpl* eggs
uovo *m* egg
  uovo di Pasqua Easter egg
  uovo sodo hard-boiled egg
uragano *m* hurricane
urgente urgent
usare to use
uscire to go/come out

USCITA exit/gate

  uscita di sicurezza emergency exit
USL *abbrev. of* Unità Sanitaria Locale
uso *m* use
utile useful
uva *f* grapes

V

va bene all right *(agreed)*
vacanza *f* holiday(s)
  vacanze estive summer holidays
vaccinazione *f* vaccination
vagina *f* vagina
vaglia *m* money order
vagone *m* carriage ; wagon
  vagone letto sleeper
  vagone ristorante restaurant car
valanga *f* avalanche
valico *m* pass *(mountain)*
valido(a) valid

VALIDO FINO A... valid until...

valigia *f* suitcase
valore *m* value; worth
di valore valuable
valuta *f* currency
valvola *f* valve
varicella *f* chickenpox
vasetto *m* jar
vaso *m* vase
vassoio *m* tray
vecchio(a) old
vedere to see
vedova *f* widow
vedovo *m* widower
vegetaliano(a) vegan
vegetariano(a) vegetarian
veicolo *m* vehicle
vela *f* sail ; sailing
veleno *m* poison
velenoso(a) poisonous
veloce quick
velocemente quickly
velocità *f* speed
vena *f* vein
vendere to sell

VENDESI for sale

vendita *f* sale
vendita al minuto retail
vendita a rate hire purchase

VENERDÌ Friday

venerdì santo Good Friday
Venezia *f* Venice
venire to come
ventaglio *m* fan *(hand-held)*
ventilatore *m* electirc fan
vento *m* wind
verde green
verdura *f* vegetables
verità *f* truth
vermut *m* vermouth
vernice *f* paint
verniciare to paint
vero(a) true ; real ; genuine
versamento *m* payment ; deposit
versare to pour
vertice *m* summit
vescica *f* blister
vespa *f* wasp
vestaglia *f* dressing gown
vestirsi to get dressed
vestiti *mpl* clothes
vestito *m* dress
vetrina *f* shop window
vetro *m* glass *(substance)*
via *f* street ; by *(via)*
per via aerea by air mail
viaggiare to travel
viaggiatore *m* traveller
viaggio *m* journey ; trip ; drive
viaggio d'affari business trip
viaggio organizzato package tour
viale *m* avenue
vicino (a) near ; close by
vicolo *m* alley ; lane
vicolo cieco cul-de-sac
videocamera *f* videocamera
videocassetta *f* videocassette
videogioco *m* computer game
videoregistratore *m* video recorder

VIETATO forbidden

vietato accendere fuocchi do not light fires
vietato fumare no smoking
vietato l'ingresso no entry
vietato ingresso veicoli no entry for vehicles
vietato scendere no exit

VIGILI DEL FUOCO fire brigade

vigilia *f* eve
Vigilia di Natale Christmas Eve
vigna *f* vineyard
vincere to win
vino *m* wine
vino bianco white wine
vini da pasto table wines
vino da tavola table wine
vini pregiati quality wines

V

vino rosso red wine
violentare to rape
virus *m* virus
visita *f* visit

VISITE GUIDATE guided tours

visitare to visit
vista *f* view
visto *m* visa
vita *f* life ; waist
vita notturna night life
vitamina *f* vitamin
vite *f* vine ; screw
vivere to live
vivo(a) live ; alive
voce *f* voice
volante *m* steering wheel
volare to fly
voler dire to mean *(signify)*
volere to want
volo *m* flight
volo di linea scheduled flight
volo charter charter flight
volta *f* time
una volta once
due volte twice *(etc)*
voltaggio *m* voltage
vomitare to vomit
vongola *f* clam
vostro(a) your ; yours
vulcano *m* volcano
vuoto(a) empty

Z

zanzara *f* mosquito
zanzaria *f* mosquito net
zia *f* aunt
zio m uncle
zona *f* zone
zona blu restricted parking zone
zona pedonale pedestrian
zucchero *m* sugar
zucchini *mpl* courgettes
zuppa *f* soup
zuppa inglese type of trifle

V

NOUNS

In Italian all nouns are either masculine or feminine. Where in English we say **the apple** and **the book**, in Italian it is **la mela** and **il libro** because **mela** is feminine and **libro** is masculine. The gender of nouns is shown in the article (**il**, **la**, **un**, **una**, *etc.*):

THE

masc. sing.	**il** **l'** *(+vowel)* **lo** *(+z, gn, pn, ps, x, s+consonant)*	*fem. sing.*	**la** **l'** *(+vowel)*
masc. plur.	**i** **gli** *(+vowel, +z, gn, pn, s+consonant)*	*fem. plur.*	**le**

A, AN

masc.	**un** **uno** (+z, gn, pn, s+consonant)	*fem.*	**una** **un'** *(+vowel)*

NOTE: definite articles (**il**, **la**, **i**, **le**, *etc.*) used after the prepositions **a** (**to**, **at**), **da** (**by**, **from**), **su** (**on**), **di** (**of**, **some**) and **in** (**in**, **into**) contract as follows:

a + il = al	**da + il = dal**	**su + il = sul**
a + lo = allo	**da + lo = dallo**	**su + lo = sullo**
a + l' = all'	**da + l' = dall'**	**su + l' = sull'**
a + la = alla	**da + la = dalla**	**su + la = sulla**
a + i = ai	**da + i = dai**	**su + i = sui**
a + gli = agli	**da + gli = dagli**	**su + gli = sugli**
a + le = alle	**da + le = dalle**	**su + le = sulle**

di + il = del	**in + il = nel**
di + lo = dello	**in + lo = nello**
di + l' = dell'	**in + l' = nell'**
di + la = della	**in + la = nella**
di + i = dei	**in + i = nei**
di + gli = degli	**in + gli = negli**
di + le = delle	**in + le = nelle**

e.g. **alla** casa (**to the** house) **sul** tavolo (**on the** table)

PLURALS

For most nouns, the singular ending changes as follows:

masc. sing.	*masc. plur.*	*example*	
o	**i**	**libro**	**libri**
e	**i**	**padre**	**padri**
a	**i**	**artista**	**artisti**

NOTE: nouns ending in **e** can be either masculine or feminine. In the plural they all end in **i**, e.g.

la televisione	**le televisioni**
il mare	**i mari**

NOTE: most nouns ending in **co** and **go** become **chi** and **ghi** in the plural to keep the **c** and **g** hard sounding. Some exceptions occur in the masculine, e.g. **amico** – **amici**

fem. sing.	*fem. plur.*	*example*	
a	**e**	**mela**	**mele**
e	**i**	**madre**	**madri**

NOTE: nouns ending in **ca** and **ga** become **che** and **ghe** in the plural to keep the **c** and **g** hard sounding. Nouns ending in **cia** and **gia** often becomes **ce** and **ge** to keep the **c** and **g** soft sounding.

ADJECTIVES

Adjectives normally follow the noun they describe in Italian, e.g. la mela **rossa** (the red apple)
Some common exceptions which precede the noun are:
bello beautiful, **breve** short, **brutto** ugly, **buono** good, **cattivo** bad, **giovane** young, **grande** big, **lungo** long, **nuov**o new, **piccolo** small, **vecchio** old
e.g. una **bella** giornata (a beautiful day)

Italian adjectives have to reflect the gender of the noun they describe. To make an adjective feminine, an **a** replaces the **o** of the masculine, e.g. ross**o** – ross**a**. Adjectives ending in **e**, e.g. **giovane**, can be either masculine or feminine. The plural forms of the adjective change in the way described for nouns (above).

MY, YOUR, HIS, HER, OUR, THEIR

These words also depend on the gender and number of the noun they accompany, and not on the sex of the 'owner'.

	with masc. sing. noun	*with fem. sing. noun*	*with masc. plur. noun*	*with fem. plur. noun*
my	**il mio**	**la mia**	**i miei**	**le mie**
your *(polite)*	**il suo**	**la sua**	**i suoi**	**le sue**
your *(familiar)*	**il tuo**	**la tua**	**i tuoi**	**le tue**
your *(plural)*	**il vostro**	**la vostra**	**i vostri**	**le vostre**
his/her	**il suo**	**la sua**	**i suoi**	**le sue**
our	**il nostro**	**la nostra**	**i nostri**	**le nostre**
their	**il loro**	**la loro**	**i loro**	**le loro**

PRONOUNS

SUBJECT		OBJECT	
I	**io**	me	**mi**
you	**lei**	you	**la**
he	**lui/egli**	him	**lo/l'** *(+vowel)*
she	**lei/ella**	her	**la/l'** *(+vowel)*
it *(masc.)*	**esso**	it *(masc.)*	**lo/l'** *(+vowel)*
it *(fem.)*	**essa**	it *(fem.)*	**la/l'** *(+vowel)*
we	**noi**	us	**ci**
you	**voi**	you	**vi**
they	**loro**	them *(masc.)*	**li**
(things:masc)	**essi**	them *(fem.)*	**le**
(things:fem.)	**esse**		

The object pronouns shown above are also used to mean **to me, to us**, etc., except:

to him/to it	= **gli**
to her/to it/to you	= **le**
to them	= **loro**

Pronoun objects (other than **loro**) usually precede the verb:

lo vedo	but	**scriverò loro**
I see him		I will write to them

When used with an infinitive (the verb form given in the dictionary), the pronoun follows and is attached to the infinitive less its final *e*:

voglio comprarlo — I want to buy it

Subject pronouns (**io**, **tu**, **egli**, etc.) are often omitted before verbs, since the verb ending generally distinguishes the person:

parlo	I speak
parliamo	we speak
parlono	they speak

Lei is the polite form for **you**; **voi** is the plural form. **Tu**, the familiar form for **you**, should only be used with people you know well, or children.

VERBS

There are three main patterns of endings for verbs in Italian – those ending **-are**, **-ere** and **-ire** in the dictionary. Two examples of the **-ire** verbs are shown, since two distinct groups of endings exist. Subject pronouns are shown in brackets because these are often not used:

	PARLARE	TO SPEAK	VENDERE	TO SELL
(io)	**parlo**	I speak	**vendo**	I sell
(tu)	**parli**	you speak	**vendi**	you sell
(lui/lei)	**parla**	(s)he speaks	**vende**	(s)he sells
(noi)	**parliamo**	we speak	**vendiamo**	we sell
(voi)	**parlate**	you speak	**vendete**	you sell
(loro)	**parlano**	they speak	**vendono**	they sell

	DORMIRE	TO SLEEP	FINIRE	TO FINISH
(io)	**dormo**	I sleep	**finisco**	I finish
(tu)	**dormi**	you sleep	**finisci**	you finish
(lui/lei)	**dorme**	(s)he sleeps	**finisce**	(s)he finishes
(noi)	**dormiamo**	we sleep	**finiamo**	we finish
(voi)	**dormite**	you sleep	**finite**	you finish
(loro)	**dormono**	they sleep	**finiscono**	they finish

IRREGULAR VERBS

Among the most important irregular verbs are the following:

	ESSERE	TO BE	AVERE	TO HAVE
(io)	**sono**	I am	**ho**	I have
(tu)	**sei**	you are	**hai**	you have
(lui/lei)	**è**	(s)he is	**ha**	(s)he has
(noi)	**siamo**	we are	**abbiamo**	we have
(voi)	**siete**	you are	**avete**	you have
(loro)	**sono**	they are	**hanno**	they have

	ANDARE	TO GO	FARE	TO DO
(io)	**vado**	I go	**faccio**	I do
(tu)	**vai**	you go	**fai**	you do
(lui/lei)	**va**	(s)he goes	**fa**	(s)he does
(noi)	**andiamo**	we go	**facciamo**	we do
(voi)	**andate**	you go	**fate**	you do
(loro)	**vanno**	they go	**fanno**	they do

	POTERE	TO BE ABLE	VOLERE	TO WANT
(io)	**posso**	I can	**voglio**	I want
(tu)	**puoi**	you can	**vuoi**	you want
(lui/lei)	**può**	(s)he can	**vuole**	(s)he wants
(noi)	**possiamo**	we can	**vogliamo**	we want
(voi)	**potete**	you can	**volete**	you want
(loro)	**possono**	they can	**vogliono**	they want

g r a m m a r

	DOVERE	TO HAVE TO (MUST)
(io)	**devo**	I must
(tu)	**devi**	you must
(lui/lei)	**deve**	he/she must
(noi)	**dobbiamo**	we must
(voi)	**dovete**	you must
(loro)	**devono**	they must

PAST TENSE

To form the simple past tense, I spoke/I have spoken, I sold/I have sold, etc. combine the present tense of the verb **avere** – to have with the past participle of the verb, e.g.

ho parlato	I spoke/I have spoken
ho venduto	I sold/I have sold

PARLARE (past)		VENDERE (past)	
ho parlato	I spoke	**ho venduto**	I sold
hai parlato	you spoke	**hai venduto**	you sold
ha parlato	(s)he spoke	**ha venduto**	(s)he sold
abbiamo parlato	we spoke	**abbiamo venduto**	we sold
avete parlato	you spoke	**avete venduto**	you sold
hanno parlato	they spoke	**hanno venduto**	they sold

DORMIRE (past)		FINIRE (past)	
ho dormito	I slept	**ho finito**	I finished
hai dormito	you slept	**hai finito**	you finished
ha dormito	(s)he slept	**ha finito**	(s)he finished
abbiamo dormito	we slept	**abbiamo finito**	we finished
avete dormito	you slept	**avete finito**	you finished
hanno dormito	they slept	**hanno finito**	they finished

NOTE: not all verbs take **avere** (**ho**, **hai**, etc.) as their auxiliary verb, some verbs take **essere** (**sono**, **sei**, etc.). These are mainly verbs of motion or staying, e.g. **andare–to go**, **stare–to be** (located at):

e.g. **sono andato** — I went
sono stato a Roma — I was in Rome

When the auxiliary verb **essere** is used, the past particple (**andato**, **stato**) becomes an adjective and should agree with the subject of the verb, e.g.

sono andata — I went *(fem. sing.)*
siamo stati — we went *(masc. plural)*